# RECONSIDERING SEX
# CRIMES AND OFFENDERS

# RECONSIDERING SEX CRIMES AND OFFENDERS

## Prosecution or Persecution?

*Lisa Anne Zilney and Laura J. Zilney*

**PRAEGER**

*An Imprint of ABC-CLIO, LLC*

A B C 🌐 C L I O

Santa Barbara, California • Denver, Colorado • Oxford, England

**Library of Congress Cataloging-in-Publication Data**
Zilney, Lisa Anne.
    Reconsidering sex crimes and offenders : prosecution or persecution? / Lisa Anne Zilney and Laura Zilney.
        p. cm.
    Includes bibliographical references and index.
    ISBN 978-0-313-34857-0 (alk. paper) — ISBN 978-0-313-34858-7 (ebook)  1. Sex offenders—Legal status, laws, etc.—United States. 2. Sex crimes—United States.  I. Zilney, Laura J. II. Title.
    KF9325.Z57 2009
    345.73'0253—dc22                                    2009022952
13  12  11  10  09      1  2  3  4  5

This book is also available on the World Wide Web as an eBook.
Visit www.abc-clio.com for details.

ABC-CLIO, LLC
130 Cremona Drive, P.O. Box 1911
Santa Barbara, California 93116-1911

This book is printed on acid-free paper. ∞
Manufactured in the United States of America

*In memory of Leviathan (1996–2009),*
*for years of playful companionship and a lifetime of loving memories.*
*—Lisa*

*To G for showing me another way of thinking.*
*—L.J.*

# CONTENTS

# ACKNOWLEDGMENTS

We are grateful to our Praeger editors for seeing the manuscript through the production process. We are grateful to Gregg Barak (Eastern Michigan University) for encouraging the current project as an outgrowth of his *Battleground: Criminal Justice* (Greenwood Press, 2008) project. Despite all of the input, any errors in interpretation remain our own.

# INTRODUCTION

Sex offenders are one of the most despised groups of people in American society—along with terrorists and perpetrators of genocide. But what do we really know about sex offenders? Is the information we possess based on fact or fiction? Unlike media accounts, we cannot identify sex offenders by the way they look, how they dress, or their IQ. If we cannot easily pick sex offenders out of a crowd, how do we know who they are, how dangerous they may be, and how to protect ourselves from these "predators"?

This book is written from two varied perspectives: that of a sexologist and that of a criminologist. The sexologist (and parent) has worked with persons who have offended sexually for more than 10 years and has found these individuals to be average people: sales representatives, engineers, tradespeople, truck drivers, office workers, and professionals. Their backgrounds and intelligence are as diverse as their professions. As a clinician, she strives to be positive in her approach; knowing that sex offenders are people who make mistakes like everyone else, but their mistakes are sexual ones that have ramifications for other individuals. Consequently, their therapy involves redirecting socially inappropriate sexual behavior to a positive and consensual outlet without the use of shame or threats of prison and loss of family. On the other hand, as a parent, if someone were to hurt her child, she would seek vengeance; she would want to see them suffer as they made her child suffer. Needless to say, this is a difficult balancing act.

The other author of this book is a professor and studies sex offenders from an academic and theoretical perspective. She does not work with persons who have offended sexually in a clinical sense but examines the backgrounds of those who have been charged and convicted in the larger social context of the criminal justice system. Hers is a different perspective simply because a face has not been put to the offenders involved. Her attitude is more conservative than that of a sexologist, although it is tempered by in-depth knowledge of the myriad of structural and individual reasons that individuals commit crimes, either sexual or otherwise.

If someone commits a nonconsensual sexual act, they should be punished. Note the specific mention of *nonconsensual* acts, as many individuals are charged, convicted, and required to register for life as sex offenders for acts that were *consensual*. Also note that we do not necessarily conclude that persons who have offended sexually should be sent to prison for life or that prison should even be a requirement in all circumstances. In fact, prison is only effective for the very small fraction of offenders who are incapable of responding to treatment, such as those who have committed violent sexual offenses or long-term offenders with no desire to change their behavior. These are important distinctions and ones that cannot be overstated. Not all sex offenders are created equal. Sex offenders are fathers, our brothers, our uncles, our mothers, our sisters, and our cousins. They are people we have in our lives right now, people we love very much. We know they are good and decent individuals who have made a mistake. We have to remember that people are worth more than the worst thing they have done in their lifetime.

There is no black-and-white rule that can be drawn as to how to treat offenders legally, professionally, academically, and morally because they are as different as the crimes they have committed. Would a parent feel the same if someone exposed themselves to their child as opposed to raping the child? What if the child was shown sexually explicit materials but was not touched? Would the parent's sense of anger and violation be different? Would the parent think to themselves, "At least my child wasn't raped, killed, or kidnapped—it could be worse?" From the perspective of a sexologist, while the treatment plans would be varied for the type of crime committed and the background of the person involved, there would be no distinguishing between offenders, no categorizing of offenders or placing them in a hierarchy from "bad" to "worse." In treatment, this is beneficial in helping individuals realize that their actions impact others and that they can learn from the experiences of other offenders in treatment. Thought processes are similar for voyeurs, exhibitionists, rapists, and child offenders, so if individuals can see a bit of themselves in others and how that behavior is perceived, it can be a great catalyst for change.

This book is primarily about people who have committed consensual or nonviolent behaviors that have resulted in significant punishment. It is about learning who sex offenders are and critically analyzing why they are treated so harshly in society. Chapter 1 sets the stage for this analysis by providing a historical foundation for examining sex offenses and sex offenders. We look at how religion has shaped our modern understanding of what constitutes a sex offense and how those who commit such offenses should be managed. We learn that religion helped to define sex offenders and that the medical community then stepped in to typologize and "treat" these individuals. This began with behaviors considered religiously immoral and shifted to identifying, labeling, and treating people who acted sexually in ways that society regarded as a nuisance.

Chapter 1 also examines the role of academia in defining and studying sex offending and offers explanations for the etiology of this important social issue.

Chapter 2 provides an in-depth analysis of various types of sex offenders that come to the attention of law enforcement to help us understand how many offenders we have in our midst. Moreover, it looks at the recidivism rates of offenders and examines whether there is a "typical" sex offender. Though research has indicated that most individuals have participated in a sexual act that is illegal (such as engaging in sexual activity in a public place, or urinating in public), most people have not been caught or punished for this behavior. Basically this means that those imprisoned are actually a very small fraction of those who have committed a sex offense. Those who get caught for crimes are often from lower socioeconomic backgrounds, may be from minority racial or ethnic groups, and often conform to stereotypical images of sex offenders.

Chapter 3 outlines the variety of laws the United States has imposed to deal with sex offenders. This chapter demonstrates that laws have changed to reflect the changing morality of America. Early sex offender laws targeted behaviors considered immoral, if not disgusting, to many people: homosexuals were the initial targets as it was believed they raped children, thus turning them gay. This seems utterly ridiculous to us now, but think of the current laws that focus on "stranger danger"—the lone male in a trench coat, walking around our neighborhoods assaulting people. Most sex offenses are committed by people we are related to or acquainted with, so why do politicians and the media focus almost exclusively on stranger assaults? First, they are sensational and make for compelling news stories. Society likes to read about how danger lurks in faraway places, thus reinforcing a sense of safety with those we know and love. Second, it is an easy political target: create a political buzz by being tough on crime. Third, it distracts the public from political mismanagement and social unrest. Crime legislation tends to create an "us" versus "them" mentality, thus establishing rifts among groups in society as opposed to focusing on the structural issues that lead to crime. Fourth, it may be a kneejerk response to a highly publicized tragic event, such as the rape and murder of a child by a repeat offender. While legislation may satisfy the public's immediate demand for justice, it virtually always lacks any basis in reality in terms of eradicating sexual violence at its source.

Chapter 4 looks at the practical application of the laws created to deal with sex offenders. Several case studies are examined that elaborate residency restrictions, civil commitment, and the death penalty. Each of these is a highly controversial control on sexual offenders, although we will see that some of these can have very negative consequences. This chapter also examines the media phenomenon of *Dateline's To Catch a Predator*

Chapter 5 discusses so-called sex crimes that are consensual but distasteful to many members of society. Oral sex, homosexuality, prostitution, sadomasochism, statutory offenses, bestiality, polygamy, and select types of incest are reviewed. Case studies are included in order to demonstrate that average people are being unfairly targeted by law enforcement and forced to pay for their sexual indiscretions for the rest of their lives. This theme is continued into

Chapter 6, which looks at the history of sexually explicit materials. We will learn that erotica has a long and colorful history and that it has been a cornerstone for challenging the status quo. This chapter examines adult and child sexually explicit materials, as well as Internet-based crimes.

Chapter 7 changes direction and looks at nonconsensual acts such as voyeurism, exhibitionism, sexual assault, and rape. This chapter seeks to challenge the common understanding of what a nonconsensual crime is, who is punished for these types of offenses, and the typical lengths of punishment. The book concludes with Chapter 8, which seeks to answer several remaining questions about sexual offenses and offenders. The chapter aims to dispel several common myths, such as: Are strangers the greatest source of danger? Do sex offenders keep reoffending and therefore pose a great risk to community safety if they are not indefinitely confined? Does community notification and registration increase community safety? And, do residency restrictions increase community safety?

What we have attempted to do by writing this book is to weave together a story to help you understand why members of society think and feel the way they do about sex crimes and sexual offenders today. It is not acceptable to take what our political, medical, religious, and academic leaders say at face value. We must critically analyze the laws that are being implemented on our behalf because it is very likely we are doing things in our bedrooms that could land us in jail! What society considers a socially acceptable behavior has changed dramatically throughout history, so what we consider immoral or illegal today may one day be decriminalized. This certainly has been the case for homosexuality (to an extent), premarital sex, oral sex (in most states), anal sex (in most states), as well as having multiple sexual partners. This book is written from a sex-positive perspective, meaning that we believe that sex in all its varied forms is good and good for you, so long as it is consensual and between equals. We believe the government has no place dictating what we can and cannot do inside our bedrooms. Enough with putting scarlet letters on people for doing what many others have done or continue to do with consensual partners. Instead of focusing efforts on punishing religiously based indiscretions, society should start focusing on eradicating actual sexual violence—behaviors that are nonconsensual, abusive, and harmful to society as a whole. This will require significant work and the cooperation of the legal, medical, and academic communities to help translate the structural causes of sexual violence into practical and flexible legislation. It is our hope that as you read this book you will become more cognizant of the complexity of this highly charged issue and remember that a person should not be defined by their worst action or behavior in life!

# PART I

# EXPLAINING SEXUAL OFFENDING

CHAPTER 1

# RELIGION, MEDICINE, AND SOCIAL SCIENCE

When thinking about sexual offending and sexual offenders the topics of religion, medicine, and academics probably do not come immediately to mind. Yet all three areas influence this highly charged topic and have done so historically. Each has played a role in defining the types of behavior that are considered "abnormal" and "deviant," and each has helped identify ways in which treatment of offenders should occur. Labels such as "sinner," "deviant," "pervert," "evil," and "unnatural" have been used by religion, medicine, and academia to create a separation between "us" and "them." The ultimate purpose has been to clearly demarcate how "good and moral" people behave versus those that are "immoral." One major problem with this distinction is that the definitions of offending behaviors have changed dramatically throughout history, and America has witnessed a huge shift in cultural norms in reference to behaviors that were once considered sexually offensive, such as homosexuality, oral sex, anal sex, and sex before marriage. How have religion, medicine, and social science shaped our understanding of sexual offending and sex offenders, and what impact does that have on our society today? These complicated and challenging questions will be examined by reviewing the sexual history of Judeo-Christianity, discussing the main medical text on sexuality (the *Diagnostic and Statistical Manual of Mental Disorders*), and exploring the various theories in social science used to understand sexual offending.

## Religion

American society is founded on the principles espoused by the Judeo-Christian perspective. These principles form the basis of the Constitution and federal and state laws. Notions of morality and deviant behavior stem in large measure from religious doctrine, yet many Americans would be surprised to learn that most of what the Bible and Torah preach about sex is actually positive and empowering. The Song of Songs celebrates all sorts of loving, sexual relationships between consenting adults. In fact, passages that specifically prohibit sexual acts represent less than 0.03 percent of the verses in the Hebrew and Christian testaments.[1] Sexual sin is more often defined as abuse or exploitation, such as when there is a lack of consent.[2] Thus, the Bible is not to be interpreted as a sexual code of conduct, but as a guide to how people should behave toward each other in all facets of life, including the sexual. This raises the question: how did society manage to focus on the few sex negative messages in religious texts and incorporate them into laws?

If you read the scriptures, it becomes evident that very little sexual behavior is prohibited, and the behavior that is listed addresses cultural issues present in Christian societies thousands of years ago. Historically, it was important to ensure the continuation of Christianity and Judaism through the generations; thus, homosexual behavior was considered immoral. It was also important to be able to trace lineage and ensure the propagation of healthy offspring; thus, certain forms of incest were also prohibited. After the importance of these issues faded, church leaders sought to establish concrete rules upon which the faiths would be based. For Christians, this meant that the church created Canonical Laws. Some of these laws dealt specifically with sex and sexuality and prohibited all behaviors that did not lead to procreation within the confines of heterosexual marriage. This meant that oral and anal sex, masturbation, and fantasy were not allowed, regardless of whether the parties were in a committed relationship.

The Torah, however, was somewhat more permissive in that it allowed behaviors that did not lead to procreation within marriage so long as the couple had children. Sex was not considered sinful or harmful, but there was a belief that it must be controlled and satisfied in a religiously appropriate way at a proper time and place. For the Jewish, debates surrounding sexuality began as early as 325 A.D. when rabbis argued over issues such as marriage eligibility, what sex acts were permissible, what sexual partnerships were allowed, and what role women should play in religious leadership. Similar to the Bible, the Torah is not to be taken literally but instead is to be used as a reference. Unlike Christians, however, followers of Judaism do turn to the Torah for information on sexual enjoyment, the concept of modesty, and how to translate these notions into practice. Importantly, both the Bible and the Torah do not prohibit many acts considered sexual offenses today, such as child sexual abuse, rape, exhibitionism, and voyeurism.

The church developed sexual rules for a variety of reasons. First, rules were a way to distinguish believers from nonbelievers. This in essence, created an "us" versus "them" mentality that is still prevalent. Believers can be redeemed so long as they follow church rules, but nonbelievers are subject to eternal damnation. Second, rules were a way for the church to control its members, especially members of the lower classes. For instance, in the seventeenth century, the church changed its rules related to confessionals and required all Christians to disclose not only the sexual acts in which they participated, but also their sexual thoughts and fantasies. This shift in church policy coincided with a new interest by the state to have laws regulating sexual behavior. Taking the lead from the church, the law now began to monitor all things sexual and administer punishments for what it considered to be inappropriate behavior. Controlling sexuality was a way to ensure that Christians would continue to reproduce and guarantee the next generation of followers.

With theologians constructing church laws (as opposed to actual scriptures informing church laws), how can we learn the stance of Christianity on sex and sexuality? This is definitely a challenging question, and the most obvious place to turn is the scriptures. However, scriptures were written in a time period that is completely foreign to our understanding today. To take the scriptures at face value would not be appropriate. Literal interpretations of the Bible would result in a ban on divorce, sex during menstruation, and remarriage, yet it would allow polygamy, prostitution, and the subordination of women. Obviously, the behaviors considered problematic in biblical times are fairly commonplace today. At this point, church theologians developed policies prohibiting certain behaviors, not because God commanded so, but because the church made a conscious decision to deem certain acts immoral.

Consider this: no new sex acts have been created since the Bible was written, and behaviors we now regard as illegal and immoral have been practiced for thousands of years in hundreds of cultures. So what makes these behaviors worse now than they were years ago? Generally speaking, behaviors become troublesome when they threaten the status quo—meaning that they challenge how society functions. This is the main reason that the church is so much against homosexuality and why, in America, homosexuality was illegal until just a few decades ago (and some "homosexual" acts, such as anal or oral sex, are still illegal in some states). Having sex for pleasure and not to procreate threatened the sanctity of marriage; although this could be said for most heterosexual couples today as well!

In biblical times, clear social and gender roles were used to prevent people from challenging the authority of the church or state. Interestingly, words like "sodomite" only appeared in the 1611 King James version of the Bible, and the term "homosexual" was not even coined until the nineteenth century. Therefore, it can be easily established that church doctrine about certain sexual behaviors has not been communicated by God, but has been developed recently by church leaders. These policies more accurately reflect the social mores of English society than actual religious teachings. Moreover, the Old and New Testaments are often contradictory in their teachings, with the New Testament (as communicated by Jesus) much more focused on love, acceptance, and forgiveness than the Old Testament.

The point of reviewing the history of sexuality in the church is not to demonize Christians for church doctrine on sex, but to demonstrate that even the views of the church change as society changes. Thus, it is not acceptable to literally interpret a document written thousands of years ago and apply it to the current day. In fact, most of the church's policies on sex were initially drafted in the fifth century under St. Augustine. This is when the focus of debate shifted, and married procreative sex came to be the idealized form of sexuality that all Christians were to aspire to (sex for the purposes of having a child).[3] This policy became so popular that hundreds of years later when the American colonies were being settled, it was brought over as the dominant ideology. The Puritans used it as the basis for their laws prohibiting all alternative sexualities, meaning any activity outside the confines of marriage and even some sex within marriage![4] With the help of the Puritans, a certain type of sexuality became the benchmark for the moral health of Christian communities and nations. Anyone deemed to be practicing an alternative sexuality was publicly named a sex offender by Puritans,[5] and ostracized in the same manner that we do today with sex offender registries.

How do we get from church policy to current laws? The church has always been effective at identifying what it considered to be deviant behavior and associating deviancy with sinfulness. As one scholar describes it:

> First, Christianity's influence over American society is strong, whether the currents of influence flow one way or two. Second, Christianity's influence over societal norms is felt most strongly in the realm of sexuality, specifically in regards to establishing a dominant/normative sexuality as well as alternative, deviant sexualities that exist outside of the norm. It can scarcely be denied that biblical sexual prohibitions have had a major effect on Western law. It is largely by biblical precepts that society today condemns adultery, male homosexuality, bestiality, and incest. Moreover, many criminal laws have at least partly religious origins. No area of criminal law feels Christianity's influence more than that which regulates sexual activity. One need only appreciate the language of morality inherent in sex crime statutes. Words and phrases such as "indecent," "lewd," "obscene," "immoral," and "the infamous crime against nature" indicate a normative morality and Christian history.[6]

This same scholar also describes the church's involvement in the current definitions of sex crimes:

> This view of sex offenders and its truth for a few offenders does, however, serve the American Christian need to create alternate sexualities as deviant and evil. Sex crimes law prohibits a few truly dangerous and incurable offenders from acting, but under the same "sex offense" category also outlaws homosexuality, public displays of nudity, obscenity (including porn), and risqué sexual proposals. Given society's pervasive religious foundation, it is not very hard to convince the public that all of these forms of sexuality are as bad under sex crimes law as was [Megan] Kanka's rape and murder. Instead of targeting the truly dangerous individuals, therefore, sex crimes and the offenders who are caught in them range from the truly dangerous to the utterly harmless.[7]

However, a major issue with church laws, and one that has been only minimally addressed by American laws, is that there is no distinction between the severity of sexual transgressions. In other words, a homosexual is as dangerous, sinful, and immoral as a rapist, an incest offender, or an adulterous wife. But how can this issue be addressed? Should the United States look to create a hierarchy of sex offending? If we do this, how do we measure harm? As discussed later in this chapter, some scholars suggest that sex acts, like intergenerational sex, may not cause as much harm as was originally thought.

While the church did not specifically outline what constitutes a sex crime, it did play a leading role in defining what is "deviant" and "immoral." Surprisingly, this information is not located within the Bible or Torah, but is the result of church leaders developing policies on the types of sexual practices considered appropriate for their followers. Thus, we cannot use the Bible or Torah as guides to ethical sexuality, but merely as documents to be viewed within the context in which they were written and ones that preach love and mutual respect. Unfortunately, knowledge about sex and access to various sexual outlets have been used by the church to control followers and create an "us" versus "them" way of thinking. The result has been that anyone who participates in an alternative sexuality, however, that is defined at a moment in history, is labeled deviant by both the church and the state. It is at this point that the medical establishment becomes involved in "treating" the deviances identified by the church and state.

## The Medical Model

Americans hold medical doctors in high esteem, believing them to possess valued knowledge about the mind and body. Medical science, however, has barely scratched the surface of how humans function or the interplay between the brain and attitudes and behavior. Historically, the medical community has regarded socially objectionable behavior, such as various sexual activities, as mental diseases. Thus, it was only logical that the religious and legal communities would defer to medical professionals to provide treatment. Unfortunately, the medical establishment, because it lacks specialized training and education in sexuality (the cultural and behavioral elements, as opposed to the biological and physiological components), has its own biases and misconceptions. Such misconceptions included that there is a primary genetic explanation for sexual crime, that permanent drug treatment is necessary for sexual offenders, and that there is no "cure" for sex criminals, so indefinite hospitalization and/or imprisonment is required. Although these myths have been dispelled, they still hold sway and impact the creation of public policy and the treatment of those deemed sex offenders.

The medical community, outside of the few who specialized in "deviancy," became actively involved with the issue of sexual offending after World War II when society began to increasingly focus on children and childhood. Crimes against children became one of the most pressing social issues of the time, likely as a result of a renewed focus on the family after many years of violence and hardship globally. Criminal sexual psychopath laws were written to identify mental disease as the underlying cause of supposed sexual indecency, and punishments included indeterminate imprisonment and medical treatment.[8] The response of the medical community was swift and decisive. Persons convicted of sex crimes were labeled perverts and diagnosed with increasingly violent tendencies and uncontrollable urges—this diagnosis was given regardless of the sexual activity in which the "offender" participated.[9] However, at this time in history, sex crimes tended to have a moral-religious undertone, and were predominantly defined as homosexuality, transgenderism, and intergenerational sex (e.g., a 20-year-old male having sex with a 16-year-old female). Thus, the role of the medical community was overwhelmingly to eliminate the sexual behaviors that society found distasteful, and professionals advanced this goal through the use of drug therapy and other highly intrusive procedures. The result was largely a failure with extremely low success rates.[10]

Regardless of the ultimate failure of the medical community in relation to the treatment of sexual offending, a complex system of treatment modalities had been created to thoroughly establish the medical community as the ultimate authority on sexual offending.[11] The research used by the medical community to legitimate their claims is highly suspect because it is based on persons convicted of sex crimes, as opposed to all persons who have committed a sex crime. This is a major distinction and one that cannot be overstated. It is well established that those convicted represent a very small fraction of those who actually commit sexually based crimes. So why is this relevant to a discussion of the involvement of the medical community in sex offender treatment? There are two main reasons: (1) sexual behavior and what is considered acceptable behavior varies according to social class, and doctors are often from higher socioeconomic levels than those charged and convicted of sexual offenses, and (2) people from the lower social classes are overwhelmingly over-represented in prisons. Moreover, research has shown that there is no difference between how nonconvicted or criminally charged males respond to stimuli illustrating sexual coercion (e.g., rape) compared to men who are imprisoned for a sex crime.[12] The underlying premise of the medical model is that a sex offender is a stranger to his victims, is highly predatory, and suffers from some form of personality disorder or mental abnormality.[13] In essence, the medical model takes what society regards as nuisance behavior or social immorality and turns it into a mental health issue.

Case in point: *The Diagnostic and Statistical Manual* (DSM) is the text that virtually all mental health professionals and medical doctors use to diagnose and develop treatment plans for sex offenders. There is enormous controversy surrounding the *DSM*, and virtually all of its elements elicit criticism, from classifications of sexual offenses to descriptions of sexual offenses to treatment plans for sexual offenders. The main issue with the *DSM* is that it takes behaviors considered socially unacceptable and turns them into psychiatric illnesses. If 50 percent of society has participated, or regularly participates in a behavior, then it is considered "normal." This is problematic when you consider that unsafe sex, serial monogamy, divorce, infidelity, and other stigmatized behaviors are participated in by over half of all Americans. Is having unsafe sex with multiple partners whom you have known for a very short period of time morally right? Is cheating on your spouse acceptable if most people have engaged in this behavior? These questions are best debated through another venue, but the point remains clear: just because a lot of people do something does not automatically make it morally or ethically correct—and therefore not "offensive!"

The *DSM* has been used by therapists, psychologists, and psychiatrists to establish legitimacy for their respective disciplines. The emphasis is on defining and labeling people, and this is achieved through classifying individuals as "abnormal." Consequently, socially unacceptable behavior is labeled as abnormal, deviant, and abhorrent.[14] Some examples are homosexuality, sadomasochism, and intergenerational sex. Throughout most of American history, homosexual behavior has been illegal and highly stigmatized. There was a time that the religious, medical, and legal communities believed all homosexual men were pedophiles. Obviously, we now know that this is not true, but the thought of homosexuality is still upsetting to many segments of our society. For these reasons (and because less than half the population admitted engaging in such behavior), homosexuality was listed as a mental disorder in the *DSM*. People charged with sodomy or gross indecency, the most common charges associated with homosexuality, were often committed to mental institutions for treatment. Sadomasochism is another example that research indicates is part of the vast majority of sexual unions at some point now.[15] Most couples incorporate biting, scratching, or spanking into their sex lives . . . so is this behavior deviant? If it occurs consistently or if you have fantasized about it consistently over the course of six months or more, then according to the *DSM*, it is indeed deviant! The last example, intergenerational sex, is much more controversial. Historically, it has been socially acceptable for adolescents to engage in sexual relations with older partners, especially young females with older men. It was not unusual to have a young woman marry and assume the responsibilities of motherhood after the death of an older man's wife. So why is it considered child abuse for a teenager to have sex with a person in their twenties, thirties, or older? Biologically, teenagers are physically capable of having sexual relations and reproducing, so why is this not socially acceptable? Is it more socially acceptable if the adult is a female and the teenager is a male?

The *DSM* contains over 40 sexual behaviors that are regarded as psychiatric, and this has enormous implications for people labeled with a sexual disorder. Being labeled impacts one's access to insurance, employment, and security clearances. The behaviors contained within the *DSM* are socially constructed, meaning that they are not *inherently* wrong or bad. They have been identified as "abnormal" by medical doctors and are subject to change at any time in history. As mentioned previously, homosexuality was considered a mental illness and listed in the *DSM*, and only through much lobbying and advocacy was it removed from the *DSM*. However, the fight continues to remove cross-dressing and other similar behaviors from the *DSM*. More importantly, though, behaviors that most Americans would agree are morally wrong and violate human rights, such as rape, are not listed in the *DSM*. Obviously, this is very controversial as consensual activity between adults is listed as abnormal and requiring medical intervention, whereas raping someone is not.

### *Who Has Influenced the Making of a Sex Offender?*

Thus far, we have examined the medical model and how it poses problems in the treatment of sex offenders. Another part of history that is important to review are some of the influential people who first studied human sexuality and helped label the behaviors currently regarded as criminal. Although at first it may appear that psychology and psychiatry are the main disciplines related to this topic, the most influential and far-reaching field is sexology. Sexology is the study of what people do sexually, their attitudes about sex and sexuality, and the connection between attitudes and behaviors. We will be looking at four predominant sexological thinkers and researchers to help illustrate how viewpoints on sexual offenders have changed. The thinkers are Sigmund Freud, Richard von Krafft-Ebing, Alfred Kinsey, and Wardell Pomeroy.

Sigmund Freud is best known as a psychoanalyst and a creator of modern talk therapy, but he was also a sexologist and wrote extensively about human sexuality. Freud focused most of his sexological writing on what he considered deviant behavior, such as bestiality (sexual activity with animals), homosexuality, viewing sexually explicit materials, and exhibitionism. In his earlier work, Freud was extremely conservative in his views and believed that most violent crime, especially of a sexual nature, was the result of homosexuality. He popularized the belief that all homosexuals are child molesters and in this sense did a great disservice to the academic world. Unfortunately, Freud used his position as a scholar and therapist to give legitimacy to ideas that were not founded on any type of empirical data or research. For Freud, anything outside of penis-vagina sex was considered abnormal and a possible area of concern.[16]

However, as Freud aged and started corresponding more frequently with other sexological scholars, his positions on sexual deviancy became more liberal. Freud drafted letters and articles about how certain sexual behaviors he once deemed extremely deviant, such as fetishism (a fixation on objects), were completely benign if the person could still enjoy sexual relations with others. Unfortunately, such writings rarely made it into the public domain, and religious and legal leaders as well as other medical professionals still contended that certain solo sexual behaviors, such as fetishism and masturbation, were gateways to increasingly violent sexual assaults.

One of Freud's most profound comments was his description that everyone could be classified as a sex offender—a point reiterated with much controversy decades later by Alfred Kinsey:

> If circumstances favor such an occurrence, normal people too can substitute a perversion of this kind for the normal sexual aim for quite a time, or can find place for the one alongside the other. No healthy person, it appears, can fail to make some addition that might be called perverse to the normal sexual aim; and the universality of this finding is in itself enough to show how inappropriate it is to use the word perverse as a term of reproach.[17]

By the end of his career, Freud had concluded that the definition of perversity had to be narrowed to ensure the medical and legal professions were not targeting all socially undesirable behaviors. Consequently, he argued for a definition of perversity based on a person's inability to maintain familial or social relations, employment, or recreation, and it applied only if their fixation was their sole sexual interest. In this way, Freud was a trailblazer for advocating for a more narrow definition of sexual offending and one that could be customized to the accused.

Freud corresponded regularly with Richard von Krafft-Ebing, a leading sexologist of the nineteenth and twentieth centuries. Krafft-Ebing wrote extensively on all things related to sex and was the author of the first comprehensive classification manual for sexual disturbances entitled *Psychpathia Sexualis*. This book was published in 1906 and provided the foundation for the *DSM*. It was used extensively by the medical and legal communities in dealing with people who were charged with sexually based crimes.[18] Similar to Freud, Krafft-Ebing was extremely conservative and held strict Victorian notions about normal and abnormal sexual behavior, believing that sexual behavior that did not lead to procreation was perverse and subject to penalty.[19] To his credit, he did shine a bright light on behaviors that were never before publicly discussed and outlined what he considered to be the causes and best treatments for a variety of sexological disorders.[20] On the other hand, he made popular the belief that sex criminals had uncontrollable sexual urges and needed to gratify those urges through the use of violence. Moreover, he contended that men with high sex drives were the people who committed incest, adultery, child abuse, rape, and public masturbation.[21] For Krafft-Ebing, the source of offending rested in mental illness, likely inherited or caused by masturbation.[22] Obviously, the (mistaken) notion that masturbation causes harm is very old indeed!

Krafft-Ebing is a highly controversial figure within sexology. He has caused much harm by labeling behaviors he considered to be offensive as criminal and abnormal—and these labels still exist today! For a profession that prides itself on being sex positive, this founding member who has left such a negative legacy is troubling. However, what it really demonstrates is: (1) people have been having sex in numerous ways

---

**What Do You Think?**

Masturbation has been blamed for a whole host of social problems and was believed to be the cause of most mental diseases. Religious leaders regarded masturbation as a source of evil because it provided sexual gratification and did not lead to procreation. The medical community and many sexology scholars considered masturbation a gateway to other mental illnesses as well as crime. Just as the medical community believes today that smoking marijuana will lead to drug addiction and the use of "harder" drugs, it was believed years ago that masturbation caused retardation, hypersexuality, and sexual violence. Recently, some sexologists have actually been using masturbation as part of the treatment plan for persons who have offended sexually to help them realign their sexual fantasies to socially and legally appropriate stimuli. This method remains controversial. Did you know there are many advantages of masturbation? Some advantages include:

- It helps people to understand that sex is a good thing and not something to feel guilty about.
- It makes a person a better lover because they know what they like and what feels good and can translate that into sex in relationships.
- It allows people to avoid dependance on others for their sexual gratification.
- It lets people have an active sex life who are otherwise uninterested or inhibited or who have handicaps (mental or physical) that would prevent them from finding partners.
- It provides physical and mental release from stress or physical tension.
- It is the safest sex possible.
- It is a sex drive equalizer within relationships.
- It can provide an outlet for sexual feelings that are not reciprocated.

What do you think? Is masturbation immoral or sinful, or is it an innate way to receive sexual satisfaction and release tension?

for centuries, so much so that it has been deemed worthy of study, and (2) behaviors considered unusual at one point in history are considered illegal or perfectly acceptable in another. Thus, what Krafft-Ebing taught is that sex offending is socially constructed, and the treatments designed for offenders are equally as varied. Krafft-Ebing believed that offending behaviors could be stopped through masturbation prevention (e.g., steel devices that would prick the penis of a male when it became erect, or through removing or burning the clitoris in women), through hypnotic suggestion or through good hygiene (side note: Victorian times linked hygiene—read poverty—with sex crimes).[23] Krafft-Ebing proved right in his assertion that sex crimes are the result of emotions being redirected to a sexual outlet. In other words, a person is unable or unwilling to experience his emotions and instead seeks sex to compensate. He also put forth the notion that there is a difference between offenders who commit sex crimes because the opportunity arises and those who plan their crimes in advance. These notions continue to be recognized in the law today and play a role in sentencing.

The academic discipline of sex came to a halt with World Wars I and II and Hitler's destruction of much of the sexological materials written by the leading scholars of the time. During the mid to late 1940s, sexology experienced a resurgence with the work of Alfred Kinsey and his research team. Kinsey conducted the most comprehensive cataloging of sex behaviors, an accomplishment that is unmatched to this day. Kinsey and his colleagues interviewed thousands of men and women about their sexual behaviors and learned that many people have engaged in sexual acts, such as bestiality or homosexuality, that were illegal at the time.[24] Moreover, he challenged the public about the supposed harm caused by certain sexual activities, such as intergenerational sex, as his research demonstrated that most people felt no lasting negative effects from such contacts.[25]

Kinsey spoke out boldly against sex crimes legislation: ". . . poorly established distinctions between normality and abnormality lead to the enactment of sexual psychopath laws which are unrealistic, unenforceable, and incapable of providing the protection which the social organization has been led to believe they can provide."[26] He also believed that sex crimes and sex criminals were socially constructed and that arrests had more to do with the sexual attitudes and behaviors of law enforcement personnel than actual offending behaviors.[27] His research revealed that less than 1 percent of individuals who commit sex crimes are ever charged, prosecuted, or convicted, and that to have effective sex crimes legislation, it was necessary to compare and contrast those convicted with those who committed sex crimes but were never brought to the attention of law enforcement.[28]

Kinsey managed to bring to public attention the myriad of sexual behaviors in which people participated. Unfortunately, Kinsey failed to ask in-depth questions about select behaviors such as group sex, sadomasochism, and voyeurism because he was uninterested in these acts academically.[29] The result was that society was led to believe these behaviors were abnormal or somehow wrong—views that still exist today. More importantly, by demonstrating that people engage in a wide variety of sexual activities, Kinsey challenged lawmakers to justify their reasons for the illegality of such behaviors. This helped push forward the gay rights movement and emboldened the sexual revolution that was to come in the following decades.

One of Kinsey's lead researchers was Wardell Pomeroy, and he continued to conduct significant sexological research after parting ways with Kinsey. Along with fellow researchers from Kinsey's team, Pomeroy led the first and only comprehensive study of convicted sexual offenders. Unlike studies today that involve a few dozen or a hundred subjects, Pomeroy and his team interviewed over 1,500 convicted sex offenders and took detailed sexual histories of the participants. He then compared the responses of the convicted offenders with those who had committed the same crimes and had not been caught, as well as a control group of men who had not committed any sexual offenses. The research led to the first typology of sex offenders and was intended to lead public policymakers into making more informed sex crimes legislation. As a result of this research, a new definition of sex offender was offered, which stated that a sexual act must be committed for "immediate sexual gratification" that goes against what is sexually acceptable to society, is legally punishable, and results in a legal conviction.[30] To illustrate the reasoning behind the proposed definition, the following example was offered:

1. A truck driver in a roadside café seats himself in a booth, gives the waitress his order, and as she turns to depart, pats her on the buttocks. The other drivers who witness this are not offended, nor is the waitress, who is either inured to such behavior or interprets it as a slightly flattering pleasantry.
2. The same behavior occurs in a middle-class restaurant. The waitress feels that an indignity has been committed upon her person, and many of the witnesses consider it an offensive display of bad manners. The offender is reprimanded and asked to leave.
3. A man bestows the same pat upon an attractive but unknown woman on a city street. She summons a nearby policeman, some indignant witnesses gather to voice their versions of the offense, and the man is ultimately charged with a sexually motivated assault.[31]

As can be seen, the context of the sexual act is extremely important in determining whether it is criminal or not. Too frequently, however, American laws fail to take into account the context of an act and instead are based solely on a black-and-white notion of appropriate versus inappropriate sexual behavior. Pomeroy's efforts were a huge contribution to the field, as they challenged lawmakers to be more cognizant of the variances in sexual behavior and morality among different social classes, religions, and genders. In combination, Sigmund Freud, Richard von Krafft-Ebing, Alfred Kinsey, and Wardell Pomeroy have made significant contributions to societal understanding of sexual behaviors and the definition of a sexual offender.

## How Do Social Scientists Explain Sexual Offending?

Social science theories from sociology or criminology have not been as widely applied to the understanding of sexual offenses and sexual offending as psychological theories or even feminist theories. Despite this lapse thus far, a number of criminological theories that have their roots in sociology can provide relevant explanations for sexual offending. As disciplines, sociology and criminology suggest that social problems are rooted in the structural elements of society. Therefore, individual factors cannot explain social issues; instead a societal explanation is required. It is believed that social and cultural factors influence our attitudes toward sexual offenses, what we consider a sexual offense, how we view sexual offenders, as well as the significance of sexual offenses as a problem in American society. Generally, sociologists and criminologists focus on the social environment of the offender and social interaction patterns in specific situations. The social scientific theories relevant to sexual offending that will be discussed are social learning theory, social control theory, rational choice theory, and social reaction theory.

### Learning from Associates: Social Learning Theory

According to social learning theorists, people learn behavior through imitation from their closest associates. We learn to tie our shoes from our sister or to ride a bicycle from a parent. In a similar fashion, we also learn attitudes that are either favorable or unfavorable to inappropriate sexual behaviors and interaction from those we grow up with and those we are close to. Social learning theorists believe that sexual beings are not born; they are created through influences after birth. Sexually inappropriate behaviors are believed to be "learned" as a result of being sexually abused as a child or viewing sexual abuse in the home or elsewhere. One of the most well-known social learning theorists, Edwin Sutherland, used the term "differential association" to refer to the fact that the key factor in whether or not someone would participate in a deviant behavior was the group of individuals with whom they associated.[32] In essence, if the people a person associates with have favorable attitudes toward deviance and there are more favorable consequences to deviant behavior, then an individual is more likely to engage in this behavior. Social learning theory argues that deviant behavior, including sexual offending, is a learning process that can affect anyone in any culture, and that the skills and motives behind deviance are learned as a result of contact with values, attitudes, and definitions favorable of such behavior. Using the logic of this theoretical approach, a person would engage in sexual offending behaviors as long as they are surrounded by "pro-deviant" values and behaviors that are not matched or exceeded by more "traditional" values and behaviors. That is, people may engage in sexual offending behaviors as adults if they are surrounded by family and friends who are supportive of rape myths and are disrespecting of women, if they grew up in a household in which there was sexual abuse, and if they do not have other friends or venues in their life to convey to them that this behavior is not appropriate. This does not guarantee sexually offensive behavior but increases the likelihood of such behavior according to social learning theorists.

In addition to the values and behaviors of close associates, rewards and punishments are also believed to play an important role in how an individual learns, according to this theory. If a specific behavior is rewarded among a group of friends, an individual is more likely to engage in that behavior in the future. Conversely, if an individual engages in a behavior and his friends look down on that behavior, he is less likely to repeat it in the future. In this way, rewards and punishments among those close to us also help shape and mold behavior according to social learning theory. So, for example, if an individual makes a disparaging remark about a woman in front of friends, and the friends respond in a chastising manner as opposed to laughing or encouraging his behavior, the individual is unlikely to repeat this behavior (at least with this group of friends). The strongest influence on behavior during the formative childhood years comes from the family, which provides the foundation for the "intergenerational cycle of violence theory." This theory suggests that violence, including sexual offending, is passed from generation to generation via a repetitive cycle within the family. However, the problem with explaining sexual offending using this theory is that while many sexual offenders experience sexual abuse during their childhood, many more individuals who were sexually victimized as children grow into functional adults who never sexually victimize another individual. Social learning theorists would suggest that these individuals who do not mature into sexual offenders surrounded themselves with associates and friends later in life that did not support a deviant lifestyle. Therefore, they were able to overcome the messages sent to them during their childhood. Unfortunately, when considering the significance of the childhood years on formative development, this explanation is somewhat problematic.

In addition to family and friends, social learning theorists also acknowledge that the larger society can contribute to learning attitudes that are "pro-deviant" regarding sex, through television, films, video games, music lyrics, music videos, sexually explicit material (pornography), or the like. The closer an individual's lifestyle and history matches this "pro-deviant" societal view, the more likely they are to engage in inappropriate sexual behavior. Of course, there are many "traditional" messages put forward in this same medium, so it is often a matter of the individual seeking out messages that conform to beliefs that they already possess on some level (as in the case of pornography). Social learning theory purports that an individual can learn "pro-deviant" values and behaviors from a variety of sources, including family, friends, and societal messages. These messages contribute to offenders becoming desensitized to deviant acts so they no longer perceive the behavior as morally wrong.

### The Influence of Culture: Social Control Theory

Many individuals engage in crime or deviance because it results in some sort of reward, whether it is a psychological benefit, an emotional benefit, or a sexual benefit of sorts. For social control theorists, the deterring factor for some individuals is either a high level of self-control or their commitment to a sense of conformity in society. In other words, social control theorists believe that some people choose to obey the rules because they are controlled by their attachment and association to conventional society. Applied to sexual offending, social control theorists would suggest that society has constructed a continuum of sexual behaviors that are considered appropriate or inappropriate, and the vast majority of individuals choose not to violate social norms. As such, the question for social control theorists becomes: why do some people follow the rules and others do not?

The most prominent social control theorist is Travis Hirschi.[33] He suggests that each individual has the potential to become a deviant, but most individuals maintain control over themselves because they fear damaging the relationships they share with the friends and family close to them. Thus, the way to decrease the likelihood of deviance is to increase a person's involvement in conventional activities in society, which can strengthen that person's bonds to traditional society. In the late 1960s, Travis Hirschi outlined four main elements that he believed would bond an individual to society: attachment, commitment, beliefs, and involvement.[34] Attachment involves a person's connection with family, friends, and the community, which serves to build respect for other individuals as well as for society's norms. Second, the level of commitment a person has to society is believed to be related to their likelihood of engaging in deviance: the more committed an individual is to society and its goals and beliefs, the less likely that individual is to risk their position in society by engaging in deviance. Hirschi's third element, beliefs, represents a tie to conventional values such as honesty, morality, fairness, and responsibility. The more likely an individual is to support these traditional values, the less likely they are to violate society's norms. Finally, involvement refers to an individual's investment in the community's activities in terms of sports, community organizations, or social clubs, which often leave little time for involvement in deviance. These four elements, according to Hirschi, serve to bond an individual to society and decrease the likelihood of their engaging in acts of deviance, including sexual deviance, because they do not want to risk their position in the community or risk their relationships with family and friends.[35]

Building on social control theory, Travis Hirschi worked with Michael Gottfredson in 1990 and suggested that those individuals with low self-control or those lacking entirely in self-control, if provided the opportunity, were the most likely to engage in crime.[36] They suggested that individuals with little to no self-control were impulsive, more likely to take risks, and shortsighted. All of these factors made these individuals more likely to engage in deviance if provided the opportunity and to engage in a variety of offenses. Interview data has confirmed this suggestion and the importance of opportunity for sexual offenders, with those incarcerated for sexual offenses admitting to a history of both sexual offenses and nonsexual offenses,[37] although pedophiles as a group seem to be less "generalist," meaning they are less likely to engage in a variety of criminal offenses.[38]

According to social control theorists, the way to reduce sexual offenses would be for society to widely condemn these behaviors and be committed to investigating and prosecuting these claims in a manner that provides swift, certain, and proportional punishment by the criminal justice system. This systematic response would create a situation in which an offender would be deterred from committing an offense due to the loss of bonds and humiliation by family, friends, and the community.[39]

### Individual Decisions: Rational Choice Theory

The U.S. criminal justice system works on the assumption that individuals make rational decisions and that they can therefore be deterred by the "threat" of punishment. The justice system assumes that before an individual engages in a criminal act, he considers the possible punishment that could result from that act and decides to engage in the behavior anyway after a careful consideration of the pros and cons. There are two types of deterrence: specific deterrence and general deterrence. Specific deterrence seeks to deter an individual who has already committed a crime from committing another offense once released from prison. For example, an individual who has committed a sexual offense and served his time in prison is then given community supervision for life upon his release in order to deter him from committing a subsequent offense. General deterrence seeks to deter those "potential" offenders in society by making "examples" of individuals who have committed a crime, thereby instilling the fear of punishment. For example, potential offenders can be deterred from committing a sexual offense (according to the general deterrence model) because they have seen the severe punishment of individuals convicted of similar offenses. Some potential offenders, however, do not view the potential punishment as severe because they do not believe they will get caught. For example: one man imprisoned for rape said: "At the time I didn't think of it as rape, just [sex] ... but I knew I was doing wrong. But I also knew most women don't report rape and I didn't think she would either."[40] Another man convicted for rape expressed a similar sentiment: "I knew what I was doing. I just said, the hell with the consequences. I told myself what I was going to do was rape ... but I didn't think I would go to prison."[41] The comments of each of these men illustrate their rational calculation prior to committing a sexual offense. Each man acknowledged that he knew the act was wrong, but neither felt the potential costs or the likelihood of getting caught was significant.

The question for rational choice theorists, however, is: why are some individuals deterred (either by specific or general measures) and other individuals are not deterred? A number of factors go into an individual's calculation of whether or not to engage in crime. Most simply, an individual weighs the pros and cons in a cost-benefits analysis prior to the commission of a sexual offense. If, in the mind of the potential offender, the benefits of the offense outweigh the potential risks, they are likely to engage in crime. In order to deter an offender from committing a crime, punishment in the criminal justice system must be *perceived* as swift, certain, and severe enough to offset the benefits of a crime. With sex crimes, there are also additional factors to consider, such as moral inhibition that the individual must overcome, lowered self-control, a lack of empathy that must be present, and a physical and/or psychological pleasure that is often associated with this type of offending. These are termed extra-legal factors (aside from the considerations of punishment by the criminal justice system) that a potential offender considers when weighing the costs versus the benefits of sexual offending. In addition, there are situational factors that are analyzed, such as whether or not there is a victim that is deemed appropriate and whether there is an opportunity to offend against this victim. Based on factors such as prior experience with the criminal justice system (specific deterrence) or knowing other offenders involved in the criminal justice system (general deterrence), along with individual psychological processes and situational context, rational choice theorists suggest that the offender makes a rational choice or calculation to commit an offense.

Studies have been conducted which support that sexual offenders are both rational and calculating in the commission of their offenses.[42] For example, research on rapists has suggested that the offense and victim may be planned,[43] and that some rapists have a preplanned script that they follow during an attack.[44] Studies that evaluate decision making among men who sexually abuse their female children suggests that offenders weigh opportunities and consider victim characteristics and risk factors prior to offending.[45] Perhaps one drawback of rational choice theory is that it is very subjective; what one offender may consider a "benefit" of offending, another may consider a "risk." As such, it is very individual in scope and is therefore not very useful in creating broad policy solutions to sexual offending.

### What's in a Label? Social Reaction Theory

Labeling theory (also called social reaction theory) asserts that there are some behaviors (and therefore the individuals who commit such behaviors) that are likely to be labeled negatively by society and by the criminal justice system. This label results in an individual being stigmatized by traditional society. The result is a negative societal response, which often fuels the individual's return to the questionable behavior. Social reaction theorists suggest that the meanings we assign to events and behaviors are shaped by our social and cultural experiences, so that what is acceptable at one time and place may be entirely unacceptable at another time and place.

Using sexual offending as an example, the stages of the labeling process are traditionally as follows. First, an individual commits a sexual offense. This theoretical approach does not attempt to explain the initial motivation for an offense, so the reasons why an individual would commit this type of offense could be varied. Second, this individual's behavior is brought to the attention of others or to the attention of the criminal justice system. Third, some (but not all) of the individuals who commit a sexual offense are officially labeled as criminals. They are labeled through the process of being arrested and formally charged by the criminal justice system and may be further labeled by widespread media exposure. As elaborated earlier, if the victim was a stranger, the likelihood of arrest is substantially higher. In addition, other individuals may officially be labeled through registration and notification procedures. A man convicted of attempted sexual abuse of a minor illustrates the impact of a stigma:

> There is so much stigma I hardly know where to begin. People look at child sex offenders as a hideous monster kind of thing. They don't want to be near you. People act like they [sex offenders] are like on the verge of just, like they are lust-crazed animals and I don't think that is the case . . . It can be anybody. I mean, it can be your priest, it can be your gardener, it can be anybody, you know . . . it could be you. I never pictured myself as a monster . . . I do see myself as a child molester. I don't see myself as the monster at all, but I see that people will view me that way.[46]

Another perpetrator convicted of a sexual offense against a minor female said:

> My biggest concern about this whole thing is that I did not want to be labeled as a sex offender. I mean, I recognize I am a sex offender. I committed a sex offense against a minor. But, I did not want to be *publicly* labeled as a sex offender . . . Why don't they label other offenders? Drunk drivers kill people every day but they are not labeled like sex offenders are.[47]

Conversely, other individuals (primarily offenders who are acquainted with their victim or are a family member of the victim) are not as often officially labeled or brought to the attention of the criminal justice system and avoid entirely the stigma associated with the commission of such an offense. In the fourth stage, the individuals who were labeled for engaging in a criminal sexual offense are now viewed negatively by conventional society, and they are viewed with disrespect and distrust by the larger community. Especially in the case of sexual offenders, society has an extremely negative reaction to this type of offense and, as such, to this type of offender. The longer and more frequently an individual is exposed to this negative label, the more likely he is to come to accept and internalize it. The fifth stage, and part of the internalization of the negative label, is when the individual starts to accept the stigma that has been associated with his offense and begins to regularly associate with others who have been similarly labeled. Once individuals accept their negative label and the stigma associated with this label, it may also decrease the ability to reintegrate these individuals into the community successfully and have the unforeseen consequence of increasing the likelihood that these persons will commit another sexual offense.

Using labeling theory to talk about sexual offending would involve exploring the ramifications of an individual being labeled publicly as a sexual offender. What happens if a person's sexual offenses are made public? What if an individual's picture is posted on a sexual offender Web site for others to find, and now his family and friends and co-workers know of his offense? What if his picture is on a poster in local supermarkets and other venues? How do these actions, this labeling, affect the ability of an individual to reintegrate successfully into a community? According to social reaction theorists, once an offense has been widely revealed and an individual is labeled by others as deviant or criminal, they are more likely to repeat the behavior because they have internalized the personality characteristics that other people expect. As such, the likelihood of subsequent sexual offenses could be decreased if society and the criminal justice system did not publicly label individuals through the use of community notification policies that have a potentially stigmatizing effect. Social reaction theory shifts the focus away from the question of why an individual would commit a sexual offense to society's reaction to sexual offenders. Labeling theorists attempt to address questions such as: Why are certain sexual offenses not pursued as vigorously by the criminal justice system as other sexual offenses? Why do some sexual offenders become publicly stigmatized and labeled, yet others engaging in the very same behavior avoid the societal stigma? How does labeling of individuals affect their lives and their choices for the future? Labeling theory raises some extremely interesting and important questions surrounding sexual offenses.

## How Do Sexologists Explain Sexual Offending?

The study of human sexuality is a highly valuable and extremely complex area of inquiry because sex is not just biological and physiological, it is also emotional, cultural, and often gender specific. Sexology is a discipline that examines both what people do sexually, and also how they feel about their behavior. Unlike other disciplines, sexology is a combination of research, education, and clinical applications, meaning that sexologists also see clients about their sexual concerns as opposed to just studying those concerns academically. Although sexology has been in existence for over 100 years, there is great debate among its practitioners as to whether there is one unifying theory to explain all things sexual. Despite this debate, all sexologists accept one fundamental principle: sex is good and good for you, and it must be described in positive terms without the use of labels. Why is this explanation necessary? When it comes to dealing with persons who have offended sexually, sexologists do not use labels to describe the individuals. Terms like "deviant," "pervert," "predator," "immoral," "evil," or "abnormal" are shunned because they have such a profound influence on how people are treated by society and how those labeled respond to treatment. Instead, the phrase "person who has offended sexually" is used because it humanizes the person and separates the person from their behavior. Here is an analogy to help illustrate this point: a group of friends go out for a night on the town; they have some beers and smoke marijuana. They are all feeling good and having fun, and then as a joke a few of them decide to flash a passerby. Would we call these friends alcoholics? Drug addicts? Sex offenders? Probably not, despite the fact that they are committing at least two illegal acts by smoking marijuana and participating in gross indecency. Labeling these individuals as sex offenders would have significant repercussions socially and would follow the group of friends for their entire lives.

There is some general consensus in the field of sexology that people's attitudes about sex do not align with their behaviors. Kinsey proved this empirically in his two groundbreaking studies on the sexual behavior of men[48] and women.[49] Basically, Kinsey found that people are conservative in their attitudes but liberal in their behavior. Kinsey and his research team discovered that many people routinely participate in illegal sexual activities, such as oral and anal sex and intergenerational sex. He learned that such behaviors are engaged in by all social classes and educational levels, and that there is a significant gap between what is culturally and religiously sanctioned and what actually occurs. To help understand how sexology views sexual offending, we will look at two theoretical frameworks: the socio-sexual response cycle and sexual anthropology.

### Socio-Sexual Response Cycle

The Socio-Sexual Response Cycle (SSRC) is used as a clinical model in sexology to help people understand their sexual decision making. The SSRC examines how people respond to sexual stimuli within their social environment (e.g., social class, gender, educational level) and how people subsequently manage their sexuality. The model suggests that each sexual encounter is composed of a series of decisions with multiple options available. Each time sexual stimuli is presented, a person negotiates their sexual choices both internally and externally. In other words, a person must decide if and when to proceed with a sexual situation and must also speak with their potential sexual partner about whether they want to proceed and with what types of activities. It is a holistic approach that encompasses both desire and the consideration of options. For persons who have offended sexually, the crime occurs during the phase in which they are considering their options . . . when they decide to proceed without the consent of their potential partner.[50]

Society condemns many sexual activities that average people routinely perform so sexology advocates for more expanded definitions of sexual options so that inappropriate sexual behaviors become unnecessary.[51] The SSRC is used in clinical settings to give persons who have offended sexually permission to be sexual in socially acceptable ways by providing them with additional sexual outlets they may have previously been unaware of by using fantasy to formulate consensual activities.[52] Sexologists use the SSRC to take these newly created fantasies based on consensual activity and transfer them to reality. This is accomplished by taking detailed sexual histories of offenders in order to understand what they have read, watched, and been exposed to, as well as to understand the thought processes that influence them most profoundly.[53]

Basically, the SSRC forces people to identify what they want sexually, advocates communication of these desires to potential partners, and then promotes negotiation with potential partners about the specifics. This is an exercise in good relationship communication, and one that we all should be having with our sexual partners—but unfortunately, it is one that very few of us are comfortable with. For offenders, identifying what they want is fairly straightforward, it is asking and gaining consent that is often problematic. Most persons who offend sexually are good people who have made mistakes: they have taken the easy route by assuming that because a person smiles, engages in conversation, kisses them, or wears provocative clothing that their behavior is equivalent to consent. Society has fostered a lot of these notions by sexualizing almost everything from deodorant to shoes to watches. Think back to the controversy in the 1980s when feminists fought to have sexual harassment and date rape defined as criminal and to incorporate rape shield protections into the law. It was only a short time ago that most of society believed that a woman was asking to be raped if she was out at night alone, had multiple sexual partners, or wore revealing clothing. Indeed, some still believe these rape myths! The point here is that

### The SSRC in Practice

John is out on a third date with Joanne. He is really attracted to her and thinks that she is to him as well. He planned a special evening with dinner, dancing, and wine back at his place. Joanne is enjoying the evening and agrees to go back to John's place for some wine. She likes John and thinks there is a real possibility of a relationship. Back at John's house, they enjoy a glass of wine and some conversation about their childhoods. Joanne places her hand on John's knee, which he sees as an opportunity to get more sexual. He leans over and kisses her. Joanne responds and kisses John back. But when John moves his hand over Joanne's breast, she moves away. She tells John she must go home because she has to work tomorrow. John thinks Joanne is playing hard to get and really wants to stay and have sex. He leans over to kiss her again, but she moves away again and starts to get off the couch. John grabs her arm, forcing her on the couch again, and begins kissing and fondling her. Joanne is upset, but John does not stop and proceeds to have sex with her. What are the decisions John made in this encounter that led to Joanne's rape?

attitudes that sex offenders hold are not that different than those held by the rest of society. The difference lies in the fact that offenders act on their attitudes whereas the rest of us are socially constrained. The SSRC is useful because of its underlying premise that all sexual acts are planned and conscious and that each partner is making choices throughout the entire encounter. As a result, offenders must be taught to identify the choices they made that placed them in a situation to offend, become aware of their sexual fantasies, develop the necessary skills to recognize socially acceptable sexual cues, and learn to communicate with potential partners throughout the sexual act.

### Sexual Anthropology

Another framework to help explain why people offend sexually is sexual anthropology (SA). This theory states that we must fully understand all types of sexual behaviors, especially those at the margins of society, in order to better understand the average sexual behavior. This framework uses two main concepts: (1) cultural relativism, and (2) symbolism. Simply put, cultural relativism means that we can only understand a culture, or subculture, on its own terms. In other words, Americans cannot look at Thailand and their general acceptance of intergenerational sex and say it is evil when we are not familiar with that culture or the history that led to their belief systems. Symbolizing occurs when a researcher participates in the behavior they are studying in order to gain an understanding of how it developed its meaning. What SA has demonstrated is that there is only one universal characteristic common to all cultures, and that is control over sexual behavior. Regardless of where you look, cultures all over the world control the types of sexual behaviors engaged in and who engages in them. SA also teaches us that once a culture compartmentalizes a behavior, this has the effect of normalizing that behavior. So when we label someone a pervert or deviant for having performed a sexual act that is against social norms, it has the effect of turning them into the "other"—the one to be leery of, the one who goes against what we regard as normal. This also reinforces our behavior as "normal," and we use that as justification for our own sexual proclivities (e.g., "At least I'm not a pervert like that guy!").

Havelock Ellis, a leading sexologist, used the concept of cultural relativism in the late 1800s to explain the differing notions of modesty between African cultures and European and North American cultures. Ellis described modesty as any behavior regarded by the majority of society as acceptable. For Europeans and North Americans, that meant covering the breasts and genitals, sometimes even during intercourse! On the other hand, in some African countries, people only covered body parts they wanted to be eroticized, so the breasts and genitals were left uncovered because they were not regarded as sexual.[54] What this demonstrates is that while the concept is the same—in this case, modesty—the practice is different in different cultures, as well as across time. We do not see many individuals in African cultures walking around naked anymore! Another example of cultural relativism is the Gusii of Kenya whose women are taught to encourage men sexually and then deny them, and the men are taught to forcefully demand sex.[55] Americans would label this behavior rape, but it forms part of a highly regarded intricate mating ritual in this Kenyan culture.

Fast-forward 50 years to the research of Alfred Kinsey, and we learn that cultural relativism applies within a culture as well. Kinsey was the first to document the differences in attitudes and behaviors between social classes, among educational levels, and between women and men.[56] Kinsey discovered that in America the upper class self-defines appropriate sexual behavior, and that this definition is very different from what they consider acceptable behavior for the lower class.[57] For instance, it was demonstrated that the upper class routinely engage in oral sex, but they considered this behavior less acceptable for those from the lower class. Moreover, sexual anthropology illustrates that sexual behavior is influenced by a variety of factors, including family, economics, social organization, social regulations, political intervention, and cultural resistance.[58]

What we learn from sexual anthropology is that when people deviate from "normal" sexuality, factors such as religion, culture, and the state work together to take away control over the bodies of such individuals and then label them as deviant. A modern example would be civil commitment laws where a person is committed to a mental institution for what they might do in the future because they engaged in socially unacceptable or illegal behavior in the past. The following quote from a criminology scholar demonstrates the biased lens through which we see these labeled sex offenders:

> Most offenders commit a variety of offenses. Versatility in offending is part of a lifelong pattern in which offenders act on the spur of the moment, are hedonistic, egocentric, concrete, opportunistic, impulsive, and focus almost exclusively on immediate gratification without regard to the long-term consequences of their behavior. Because offenders are not governed by the long-term consequences of their acts, they are "likely to engage in a host of immediately pleasurable activities—from sex to drugs to assault—without pattern, rhyme, or reason."[59]

What is wrong with this statement? Why is it that the author assumes that a person who commits a sex crime is a raging criminal with no conscience? The answer lies in sexual anthropology: the author is making assumptions based on her own upbringing and generalizing them to everyone. Not all criminals are sex offenders, and not all sex offenders commit other crimes. We must look within the culture of the individual who committed the sex crime as well as their familial background to truly understand how they came to the decision to offend and ultimately how to correct the behavior and prevent future recidivism.

CHAPTER 2

# HOW MANY SEX OFFENDERS ARE THERE?

To discuss the issues surrounding sexual offenses and sexual offenders, it is important to understand how widespread the issue of sexual offending is across the United States. This chapter will examine how many sexual offenders there are in the United States and what types of sexual offenses are most common. One significant problem, however, is that between jurisdictions the definition of what constitutes a sexual offense can vary greatly, making comparisons somewhat complicated. For example, in some states consensual sodomy is illegal, whereas in other states it is legal. Another difficulty is that age of consent varies by state, ranging from 14 to 18 years. Those states with higher statutory ages of consent will likely have higher rates of sexual offense violations and therefore a higher concentration of "sexual offenders." Inconsistencies such as these in legislation impact the measurement of sexual offenses across states and contribute to confusion when attempting to compare statistics across regions. Although there are some differences between jurisdictions, most states agree that a sexual offense involves lack of consent, which generally involves (a) force or threats of force; (b) a statement by the victim that he or she does not want to participate in the activity; or (c) an individual who is unable to consent due to age, mental capacity, physical disability, or because they are under the care of the state.

To determine the number of sexual offenders and types of sexual offenses, there are two primary methods of data collection used in the United States. The first source is from arrest and conviction data obtained by law enforcement. The National Incident Based Reporting System (NIBRS) in the United States counts crimes reported to law enforcement by participating agencies. One drawback of NIBRS is that it does not include statutory sexual offenses, likely due to the varied definitions by state and of the "gray" area involved in counting these offenses. Perhaps the most problematic aspect of this source of sexual offense data, however, is that it only includes offenses reported to law enforcement. As such, this source of data overlooks the "dark figure" of sexual offenses. The "dark figure" is the number of crimes not reported to the police, and in the case of sexual offenses, there are many reasons that a victim may not report a sexual crime to the authorities. Although society has progressed significantly in dealing with issues of sexual abuse, estimates still indicate that less than 20 percent of adult women who are victims of rape choose to report the incident to law enforcement.[60] Due to increased attention to the issues of child and adult sexual abuse, the stigma associated with sexual victimization is less today than it was 30 years ago, but a stigma remains, and this keeps many victims from reporting. Reasons for not reporting include that the victim may feel shame or embarrassment, resulting in the victim not wanting others to know; the victim may not understand that they were legally sexually assaulted; a victim may not want to allege abuse against someone they know; the victim may fear there is no "proof" of rape and therefore may be less willing to report; a victim may fear the interaction with police or the process of an investigation by the criminal justice system; the victim may fear retribution by the offender; or an individual may not want the stigma associated with being labeled a victim.[61]

For children, the barriers to reporting are somewhat different. The child may not report their abuse because they feel shame or embarrassment; because the child does not want others to know; the child may not truly understand that anything "wrong" has happened; the child may fear telling a parent because threats of harm may be involved; or the abusive parent may be the child's only source of emotional support, and the child's attachment may outweigh the anger, humiliation, and self-blame. As children get older, they may not want to allege abuse against someone they know, or they may fear that there is no "proof" and therefore be less willing to report it to the authorities. Similar to an adult victim, an older child may fear the process of a criminal justice system investigation or may not want the stigma associated with being labeled a victim. For all minors, however, the challenge in reporting to the authorities is transferred to the parent(s) who are in charge of making the report. In the case of incest, the challenge of one parent reporting the other, or reporting another family member, can be extremely traumatic emotionally.

The second source of measuring sexual offenses (which overcomes some of the flaws of the National Incident Based Reporting System) is the use of the National Crime Victimization Survey (NCVS). This is a national survey conducted annually of a randomly selected population to help assess the dark figure of sexual offenses and other types of crimes. The NCVS involves participants self-reporting crimes that have impacted their lives over the previous 12 months. One potential disadvantage to this type of study is the possibility that participants may forget which incidents occurred during the last year. This may result in forgetting to report some incidents and reporting some incidents that happened more than a year ago. Victimization surveys indicate that most types of crime, including sexual offenses, are significantly underreported to the police and help to increase our understanding of the true prevalence of such offenses in society.

NIBRS studies and NCVS data provide much of the basis for the data supplied in this chapter on sexual offenses and offenders. While some information also comes from studies conducted by researchers who, for example, conduct in-depth interviews with sexual offenders, or collect data on the experience of victimization through interviews with victims, these studies are not nearly as common as NIBRS and NCVS research. The remainder of this chapter will review the prevalence in types of offenses and answer questions about the "typical" offender and the types of sexual offenses committed in the areas of child sexual offenses, adult sexual offenses, Internet sexual offenses, female sexual offenders, and juvenile sexual offenders.

## Child Sexual Offenses

Child sexual offenses may involve either contact or noncontact offenses. Contact offenses include touching or penetration (either completed or attempted penetration), or participation of a minor in prostitution or pornography. Noncontact offenses include sexual comments toward a child, voyeurism (watching), exhibition (showing) of one's genitals to a child, and sexually related contact via the telephone or Internet. Incest involves either contact or noncontact sexual abuse of a child with whom the adult is related by blood or marriage. The most frequently occurring incestuous relationship is between a father and daughter, with mother-child incest rarely reported to law enforcement officials.

To clarify language used frequently in the media, the term "pedophile" has become synonymous with "child molester," but technically this is incorrect. To be precise, pedophilia involves a sexual interest or desire in children who have not yet reached puberty. Contrary to media reports, this is rare. Child molestation is a term used to refer to incidents in which the victim is over the age of 13, but the offender is typically only 4 or 5 years older than the victim. It is not a term that has any clinical or therapeutic value. "Hebephile" is the term used for offenders who are sexually interested in minors who have reached puberty. This is the term that would therefore apply to most heterosexual men in America. Although society regularly expresses its condemnation of pedophiles and views them as mentally deranged monsters, in one study a reasonably high percentage of male undergraduate students reported an attraction to children. In this study, 21 percent admitted a sexual attraction to children who had not yet reached puberty, 9 percent admitted to sexual fantasies involving children, 5 percent admitted to masturbating to sexual fantasies involving children, and 7 percent indicated that they might engage in sexual activity with a child if there was no chance they would be apprehended and punished.[62] A review of research reveals that pedophiles are typically male.[63] Recently, in the media several cases have been reported of female teachers having sexual relations with minor boys. It is important to note that these women are hebephiles as the boys they typically abuse have reached puberty. As a group, pedophiles are usually gender specific, targeting either boys or girls but not typically both genders, as well as age specific, with a preference of about a 4-year age span.

One source of data regarding child sexual abuse is the National Child Abuse and Neglect Data System (NCANDS) collected by the U.S. Department of Health and Human Services. Data is combined from state child protective agencies and reported each year regarding child abuse, with statistics kept separately for incidents of sexual abuse. The most recent data comes from 2005 in which child protection workers investigated 83,810 cases involving sexual abuse. This amounts to 9.3 percent of all cases of child abuse that were investigated.[64] According to the Administration on Children, Youth, and Families, despite the fact that almost 83,600 cases of child sexual abuse were confirmed in 2005 (only 210 of the investigated cases were not confirmed), this was a significant decline from 2004.[65] Between 1992 and 2000, the number of substantiated child sexual abuse cases decreased by approximately 40 percent. This pattern of decline appears "real" and not a statistical "mistake" because it appeared in 26 states and in various types of research studies.[66]

Looking at NIBRS data from 1991 through 1996 can reveal more in-depth information about the victim. Of sexual assaults reported to law enforcement during this period, 33 percent involved victims aged 12 through 17, and 34 percent involved victims under the age of 12.[67] This means that 33 percent of sexual assaults reported to the police involved a victim 18 years of age or older. Of the sexual assault cases reported, 69 percent of victims under the age of 6 were female, 73 percent of victims under the age of 12 were female, and 82 percent of victims under the age of 18 were female.[68] Of those sexually victimized under the age of 6, 97 percent were victimized by a family member.[69] NIBRS data revealed that a male's risk of victimization was greatest at age 4, and a female's risk of victimization was greatest at age 14. Further, sexual assault of an individual prior to the age of 18 is a significant variable in increasing one's likelihood of being sexually assaulted as an adult by a different sexual offender.[70] Research has not fully elaborated the rationale behind this increased likelihood of repeated victimization, although factors such as low self-esteem or associating with those involved with criminal activities may play a role in further victimization.

## Adult Sexual Offenses

Myths surrounding the sexual assault of women, called "rape myths," continue despite the work of feminists and activist groups that began in the 1960s and 1970s. These myths fuel the underreporting of sexual offenses, are often believed by both women and men, and influence both reporting of offenses as well as criminal justice responses. Such myths include: "yes means no and a woman will eventually give in," "on some level women want to be raped," "if a woman really wanted to defend herself against a rapist she could," "she was asking to be raped because she was alone in a specific place or wearing a specific outfit," or "many women lie about being raped because they regret having sex with a specific individual." Each of these myths brings further shame to the victim and therefore discourages many women from reporting.

Types of offenses included in the category of adult sexual offenses include sexual assault or rape by a stranger, by an acquaintance or date, by a spouse, or a rape that occurs in jail or prison. These offenses may include completed or attempted rape, completed or attempted sexual coercion (which involves manipulating or threatening someone into engaging in sexual contact), or completed or attempted sexual contact. The Uniform Crime Report measures discussed here (as measured by NIBRS) defines forcible rape as "the carnal knowledge of a female forcibly and against her will . . . assaults and attempts to commit rape by force or threat of force are also included; however, statutory rape (without force) and other sex offenses are excluded."[71] The Uniform Crime Report measures the number of forcible rapes per 100,000 females in the population as a way to measure change across time. This is more accurate than counting the number of rapes that occur each year, because each year the number of females in the population also changes. Beginning in 1992 and continuing through 2006, a steady decline in the rate of forcible rapes occurred in the United States.[72] The 1992 rate was 42.8 forcible rapes per 100,000 female inhabitants in the population, which had declined to 30.9 per 100,000 in 2006. When examining sexual assault statistics by region, there is some variation with 38.6 percent of all forcible rapes occurring in the South, 25.4 percent in the Midwest, 23.9 percent in the West, and 12.2 percent in the Northeast.[73] These statistics tend to fall in line with crime rates generally as the South tends to have the highest rate of violent crime.

An analysis of victimization surveys reveals that reporting of sexual assault varies by racial and ethnic groups. Forty-four percent of Caucasians sexually assaulted reported the crime to law enforcement, compared to only 17 percent of African Americans. Reporting also varies by age, with those ages 35 to 49 most likely to report an assault.[74] Research that examines why a woman would choose not to report a sexual assault reveals that 22 percent indicate it is because the event is a private matter, and 18 percent suggest they reported the incident to a different official (for example, a religious figure or school administrator).[75] Of those who did report the crime to law enforcement, 17 percent made the decision in order to prevent the offender from committing a future offense.[76]

Of cases reported to law enforcement, the victim knew the offender 65 percent of the time. In all reported rape and sexual assault cases of a black victim, the offender was also African American. When the victim was Caucasian, 45 percent of offenders were white, 34 percent were black, and 20 percent were of a different race. Approximately 83 percent of the time, there was a single offender involved in the assault. In approximately one-fourth of the assaults, the offender was believed to be under 21; about one-fourth of the time, the offender was perceived to be between 21 and 29; and about half of the time, the offender was believed to be over the age of 30.[77] However, if an assault was the relatively rare occurrence that involved more than one offender, 72 percent of the time the offenders were believed to be under the age of 21. As is typically perceived to be the case, in 98 percent of the rape cases, the offender was male.[78] Most frequently the offender was not under the influence of alcohol and/or drugs (only 36 percent of the time the offender was intoxicated), and in 85 percent of assault cases, the offender subdued the victim without the use of a weapon.[79]

Because rape is such an underreported crime, statistics reveal an inaccurate picture of the "typical" victim in the same way that statistics reveal an inaccurate picture of the "typical" (i.e., reported/arrested) offender. Studies reveal that sexual assault can cross all race and class lines; however, the victim who most typically comes to the attention of law enforcement or researchers is from an economically disadvantaged home, is separated or divorced, and lives in an urban area in the southeastern part of the United States.[80] It is extremely important to keep in mind, however, that the offenses most likely to be reported to law enforcement (approximately 75% of victims report stranger rapes) are not the offenses most likely to occur (65% of offenders know their victim)![81]

## Internet Sexual Offenses

Sexual offenses that involve the use of the Internet are a relatively recent phenomenon, which makes estimating the number of individuals that fall victim to online predators very difficult. To magnify the problem, this is a widely underreported crime and complex for law enforcement to detect. The World Wide Web is used for a variety of sexual purposes, including child and adult pornography, the facilitation of prostitution, and sites that cater to a variety of fetishes with the expressed goal of linking those with similar sexual preferences. Chat rooms also exist wherein potential sexual offenders can meet potential victims. While it is certainly only a rough estimate, the Texas Office of the Attorney General suggested that sexual solicitation affects one in five young people online.[82]

The research that has been conducted on individuals using the Internet for offending sexually suggests that these individuals are disturbed emotionally or psychologically, and this venue allows them to avoid confrontation.[83] Increasingly American society has become detached, and the anonymity of cyberspace provides an ideal atmosphere for sexual exploration and experimentation that has the potential to lead to manipulation or coercion. This may involve chat room behavior such as that depicted in *Dateline*'s *To Catch a Predator* series wherein agents from an organization called Perverted Justice acted as juveniles and engaged in sexual conversations with adults interested in pursuing sexual relations with minors. Law enforcement is just beginning to garner the resources to deter predators in the area of Internet sexual offenses, new laws are being enacted, and future research will likely provide better estimates of the amount of sexual offending that starts online.

## Female Sexual Offenders

Approximately 98 percent of reported sexual offenses are committed by men.[84] This means that very little is known about female sexual offenders. The most widely known study on women who committed sexual offenses was conducted in the 1980s. This research reviewed a variety of studies and estimated that 5 percent of females and 20 percent of males were victimized by a female perpetrator.[85] This is a large difference from the 2 percent estimate of female sexual offenders revealed in law enforcement data! Sexual abuse perpetrated by women could be underreported because it disproportionately involves a familial victim, which is the least reported type of sexual abuse.[86] Further, women are still the primary caretakers in American society, which involves legitimate touching of children in the form of dressing and bathing youngsters. Therefore, confusion may exist over whether or not an abusive act occurred, as some sexually abusive acts may be "dismissed" as part of routine child care. To add to this explanation, a cultural denial exists in American society as to whether a maternal figure can be abusive. Indeed, investigations of women's alleged perpetration of sexual abuse are three times as likely to be classified as "unfounded" than allegations of sexual abuse against a male.[87]

If the boy is older, the "victim" may not be so willing to identify himself as a "victim," but instead to chalk the incident up to "sexual experimentation" as opposed to "abuse." Such an incident was portrayed in the film *American Pie* in 1999 in which there were sexual encounters between adolescent boys and adult women. The young boy is often placed in a difficult emotional situation:

> Society romanticizes and minimizes the impact female molesters have on their young male victims. If a boy discloses abuse, he may not be believed. If he physically enjoyed the molestation, he does not perceive himself as a victim, despite the fact that he may be suffering from the effects of abuse. Many will suggest that he should have enjoyed the experience. If he did not enjoy aspects of the abuse, he may fear that he is homosexual. Either way the young male victim of the older female is placed in an untenable position.[88]

Because of society's misconceptions about female sexual offenders and because of the lack of reporting of offenses involving female offenders, research in this area is based on a handful of very small studies. It should be understood that these studies do not represent research on "typical" female sexual offenders; they simply represent the handful of female sexual offenders that have been studied by researchers.

The research that has been conducted on female sexual offenders reveals a patterned history of sexual abuse.[89] Another common thread is the presence of a co-offender who is typically male and is present in more than half of all such cases,[90] although recent research challenges this claim.[91] In addition, many studies find that most victims are known to the offender.[92] Generally, when people speak of female sexual offenders, it is in terms of child sexual abuse because the notion of a female raping a male is incomprehensible to many people. To be clear, as of 2000, all states have gender-neutral language with regard to statutory rape laws. This means that an adult female can be prosecuted for having sexual relations with a minor male. Conversely, if the male is 18 years of age or older, several states, including Idaho, Indiana, Maryland, Mississippi, and North Carolina, have laws that do not allow for the crime of rape to occur if the perpetrator is a female! For example, Idaho declares that rape can only be perpetrated by a male against a female: "Rape is defined as the penetration, however slight, of the oral, anal or vaginal opening with the perpetrator's penis accomplished with a female under either of the following conditions . . ."[93] Men can be raped; however, the perpetrator must be male: "Male rape is defined as the penetration, however slight, of the oral or anal opening of another male, with the perpetrator's penis, for the purpose of sexual arousal, gratification or abuse, under any of the following circumstances . . ."[94] The complexity that accompanies reporting and disclosure of sexual assault seems to be magnified when the perpetrator is a woman. Society still seems to perceive women as relatively harmless and innocent sexually. Even professionals are not immune to this stereotype, and unless this changes, underreporting will continue.

## Juvenile Sexual Offenders

Date from the Uniform Crime Report[95] revealed that 15 percent of those arrested for forcible rape in 2006 were juveniles (under the age of 18), and 18 percent of those arrested for other sexual offenses were juveniles. Knowledge regarding juvenile offenders is limited, and it is made even more complicated by the fact that it is often difficult to discern "normal childhood sexual exploration" from the behavior of a "budding sexual offender." Research finds that juvenile sexual offenders experience lowered self-esteem, poorly developed social skills, difficulty forming attachments, a higher likelihood of family problems, and substance abuse issues.[96] A major study of juvenile offenders by the National Adolescent Perpetrator Network (NAPN) that spanned 30 states found that 90 percent of juvenile offenders are male; most have committed other, nonsexual offenses; and 96 percent of the time the victim is also a juvenile.[97] Additionally, 90 percent of the victims are known to the offender, with 39 percent related by blood.[98] The average number of victims per offender was 7.7, and many juvenile offenders have experienced both physical and sexual abuse during childhood and adolescence.[99]

It cannot be overemphasized that research on juvenile sexual offenders is in its infancy. There are many contradictory findings, and much research has to be conducted before patterns are revealed and proper treatment methods can be developed. Because of the infancy of this research, a debate exists as to whether society is dealing with "children at risk" or "risky children." Are juvenile sexual offenders the "risky children" that are going to grow up to be the monstrous predators portrayed by the media, or are these juveniles "children at risk," acting out as a result of social problems that are occurring at home and in their neighborhood, such as domestic violence or substance abuse? Despite the lack of definitive answers regarding the juvenile sex offender population, there are more than 800 treatment programs across the country, and juveniles are forced into many of the same legislative rules as adult sexual offenders, such as registration and community notification in more than half the states that utilize these laws. This means succumbing to the stigma of a "sexual offender" label for an act they may have committed when they were 12 or 13 years of age. Such a policy may serve to make a "child at risk" a "risky child."

In Nevada this policy was determined to be unacceptable according to a recent court ruling. The federal Adam Walsh Child Protection and Safety Act passed in July 2006 permits offenders age 14 and older to be treated as adults for certain sexual offenses and mandates that many juveniles be included in Internet sex offender registries. In April 2008, Nevada's law (AB 579), based on the Adam Walsh Act, was ruled unconstitutional because it violated due process. Under the law, "14-year-old sex offenders can be punished as adults. But a child who is 13 years, 11 months, and 29 days can't. This age distinction, [the Judge noted], is arbitrary. Without a rational reason for the age cap, the law is a violation of due process, because part of due process is the right to rational law."[100] While the ruling will surely be appealed, it is a move in the direction of recognizing "children at risk."

## Who Is the "Typical" Offender?

Because sexual offenses are so underreported, the "typical offender" is certainly not the offender incarcerated for sexual offenses. We know that an individual is most likely to report a stranger rape (75% of victims report stranger rapes), but we also know that 65 percent of offenders know their victim! This means that the individuals incarcerated for sexual offenses are most likely there for stranger offenses, which do not represent the majority of sexual offenses that occur. For this reason, you must logically assume as you read this section on the "typical offender" that the incarcerated offender is indeed not the "typical" offender. The "typical offender" is the offender who is not reported to law enforcement, the offender who is one's father, or brother, or uncle, or priest, or cousin, or boyfriend, or neighbor. The "typical offender" is someone we know. The atypical offender, the one reported to the police, is the one to which we now turn.

Studies reveal that the type of offense most likely to be reported is one committed by a stranger and one involving violence; thus it stands to reason that the offenders in prison are those that committed offenses against strangers and offenders that were involved in crimes of higher levels of violence than is "typical." We cannot make generalizations from this data about the "average" or "typical" sexual offender who has not been caught, reported, or prosecuted. Most studies show that the sexual offender who has been brought to the attention of the authorities is male (98.6%), and about 70% of the time he is white and is usually over the age of 24.[101] Of the total 14,380,370 arrests for all crimes in 2006, there were 24,535 arrests for forcible rape and 87,252 for other sexual offenses (not including prostitution).[102] As of 2004, there were 59,700 prisoners sentenced under state jurisdiction for rape and 94,100 for other sexual assaults.[103] Of all sexual offenders incarcerated, most admitted to victimizing someone they did not know despite the fact that most victims are assaulted by someone they do know.[104] Of inmates incarcerated in state facilities for sexual assault, about two-thirds reported having a victim under the age of 18, and 58 percent of these offenders reported having a victim 12 years of age or younger.[105] Of those arrested for child sexual abuse, most offenders admitted to previous molestation of children for which they were never arrested, indicating a pattern of behavior.[106]

Once the sexual offense is reported to the authorities, approximately half of those charged with rape are released pending trial, and half of these individuals are required to post a monetary bond.[107] Approximately 80 percent of offenders pled guilty, and just over two-thirds received a prison sentence.[108] When examined in light of the total prison population, sexual offenders comprise less than 5 percent of the total correctional population in the United States. Further, while the media link serious violence and sexual offenses on a routine basis, less than 2 percent of murder cases involve any sexual assault.[109] In terms of sentencing, a significant number of offenders receive a community sentence (such as probation or intensive community supervision with treatment). Daily about 234,000 convicted sexual offenders are under the care of correctional authorities, with approximately 60 percent of these individuals under community supervision.[110] Of those sentenced to prison, the average sentence is almost 14 years, with approximately 2 percent of those convicted of rape serving a life sentence.[111] Although there are charges in the media and the general misperception that sexual assault sentences are short, a review of sentences in Washington indicates that this is not the case. In 2003 in Washington State, 27,213 felony sentences were imposed, and 1,403 involved sexual offenses. This was consistent with the national average of about 5 percent of cases involving sexual offenses.[112] The average length of sentence for all felonies was 37.3 months, and the average length of sentence for sexual offenses was 90.8 months.[113] Indeed, only murder had an average sentence length that was longer than a sexual offense.[114] Likely due in part to the war on sexual offenders waged in the media, between 1993 and 2002, the number of sexual offenders incarcerated nationally increased by 74 percent, while the overall state prison population experienced only a 49 percent increase.[115] Again, the offenders incarcerated are not the "typical sexual offenders," but the offenders who are reported to law enforcement: those offenders who commit crimes of violence against strangers. The more "typical sexual offender" is one who is not incarcerated, the offender who commits crimes against loved ones and neighbors but for reasons of shame and fear is not reported to the authorities. Due to lack of reporting, the dark figure with regard to sexual offenses is large. Experts have merely begun to scratch the surface in their analysis of sexual offenses and the search for effective methods to reduce recidivism, keep communities safe, and reintegrate ex-offenders into society. Not only does this lack of data slow the evolution of treatment methods, but it also deters lawmakers' ability to create laws based on sound science and expert analysis; instead lawmakers rely on the myths perpetuated by the media to create legislation that is ineffective and can actually serve to increase an offender's risk of recidivism. Reason and research must inform legislation to shape policies that are just for all members of the community, which include the rights of both victims and offenders. Only then will we be able to move past misguided policies based on fear and toward real community safety.

# PART II

# PASSING LAWS

# CHAPTER 3

# CREATING LAWS TO DEAL WITH
# SEX OFFENDERS

Laws to deal with sex offenders have been developed in waves throughout history, the result of panics created by a collection of serious sex offenses that occurred within a short time frame. Legislation was originally implemented on a large scale in the 1930s and was reformed for a variety of reasons during the 1960s and 1970s. This was followed by another rash of legislative controls on sexual offenders beginning in the 1990s, which continues to the present day. This chapter will examine the historical changes in sex offender legislation and explore the media's role in creating panic or hysteria in the public mind when it comes to sexual offenders. This chapter will also elaborate the varied societal responses to sexual offending.

## The Media's Role in Creating a Moral Panic

Much of the American public gets their information regarding crime from the media, so the "reality" that the media portray is extremely important because many viewers believe that what they read and see on the news is fact. With regard to sex offenses, however, the media create fear, reinforces stereotypes, and perpetuates misinformation about sexual offenders and sexual offenses.[116] The media portray a skewed "reality" that has more to do with journalistic appeal than crime fact. "Stranger-danger stories have great appeal to journalists. The random and public nature of such attacks makes every reader or viewer potentially at risk from the 'pervert on the loose.'"[117] Through the misrepresentation of news items dealing with sexual offenders and sexual offenses, the media instill a fear or "moral panic" in the public. Sexual crimes that are not sensational or violent, or those crimes that involve someone known to the victim, are viewed as "routine" and "pedestrian" and therefore not worthy of media coverage.[118] In essence, the media have the power to transform a relatively minor social problem into a major societal epidemic, and research has demonstrated that an individual's fear of crime has more to do with their television viewing than with actual crime trends![119]

> Analyses of media content demonstrate that the news provides a map of the world of criminal events that differs in many ways from one provided by official crime statistics. Variations in the volume of news about crime seem to bear little relationship to variations in the actual volume of crime between place and time. Whereas crime statistics indicate that most crime is nonviolent, media reports suggest, in the aggregate, that the opposite is true.[120]

So, if the media repeatedly show sex crimes by strangers, the public is likely to have an increased fear of being victimized sexually by a stranger, regardless of whether this is the most likely type of offender.

Applying the notion of a "moral panic" to the understanding of sexual offenses is quite useful in explaining public misunderstanding and reaction. In the 1970s, noted sociologist Stanley Cohen formulated the idea of a moral panic when he referred to:

> . . . a condition, episode, person or group of persons emerges to become defined as a threat to societal values and interests; its nature is presented in a stylized and stereotypical fashion by the mass media . . . socially accredited experts pronounce their diagnosis and solutions; ways of coping are evolved or . . . resorted to; the condition then disappears, submerges or deteriorates and becomes more visible. Sometimes the subject of the panic is quite novel and at other times it is something which has been in existence long enough but suddenly appears in the limelight. Sometimes the panic passes over and is forgotten, except in folklore and collective memory; at other times it has more serious and long-lasting repercussions and might produce such changes as those in legal and social policy.[121]

Discussing sexual offenses and society's responses to sexual offenders as a "moral panic" does not minimize the consequences to those victimized, but instead calls attention to the exaggerated and misdirected nature of societal fear. Out of this misplaced fear ineffective policies that help the public to *feel* safe, but do little to prevent sexual violence, have resulted.

As applied to sexual offending, a moral panic involves the following steps. First, sexual offenses and offenders are defined as a threat to "normal" values or interests. While there is no doubt that most sexual offenses run counter to mainstream values and beliefs, the focus in the media has been on offenses committed by strangers when statistics demonstrate that most individuals are victimized by someone known to them. When this threat is depicted in the media, it is depicted in this stereotypical form, leading the public to believe that the greatest threat of sexual violence comes from outside one's circle of friends, family, and acquaintances. The second stage of a moral panic is the rapid intensification of media interest in the issue to promote public concern. One way the media does this is to cover not only the local story of interest, but to "contextualize" the issue by relaying similar stories that have occurred across the country. As the issue of sexual offending becomes more newsworthy, these stories are covered by more stations in greater depth, leading the consumer of news to believe that the problem has become more widespread, even if this is not the case. The result is an increase in public fear. This buildup of media interest has occurred in waves in the United States, first in the 1930s and again beginning in the 1990s.

The third stage of a moral panic is when policymakers and authorities respond to the fear that has been instilled in the public. Policymakers begin to discuss how to solve the social problem, and these talks usually involve media coverage, leading to even more exposure of the issue. The solution is frequently the creation of laws to more harshly punish individuals convicted of sexual offenses. This followed the wave of media interest in sexual offenses in both the 1930s and the 1990s and indeed continues in the present day. The final stage of a moral panic is when the panic recedes as it did in the 1960s due to reforms in the laws and in attitudes toward rehabilitation of offenders. The final stage may also occur due to resulting social changes, such as a lowering of the crime rate to the extent that the public is no longer fearful (or at least to the extent that the media no longer cover the issue). Laws continue to be passed throughout the United States, and there appears to be no end in sight to the controls the public is willing to place on sexual offenders in the misdirected aim of public safety. This is compounded by the representation of offenders in crime shows:

> Crime shows rarely focus on mitigating issues of criminal behavior and are unlikely to portray offenders in a sympathetic or even realistic fashion. On television, crime is freely chosen and based on individual problems of the offender. Analysis of crime dramas reveal that greed, revenge and mental illness are the basic motivations for crime and offenders are often portrayed as "different" from the general population. . . . Viewers . . . believe that all offenders are "monsters" to be feared.[122]

And the public is fearful of those portrayed in the media as "beasts," "devils," "perverts," "fiends," or "evil persons."[123] "Citizens cannot understand a sex attack on a child, and this incomprehensibility fuels reactions of fear. . . . The attack and investigation become front-page news . . . describing the failure of the justice system to protect vulnerable persons, which fuels a strong public reaction. . . . Government officials then feel compelled to act."[124] However, it cannot be overstated that the media are not conveying "facts," but are contributing to a very skewed perception of sexual offenders and offenses. Support of laws should not be based on these skewed perceptions if the goal is to lower victimization rates and protect women and children from abuse.

## Societal Responses to Sexual Offending

Societal responses to sexual offenders have changed throughout history, essentially moving back and forth between advocating severe punishment or treatment. The four models of thought used historically in the United States are the Clinical

Model, the Justice Model, the Community Safety Model, and the Hybrid Model.[125] Each of these models views offenders and the root cause of offending differently and suggests an alternative approach to reducing sexual offending.

The Clinical Model focused on diagnoses, prognoses, and treatment. Sexual offenses were viewed as being rooted in mental health issues and therefore required intervention from medical professionals. Integral to this model was the assessment of an individual's risk, which relied on factors in an offender's history as well as current variables. Because historical and current variables were both considered in risk assessment, many individuals were considered either "moderate" or "high" risk. This model viewed the *person* as pathological, rather than suggesting that an individual had engaged in a *behavior* that was pathological. The way to reduce sexual offending, according to this approach, was indeterminate confinement in a secure mental facility for all offenders deemed "moderate" or "high" risk because it was believed that these individuals had an increased risk of recidivism. Critics argued that this approach actually resulted in longer terms of confinement for the offender than if he had simply been sentenced to prison and served his sentence in its entirety.[126] This, combined with the inexact science of risk assessment, made this approach questionable. When treatment fell out of favor, so did the Clinical Model.

The Justice Model focused on providing a punishment for the offender that was fair and "just," with the underlying assumption being that sexual offenders are deviants who deserve legal punishment. This model was not concerned with assessing the future risk of an offender but wanted simply to ensure that the offender was sufficiently punished for the current offenses he had committed. Advocates of this model recommended fixed sentencing guidelines so that sex offenses would be taken seriously at sentencing and making sure that mitigating circumstances of the offender could not result in a reduced sentence. This model is much more punitive than the Clinical Model and emphasizes the need for retribution to both society and the victim for sexual harm.[127]

As the victim's rights movement grew, the Community Safety Model took center stage in the 1980s and 1990s. This model classified sexual offenders as evil predators deserving of indefinite confinement, even if that involved violations of their constitutional due process rights along the way. This model was designed to maximize safeguards for the public and consequently severely restricted the rights of those suspected or convicted of sexually based crimes.[128] Individual rights were believed to be superseded by the greater social good, and it was argued that treatment and rehabilitation could not come at the risk of community safety.[129] This model recognizes that persons convicted of sex crimes will eventually re-enter society, so the Community Safety Model also advocates restrictions on movement, employment, and social networks in the form of laws such as residency restrictions, Internet restrictions, etc. A criticism of this model is that it has the tendency to assume guilt prior to a finding of guilt at trial. In addition, there is no recognition of the effects of stringent restrictions after release on the successful reintegration of offenders and how this may influence their likelihood of recidivism.

In recent years, the Hybrid Model is more often used by the criminal justice system when dealing with sexual offenders. This model speculates that sexual offenders have mental health issues and therefore require treatment, but it also recognizes the importance of incarceration to punish and deter offenders. The underlying assumption of this model is that sex offenders are mentally unstable, as evidenced by the fact that most illegal sexual behaviors are found within the *DSM*. In addition, however, the social good must be served by exacting a punishment from the offender for his offensive behavior. This model suggests that if treatment is available and cost-effective, it should be offered to incarcerated sex offenders. The Hybrid Model shares with the Clinical Model the critique of the inexact science of risk assessment, and some critics argue with the premise that treatment is most frequently offered to offenders only at the end of their prison term, regardless of the length of time they have been incarcerated. So an offender could have spent 10 years incarcerated without receiving any type of treatment for his sexual offending behavior, only to begin receiving treatment 2 years prior to his release. Some critics argue that at that point the therapist may have missed the window of treatment opportunity.

## Sexual Psychopath Legislation of the 1930s

Regulation of sexual behavior can be traced to the earliest civilizations, but it is important to keep in mind that as the social, moral, and political landscape of society changes, so too does the definition of a sexual offense, a sexual offender, and the socially appropriate response to such offenders. The Clinical Model was the model prevalent in the 1930s in the United States. It was thought that indefinite confinement in a psychiatric facility was the only way to deal with sexual offenders as their mental or personality disorders predisposed them to sexual crimes and violence. But who was considered a sexual offender during this historic time? Morality statutes prohibited offenses such as homosexuality, sodomy, fornication, adultery, and bestiality. Indeed, sodomy was a major offense in the 1930s and was a catch-all term used to describe consensual behaviors usually between homosexuals. The sentences for these offenses varied dramatically by state. For example, consensual sodomy in New York State carried a maximum term of imprisonment of one year in the 1940s, but it carried a potential sentence of life imprisonment in Georgia.

An examination of official statistics in the 1930s reveals an increase in sex crimes; however, most arrests were for adult consensual homosexual encounters. Therefore, much of the statistical "increase" reflects the homophobia of the time period, as opposed to an increase in real sex crimes. Beginning with the case of Albert Fish, however, there was a series of violent sexual offenses that occurred in a relatively short period of time. This rash of offenses resulted in the moral panic of the 1930s and shortly thereafter resulted in a new set of laws in response to the public outrage. The media focus on sexual violence began with the story of Albert Fish in New York State. Fish allegedly sexually assaulted, killed, and cannibalized a 12-year-old boy. Prior to his apprehension in 1934, it was believed that he violated hundreds of other children and killed as many as 15 minors. The media and the public were fascinated by his case until his execution in 1936. This case overlapped with that of a serial rapist named Gerald Thompson who was on trial in Illinois for rape and murder in 1935. The media alleged Thompson had a diary that listed the names of 83 women he wanted to sexually assault and murder. At trial, he was found guilty and was sentenced to be executed. Several years later in Washington, D.C., a 36-year-old African American taxi driver admitted to raping and choking 10 women of various ages and racial groups. This was widely reported in the media, and women were frightened for their safety. Jarvis Theodore Roosevelt Catoe, the accused, was electrocuted in 1943.

Due mostly to intense media coverage of these select cases in a relatively short period of time, the public was led to believe that there was an epidemic of sexual offending. In addition, they associated sexual offenses with serious violence and murder, although this is an extremely rare occurrence! Parents feared that there were predators like Albert Fish lurking in the streets, and "sex offender" became synonymous in the eyes of many with "child sex killer." Women feared stranger rapists and being sexually assaulted and killed by their taxi driver! These high-profile cases, despite being quite rare, fueled a conservative approach to crime control toward sexual offenders.

Although they were not commonplace, in a time of moral panic these cases were perceived as "typical sexual offenses," and individuals committing minor sexual transgressions were believed to be on a path of escalation to serious sexual perversion and violence. Caught up in this cycle of crime control toward sexual offenders, police began punishing offenses that in the past would not have resulted in arrest (petty offenses such as homosexuality, prostitution, or exhibitionism). This police activity increased the sexual offense statistics and led to the perception that the rate of sex crimes was increasing as the police focused their attention on all types of sexual offenses, driving up arrest rates. Additionally, the media were more likely to report these events and to place local crimes (regardless of how minor they were) in the context of sexual offenses nationwide, leading once again to the perception that sex crimes were increasing! The result was that the public believed there was a sex crimes epidemic as a result of increased media coverage and increased police response, rather than as a result of an *actual* increase in sex crime rates.

In the 1930s, the official response to the public's fear came in a declaration of a "war on sex crimes" by J. Edgar Hoover.[130] In this state of panic, lawmakers and the public alike lost sight of the reality that sexual homicides are very rare, and it was against this backdrop that sexual psychopath laws were created. By the late 1930s, "public indignation ha[d] reached almost a mass hysteria which ha[d] affected not only the public but also official authorities. . . . A sheriff in New York recommended shooting every child attacker on the spot."[131] The panic of the 1930s drew to a close in the early 1940s, although peaks in media coverage and hysteria over sexual offenders were noted again between 1947 and 1950 and between 1953 and 1954.[132] A 1946 article boldly suggested that "the shadow of the sex criminal lies across the doorstep of every home."[133] In an attempt to debunk the stereotypes surrounding sexual offenders that continued to be perpetuated by the media through the end of the 1940s, an article was published in

1950 by *Time* magazine. While the title of the article, "The Unknown Sex Fiend," belied its purpose; the short article in its entirety read:

> Sex crimes, flamboyantly headlined in the press, are currently troubling both public and police. After seven months of poring over statistics and case histories, New Jersey's Commission on the Habitual Sex Offender last week issued a report. One of its main conclusions: the average citizen knows little about the scope and nature of sex crimes, but he is oversupplied with misinformation on the subject. Some of the popular convictions which the commissioners would like to correct: (1) That the sex offender progresses to more serious sex crimes. Statistics clearly show that "progression from minor to major sex crimes is exceptional." (2) That dangerous sex criminals are usually repeaters. Actually, of all serious crime categories, only homicide shows a lower record of repeaters. (3) That sex offenders are oversexed. Most of those treated have turned out to be physically undersexed. (4) That there are "tens of thousands" of homicidal sex fiends abroad in the land. Only an estimated 5% of convicted sex offenders have committed crimes of violence. The commission's cool, if not too reassuring, report: "Danger of murder by relative or other intimate associate is very much greater than the danger of murder by an unknown sex fiend."[134]

It was noteworthy that this article appeared at all in the mainstream media. However, the New Jersey Commission on the Habitual Sex Offender had issued a massive report on sexual offending and sexual offenders. In response, *Time* magazine featured a ridiculously short segment of the report and essentially "undid" the findings of the experts by indicating at the end of the article that their findings were "not too reassuring."[135]

Compared to today's treatment of sex offenders, and despite public fear from media portrayals of high-profile offenses, the criminal justice system of the 1930s really did not take sex offenses very seriously. If charges were even filed, charges of rape most frequently resulted in plea bargains or convictions for assault. Statutory rape charges were overwhelmingly dismissed or reduced to a misdemeanor offense. For a less serious offense, such as indecent exposure, the likelihood of dismissal or acquittal for the accused was even greater. This was primarily because women and children held a much different role in society during the 1930s. This was a time in which men were legally permitted to rape their wives because the law viewed marriage as an indication of a lifetime of sexual consent. It was also a time in which physical corroboration of a sexual assault was necessary in a court of law. At this time, child sexual abuse was not considered a social problem.

The sexual offenders who were viewed seriously by the system were believed to be mentally ill; therefore, it was believed they should be given treatment and preventive detention in a mental health facility as opposed to incarceration in a prison. This was accomplished through the creation of sexual psychopath laws. Sexual psychopath laws provided for the *involuntary* and *indefinite* commitment of an individual who was deemed a "sexual psychopath" in a psychiatric facility. The language of these laws varied by state and was very vague. The assumption of the law was that sex offenders were driven by uncontrollable impulses and would only stop offending when the impulse to offend was eliminated through treatment. The first sexual psychopath law was passed in Michigan in 1937. It was later declared unconstitutional for violating the principle of double jeopardy and lacking the protections afforded by a jury trial. However, it was revised and approved in 1939. Several states passed laws shortly thereafter: Illinois (1938), California (1939), Minnesota (1939), Vermont (1943), Ohio (1945), Massachusetts (1947), Washington (1947), Wisconsin (1947), District of Columbia (1948), Indiana (1949), New Hampshire (1949), and New Jersey (1949). As the 1950s drew to a close, 26 states and the District of Columbia had adopted sexual psychopath legislation. A very interesting provision of these early laws was that in order to be declared a sexual psychopath in many states, an alleged offender need not have been found guilty of a sexual offense—he just had to be deemed at risk of sexual compulsivity! That alone would get him confined indefinitely for treatment under sexual psychopath legislation in many states!

Variation existed in the language of the laws by state. However, most of the sexual psychopath laws shared similar key elements. The following elements were usually included in a sexual psychopath law, although a single offender was not required to display all of these elements in order to be classified under this law: (1) a crime of a sexual nature was committed; (2) the individual's pathology was compulsive in nature; (3) there existed the assumption that the offense, or a similar sexual offense, would be repeated; (4) there existed the assumption that the individual would escalate from the offense he had most recently committed to a more serious offense; (5) there existed a potential risk to community safety; and (6) there was a belief that treatment was possible.[136] While each state sexual psychopath statute was different, an example is the 1955 California Sexually Psychopath Act:

> [S]exual psychopath means any person who is affect, in a form predisposing to the commission of sexual offenses, and in a degree constituting him a menace to the health or safety of others, with any of the following conditions: (a) Mental disease or disorder. (b) Psychopathic personality. (c) Marked departures from normal mentality. When a person is convicted of any criminal offense, whether or not a sex offense, the trial judge, on his own motion, or on motion of the prosecuting attorney, or on application by affidavit by or on behalf of the defendant, if it appears to the satisfaction of the court that there is probable cause for believing such person is a sexual psychopath . . ., may adjourn the proceeding or suspect the sentence, as the case may be, and may certify the person for hearing and examination by the superior court of the county to determine whether the person is a sexual psychopath. . . . When a person is convicted of a sex offense involving a child under 14 years of age and it is a misdemeanor, and the person has been previously convicted of a sex offense in this or any other state, the court shall adjourn the proceeding or suspect the sentence, as the case may be, and shall certify the person for hearing and examination by the superior court of the county to determine whether the person is a sexual psychopath. . . . When a person is convicted of a sex offense involving a child under 14 years of age and it is a felony, the court shall adjourn the proceeding or suspend the sentence, as the case may be, and shall certify the person for hearing and examination by the superior court of the county to determine whether the person is a sexual psychopath. . . .[137]

Presumably these statutes were to protect the community from sexually violent and psychopathic offenders who could not control their impulses, yet the laws were used to prosecute individuals for acts considered minor or even consensual today. Not all those examined by mental health professionals as "sexual psychopaths" or "sexually dangerous persons" were obviously committed, but even those who were committed were usually not involved in violent acts! More than 50 percent of the persons committed in Illinois were for acts that were minor (such as exhibitionism) but were considered morally offensive.[138] This was true in New Jersey as well where "psychiatric hospitalization...was reserved for petty sex offenders who seemed likely to escalate their crimes....Serious sex offenders were almost invariably returned to the criminal justice system for punishment."[139] Sexual psychopath laws:

> ...were passed to provide a means for dealing with dangerous, repetitive, mentally abnormal sex offenders. Unfortunately, the vagueness of the definition contained in these statutes has obscured this basic underlying purpose. There are large numbers of sex offenders who engage in compulsive repetitive sexual acts, which may be crimes, who may be mentally abnormal but who are not dangerous. The transvestite, the exhibitionist, the frotteur, the homosexual who masturbates another in the privacy of his bedroom or in a public toilet, the "peeping tom"—are typical of large numbers of sex offenders who are threatened with long-term incarceration by present [laws].[140]

In the 1930s, states that had sexual psychopath laws threatened sexual offenders with indefinite confinement more frequently than it was actually used. Indeed, most states during this period committed fewer than twenty individuals per year on average.[141]

Passage of the laws was perceived to the fearful public as an extremely positive response by government to this social problem. This was exemplified in the *Indianapolis Star* in 1948:

> Indiana today is one step nearer an enlightened approach to the growing menace of sex crimes. A proposed new law to institutionalize sexual psychopathics until pronounced permanently recovered has been drafted by a special state citizens' committee which helped the attorney general's office to study the problem. . . . Such a law should become a realistic, practical answer to the sex crime problem. This type of legislation has succeeded elsewhere and is long overdue in Indiana.[142]

Empirical research was lacking to demonstrate success of this type of legislation anywhere. This did not stop even academics from suggesting that "as we well know, some of the most heinous sex offenses on record have been committed by "fiends" whose backgrounds were marked by repeated fines and jail sentences."[143] Over and over again, these laws were passed on the basis of many faulty assumptions and media-driven panic.

Sexual psychopath legislation assumed that sex crimes were increasing rapidly and that the response of the criminal justice system was insufficient to deal with the recidivism of sex offenders. Instead of a response confined strictly to the criminal justice system, indefinite treatment was thought to be the way to "cure" offenders of their compulsions. These laws also assumed that sexual offenders "persist in their sexual crimes throughout life; that they always give warning that they are dangerous by first committing minor offenses; that any psychiatrist can diagnose them with a high degree of precision at an early age, before they have committed serious sex crimes; and that sexual psychopaths who are diagnosed and identified should be confined as irresponsible persons until they are pronounced by psychiatrists to be completely and permanently cured of their malady."[144] These are enormous assumptions to lay at the feet of the medical professionals in charge of diagnosing and treating sex offenders.

What happens, however, if these assumptions were incorrect? What if sexual offending was not a mental disorder that could be identified by mental health professionals? What if psychiatrists could not predict which sexual offenders were likely to commit violent sexual offenses and which ones would simply commit offenses society found morally objectionable, such as exhibitionism? What if the treatment methods designed by medical professionals did not work? And how would a mental health professional be able to tell when a sexual offender was "cured" of their disorder and unlikely to reoffend? There were so many questions surrounding sexual psychopath legislation, but the medicalization model and the notion of "treating" criminals were the ones that had taken hold during this historic period.

Soon, however, it came to light that offenders who were supposed to be getting treatment were not receiving any. Instead, they continued to remain confined under sexual psychopath legislation in a psychiatric facility *indefinitely*. This did not sit well with some critics and human rights advocates, and sexual psychopath laws were challenged. The U.S. Court of Appeals ruled that if an individual was deemed a sexual psychopath and held in confinement, he must be provided with treatment. If treatment could not be provided, for whatever reason, the individual could not be held. In response to this ruling, some states made legitimate efforts to improve their treatment models. Despite suggestions that improvements were made in treatment, studies estimate that fewer than 25 percent of offenders were ever "cured."[145] Applying a sexological treatment framework, in which sexuality education forms the foundation of therapy, would be significantly more beneficial because it addresses the underlying issues of sex and sexuality. Literature on treatment modalities illustrates clearly that sex and sexuality components are lacking in current treatments, and this would be a step forward for treatment in prison settings. Court rulings mandating treatment did, however, provide the foundation for much needed legal reforms.

## Reforms in Legislation

At the close of the 1960s and the start of the 1970s, many of the same concerns began to arise that present-day critics have raised regarding sexually violent predator legislation (see Chapter 4 for a discussion of current sex offender legislation). One major concern was the subjective nature of who decided on the classification of "sexual psychopath." For critics ". . . the concept of the "sexual psychopath" is so vague that it cannot be used for judicial and administrative purposes without the danger that the law may injure the society more than do the sex crimes which it is designed to correct."[146] This raises serious civil liberty concerns regarding persons who are involuntarily committed for an indefinite period of time, especially when they are committed for an offense that is merely "morally offensive" and not sexually violent. Even psychiatrists, who were generally on board with this "rehabilitative" model at the beginning, eventually became uncomfortable with the quick turnaround timeline in which they were expected to provide a diagnosis of sexual psychopathy. Mental health professionals slowly grew wary of the "sexual psychopath" terminology and the ambiguity of the concept and came to question whether "minor" sexual offenders who were being indefinitely confined to facilities would indeed graduate to violent offenses. Also problematic was that legal decisions of the early 1970s made involuntary commitment of sexual offenders very difficult unless they posed *imminent* risk of harm to either themselves or others. Under the pressure of legal changes, the ambiguity of mental health professionals, and the societal move away from rehabilitation, the sexual psychopath laws were repealed, and individuals confined under these laws were transferred to prisons.

This legislative change was one of many in the legal landscape in the 1960s and 1970s, as restrictions on morality and consensual sexual behaviors were significantly relaxed. This period was one of vast societal change and social movements for civil rights, women's rights, victim's rights, and sexual rights, as well as offender's rights. Especially notable was the influence of women's groups and victim's rights groups. In the 1970s, women's groups brought the attention of both the public and government officials to the issue of violence against women, both at home and outside the home. In terms of sexual violence, women's groups worked to challenge stereotypes about rapists as "strangers lurking in a park" and argued instead that violence occurred most frequently among those we know intimately— our friends, family, and acquaintances. Feminists wanted to convey that sexual abuse and violence could occur in a variety of situations, involve a diverse array of individuals, and did not necessarily conform to the myths that had historically pervaded societal views. Laws are important in shaping cultural perceptions; therefore, reformers sought to expand the list of potential sex crimes to include incest offenders, acquaintance rape, marital rape, rape that did not involve serious physical harm, and rape by assailants who did not fit the "stereotype" of a rapist.[147]

Another goal was to have the public view sexual violence against women as a structural problem, as opposed to an individual problem that each victimized woman should deal with by herself. Part of the work of women's groups involved reforming rape laws so that women felt less like victims in the criminal justice system and more empowered. Through legal reforms, feminists sought to "get tough" on sexual offenders by increasing the penalties for sexual offenses. This was also the first historical juncture (in the late 1970s and early 1980s) when social justice groups gave attention to the issue of child abuse and the passage of several laws to protect child safety. The reforms advocated by women's groups and victim's groups changed the trend toward decriminalization of the 1960s to the moral conservatism of the late 1970s and early 1980s.

The atmosphere started to change in the 1980s as child sexual abuse cases started to be prosecuted with some regularity. Several high-profile cases occurred in the 1980s, the most sensationalized of which was the McMartin preschool scandal in California in 1983. In brief, implicitly tied to the McMartin trial was the debate over "recovered memories" with therapists asserting that many victims repress memories of sexual abuse and may need "assistance" in recovering these events due to trauma. Critics argue that memories of sexual abuse are not really "recovered" but instead are patently false and planted by the therapist. Indeed, this was determined to be the case in the McMartin trial when all parties were acquitted of the child sexual abuse charges filed against them. This debate caused such a media stir that many (falsely) wondered if sexual abuse of women and children was really a serious problem or if many women and children were "falsifying" these memories either individually or at the "suggestion" of their therapist. This scandal set the women's movement and the child protection movement back considerably. As the 1980s ended and the 1990s began, several cases emerged in which previously convicted sexual offenders brutalized children, and these cases gained a very high profile. By this time, the public had forgotten about the emotional and financial trauma that had been inflicted against the McMartins, including years involved in needless trial and the media's rush to judgment and persecution of them for child sexual abuse. Instead, a panic of stranger danger emerged that set off a new and even tougher set of laws targeting sexual offenders.

## Legislation of the 1990s and Beyond

At a rate unprecedented at any point in history, the 1990s began a wave of panic surrounding sexual offenders and passage of knee-jerk legislation to control "sexual predators" that continues to proliferate to this day. Each of the high-profile cases that will be discussed chronologically involved the violent sexual assault and murder of a child by a stranger offender. Although each of these stories is tragic and each represents a parent's worst nightmare, cases of stranger rape and murder of a child are actually extremely rare. These cases do, however, instill fear into the public and send lawmakers scrambling to quell this fear with new legislation. Each of these tragic stories was followed shortly thereafter by legislation that was quickly put together to satisfy the public's panic. In each of these instances, the law that was created does little to help protect society from the most "typical" type of offender—the non-stranger offender.

In 1989 in Washington State, a man named Earl Shriner abducted a 7-year-old boy, brutally sexually assaulted him, severed his penis, and left him to die. Shriner had a lengthy history with the criminal justice system: he had served time in a mental facility in the 1960s for allegedly murdering a male classmate, and thereafter had been repeatedly charged with molestation (in 1977, 1987, and again in 1988). During his imprisonment, Shriner openly expressed his desires to rape and kill children, but despite these warnings, attempts to commit him to a mental health facility involuntarily were unsuccessful. After serving the entire term to which he was sentenced for sexual assault, he was released. Soon after, the attack on the young boy occurred. This case made headlines, and the public was horrified. Within six months, Washington's legislature passed sweeping new laws to control sexual offenders. They were termed special commitment laws or sexually violent predator laws.

After these laws were passed in Washington, many other states passed similar laws, all of which took effect just prior to release of an individual serving a prison term for a sexual offense. The underlying assumption of these laws is that mental health professionals can identify which sex offenders will likely recidivate and cause future harm and then treat these offenders. Sexually violent predator laws permit the state to confine offenders deemed "mentally abnormal and dangerous sex offenders" to a secure mental facility until they are deemed safe for release.[148] According to Washington State's legislation, individuals eligible for indeterminate commitment include convicted sexually violent offenders (even juveniles) whose sentence is about to expire, as well as those charged with a sexually violent offense who are found incompetent to stand trial or not guilty by reason of insanity. These laws are in many ways similar to the sexual psychopath laws of the 1930s, 1940s, and 1950s, but there are significant differences. First, the current laws do not necessarily require an offender to suffer from a "serious mental disorder." Second, the sexual behavior of the offender need not be in the "recent" past in order for the state to seek civil commitment. Indeed, an offender may have committed a sexual offense 20 years earlier, is about to be released after serving a 20-year sentence, and the state may then petition to have him confined indefinitely. Third, in many states no legitimate treatment program is required for an offender to be confined under a civil commitment statute, despite the fact that these statutes seem to herald the importance of treatment. Finally, current sexually violent predator legislation requires that an offender serve their term of imprisonment in its entirety *prior* to the state seeking civil commitment. Thus, many critics argue that "the primary goal of predator statutes is to provide a mechanism for continued confinement of sex offenders considered at risk of reoffending who can no longer be confined under the criminal justice system."[149] To many critics, this seems like double jeopardy . . . a second punishment for one offense. The Supreme Court, however, has disagreed (see Chapter 4).

Also in 1989, three boys (11-year-old Jacob Wetterling, his 10-year-old brother, and an 11-year-old friend) were confronted by a masked man with a gun while riding their bikes in St. Joseph, Minnesota. The man forced two of the boys to run and subsequently abducted Jacob, who was never found. Because there was a halfway house fairly close to the site of the abduction, there was suspicion that a previously convicted sexual offender was involved, but a suspect was never located. This was one of the few cases that did not result in immediate passage of legislation, which may be because Jacob's body was never found and the search for him was ongoing. Several years after his abduction, a federal law, the Jacob Wetterling Crimes Against Children and Sexually Violent Offender Registration Act, was named in his honor. Referred to commonly as the Wetterling Act, this law requires all states to have mandatory registration protocols that require sex offenders to register their home addresses with authorities. Access to this information varies by state and by the tier at which the offender is assessed. However, in most states this information is accessible to the general public. One of the main critiques of this law is that in many states it includes language that effectively excludes family members and close family friends from being designated sexual predators. For example, according to the Wetterling Act, a "predator" must register, and the act defines predatory behavior as "an act directed at a stranger, or a person with whom a relationship has been established or promoted for the primary purpose of victimization."[150] The rationale behind removing nonstrangers from the definition of predator, as established by two court rulings, is that an offender who targets family members or acquaintances poses less risk to the general community than an offender who targets strangers.[151] But how can this risk be measured? Do the courts contend that incest, spousal rape, and acquaintance rape are less harmful than stranger attacks? There is no existing evidence to support this position, so this law has the appearance of supporting and protecting the societal structures that cause sexual violence: lack of education about sex and sexuality, secrecy surrounding sex and sexuality, and a general devaluation of women and children in American culture.

The year was 1993, and the place was a middle-class neighborhood in California. Twelve-year-old Polly Klaas was abducted from her bedroom during a slumber party with friends. Concerned citizens searched for several weeks as her story was headline news. Richard Allen Davis, who led police to Polly's body, was eventually arrested. Prior to this offense, Davis had served 15 years for various sexual offenses but was always able to plead to offenses and avoid registering as a sexual offender. Davis was convicted and sentenced to the death penalty for the kidnapping, rape, and murder of Polly Klaas. The murder of this young girl by a repeat sexual offender outraged the public, and the media publicized the case incessantly. The result was the passage in California of Proposition 184 less than a year later with overwhelming public support. This proposition would increase penalties for repeat felony offenders. Proposition 184 is commonly referred to as "three strikes" legislation because a third felony conviction results in a sentence of 25 years to life imprisonment. The advocates of this law argue that it deters potential three-time offenders from committing their "third strike," although there is little evidence to suggest a reduction in serious crime has resulted due to this legislation.

In 1994, the rape and asphyxiation of a young girl named Megan Kanka in Hamilton, New Jersey, shocked the nation. It is believed that Megan went to the home of her neighbor, a previously convicted sex offender, under the pretense of meeting his puppy. After sexually assaulting and murdering Megan, Jesse Timmendequas disposed of her body in a nearby park. Timmendequas was on parole for a second offense against a child after he had plea-bargained to a term of 10 years imprisonment.[152] This case sparked outrage and intense media attention because the public felt as if the murder of Megan Kanka could have been prevented. Megan's mother was reported to have said: "We knew nothing about him. If we had been aware of his record, my daughter would be alive today."[153] In response to the public panic, within a month of Megan's murder, registration and community notification legislation was passed in New Jersey, and it was referred to commonly as "Megan's Law." This law became the guideline for all other states to follow, and indeed 16 states did pass similar legislation in the same year. Eventually, the federal government followed suit as well. "Megan's Law" requires sex offenders to register with the police at various time intervals depending upon their assessed tier level, and in many states law enforcement officials must notify communities when a sex offender moves into the neighborhood.

After a psychological assessment, a sexual offender is assigned a tier, ranging from 1 to 3. Tier 3 offenders are deemed the highest risk to the public, Tier 2 offenders are deemed moderate risk, and Tier 1 offenders are deemed to be the lowest risk. To notify the community that a sexual offender has moved into the neighborhood, letters may be delivered by police to various community organizations or to individual homes, Web site notification may be involved, and in some states billboard notification is possible. States such as New Jersey, Oregon, and Washington employ broad dissemination of information about offenders who are subject to community notification, including sending information to local organizations and residents, as well as the media. Other states provide more subtle notification. In states such as Connecticut, Georgia, and New York, discretion is given to probation and parole officers who can notify anyone they deem appropriate. And some states protect the privacy of offenders unless specific information is requested. In states such as Arkansas, Michigan, South Carolina, Vermont, and Virginia, information is disclosed only to individuals who submit a written request. In addition, some states, such as Delaware, label offenders with a designation of "sex offender" on their driver's license. Depending on the state and the tier, juveniles can be required to register, and registration continues even after they become adults. This is a contradiction in terms; although sex offender laws aim to provide as much exposure of offenders as possible, the juvenile justice system has historically sought to protect minor offenders. How can these goals be rationalized? For example, in New Jersey, a juvenile does not enter adulthood with a criminal record unless they are a sex offender. The sex offender registration, depending on the offense the juvenile committed, may have the offender registering long after they have reached adulthood, and sometimes even for life. One critic from the National Center for Juvenile Justice said: "Too few people understand how broad these laws are in their reach. . . . 'We've got all these ugly laws we passed when we were in a bad mood, and this is one of them.'"[154] While estimates are difficult because the ages of offenders are not tracked under the sex offender registry, it has been suggested that anywhere between 10 and 25 percent of offenders are under the age of 18. Many states have age limits, typically 14 or 15, regarding community notification laws, or these laws only apply to those convicted in adult court. A few states, however, even identify juveniles with their picture on the sex offender registry Web site: in Kansas, for example, there are pictures of sex offenders ages 11, 12, and 13.[155] Registration and notification will have a lifelong impact for these individuals.

Community notification laws have broad-based community support because the public is empowered by the sense of knowledge that is provided. However, notification that a sexual offender resides in your neighborhood may also produce a constant sense of fear. President Bill Clinton summed up the purpose of

"Megan's Law" in his presidential radio address on August 24, 1996: "Nothing is more threatening to our families and communities and more destructive of our basic values than sex offenders who victimize children and families. Study after study tells us that they often repeat the same crimes. That's why we have to stop sex offenders before they commit their next crime, to make our children safe and give their parents peace of mind."[156] From the perspective of reintegrating the offender into society, community notification laws label offenders, making it extremely difficult for them to secure housing, employment, and other opportunities. These extra stressors undermine their rehabilitative and treatment efforts. Megan's Law works if the goal is to make parents feel safe and protected from the myth of the recidivating sexual offender. The problem is that this information is not factual, and community notification laws fail to apply to the individuals most likely to take parents' peace of mind.

In 1996 in Arlington, Texas, a 9-year-old girl was pulled off her bike and forced into a truck, which then quickly sped away. Neighbors witnessed the event, and authorities followed a variety of leads without any success. Several days later, the body of Amber Hagerman was found in a drainage ditch near her home; her throat had been slashed. Although law enforcement followed leads for months, Amber's killer was never found. Out of this tragedy came the useful AMBER Alert system (America's Missing: Broadcast Emergency Response). This system provides repeated broadcasts with details of an abducted child and the perpetrator, including a physical description, vehicle description, and any other useful details. Information is broadcast via television, radio, highway notification signs, and even text message in order to garner real-time tips from the public. As of 2005, all states have an AMBER Alert system, which is most effective in recovering children who have been abducted by an individual with whom they have a relationship (e.g., custodial kidnapping). In these situations, information about the perpetrator is more readily available. The U.S. Department of Justice reports that 80 percent of abductions for which an AMBER Alert was issued have resulted in recovery of the child.[157]

Although there was a lull in high-profile sex offender cases from 1996 to about 2005, laws continued to be passed with vigor, including residency restrictions, revisions to registration requirements, revisions to community notification laws, and other community management tools to control sexual offenders. In 2005, the spotlight was on sex crimes again with the abduction of 9-year-old Jessica Lunsford from her Homosassa, Florida, home. The media coverage was intense, and three weeks after her disappearance, a neighbor and registered sexual offender came forward and admitted to sexually assaulting and killing Jessica and disposing of her body in his backyard. The perpetrator admitted to skipping out on his mandated counseling session and failing to register his address with law enforcement officials as required by registration and community notification laws. John E. Couey, the offender, who had an IQ that bordered on mental retardation. He was charged with first-degree murder, kidnapping, sexual battery, and burglary. In 2007, Couey was found guilty and, despite his borderline intelligence and the ban on execution of the mentally retarded, he was sentenced to death by a jury vote of 10 to 2.

As concerned citizens were ending their search for Jessica Lunsford's body in 2005, a 13-year-old girl named Sarah Lunde was abducted from her home in Ruskin, Florida. Because this was the second child abduction in such a short time, the media was in a state of frenzy and the public was outraged. Sadly, a week after her disappearance, Sarah's body was found in a nearby lake. Once again, the man who ultimately confessed to murdering Sarah was a convicted rapist who had previously dated Sarah's mother. Like John E. Couey, David Onstott admitted the murder to detectives, but the confession was never heard at trial because in each case the court ruled the defendant had been denied proper access to an attorney. After a 2-week trial in 2008, Onstott was found guilty of second-degree murder and sentenced to life in prison.

In response to the sexual assault and murder of Lunsford, the Jessica Lunsford Act was passed unanimously in the Florida legislature. This act provided for a 25-year mandatory minimum sentence for an individual convicted of sexual assault of a child under the age of 12. Should the perpetrator be released, he would then be subject to lifetime electronic surveillance. As of 2007, more than 30 states had followed Florida's lead and created legislation with many of the provisions of the 2005 Jessica Lunsford Act, including a mandatory minimum sentence of 25 years to life for certain sexual offenses against children. While this law can be applied to familial offenders, it is rarely used for such offenses as is the case with other types of legislation.

The Adam Walsh Act, a recent and very strong piece of legislation, was signed into law on the twenty-fifth anniversary of Adam Walsh's abduction in Florida from a shopping mall. The young boy was found decapitated 16 days later and, despite searching by law enforcement, the perpetrator was never found. In December 2008, however, the Hollywood police officially closed the investigation by attributing the murder of Adam Walsh to Ottis Toole, an individual long suspected of the crime. "Toole twice confessed to killing the boy— and twice recanted his story, saying he made it up. It could not be learned what, if any, new evidence exists."[158] Toole was a convicted pedophile and murderer who died in prison in 1996. The Adam Walsh Act is heavily supported by government funding and is perhaps most notable for the inclusion of the Sex Offender Registration and Notification Act, commonly referred to as SORNA. SORNA seeks to establish a comprehensive, streamlined, and national system for the registration of sexual offenders. The goal is for all states to have identical information about sex offenders posted online (name, address, birthdate, employment, photo, etc). SORNA organizes sex offenders into three tiers and mandates that Tier 3 offenders (the most serious offenders) update their whereabouts in person with law enforcement officials every 3 months for life, Tier 2 offenders update their whereabouts every 6 months for 25 years, and Tier 1 offenders update their whereabouts every year for 15 years. Failure to register is a felony, punishable by a fine up to $250,000 and/or imprisonment of up to 10 years. As discussed earlier with regard to Megan's Law, SORNA mandates the registration of sexual offenders as young as 14 years of age. Although due process advocates have challenged the constitutionality of the registration requirement, the courts have disagreed and upheld the law in 2008.

While laws vary by state, incest offenders are usually omitted from Web site registration, even though victim information is not provided, only the general offense the individual committed. Because the posting of offender information online, including a photo and address, could be harmful to the victim by inference, victim's rights groups have lobbied in many states to make incest offenders exempt from this type of legislation. To exclude incest offenders, however, ultimately renders the registration useless as familial and acquaintance offenders comprise the majority of sexual offenses and sexual offenders. All states in the United States must comply with the Adam Walsh Act and the provisions of SORNA by the end of July 2009 or risk a reduction in their federal grant funding. The elimination of the most frequent type of sexual victimization in this far-sweeping legislation is a huge mistake. It seems the government responds simply to fear as opposed to facts and has passed little by way of legislation to protect women and children from nonstranger offenses.

The most invasive control on sexual offenders has been the attempt to prevent future sexual offenses through castration. Involuntary sterilization of sex offenders and other habitual criminals was permitted by law in the early 1900s by many states until it was struck down by the U.S. Supreme Court in 1942. Recent laws revived this method of "treatment," and it has been mandated in several states under select circumstances. In 1996, California implemented chemical castration (the use of drugs to lower testosterone) or surgical castration laws, and several other states followed. These laws typically apply to sex offenders seeking early release from prison and require the individual to take drugs to reduce their sex drive, although no requirement exists that makes professionals available or knowledgeable in administering and monitoring this process. Indeed, Colorado's law *requires* the court to order a certain tier of child molester to take anti-androgen treatment as a parole condition without determining the medical appropriateness of the treatment for the individual offender. In Florida, qualified repeat offenders *must* be ordered by the court to submit to weekly chemical castration injections, and even first-time offenders can be sentenced to chemical castration.

While these drugs may reduce excessive sex drives or fantasies, it is important to note that they do not render the individual impotent as the name, castration, implies. These laws have several problems: The issue of consent is wrought with legal and practical ethical implications. Treatment is defined by the offense committed, not the medically appropriate use of such a treatment. Also, once an offender stops receiving injections for chemical castration, it is only a matter of months before his sex drive and testosterone levels return to "normal." In addition, except for Wisconsin, states do not provide funding for these medications, which cost between $200 and $400 per month, much more than most offenders can afford.[159] In June 2008, Louisiana passed Senate Bill 144, which on a second offense would mandate chemical castration for those convicted of aggravated rape, forcible rape, second-degree sexual battery, aggravated incest, and aggravated crimes against nature. This bill also indicated that the court may instead order physical castration, and this punishment would *not* be in place of imprisonment. Offenders are still required to serve their full term. Also, failure to present oneself for castration would result in an additional term of imprisonment of 3 to 5 years.[160] In a statement classifying sexual offenders as monsters, Governor Bobby Jindal commented: "I am glad we have taken such strong measures in Louisiana to put a stop to these monsters' brutal acts. . . . SB144 is a good bill that sends the message that Louisiana will fully punish those who harm children."[161] No one has yet been sentenced to this punishment in Louisiana, and once someone is, an appeal is likely because *Skinner v. State of Oklahoma* ruled that chemical castration violates the Equal Protection Clause of the Fourteenth Amendment if it is only provided as a punishment for certain types of crimes. It is questionable whether this bill will stand the legal test of time. Nevertheless, the governor has succeeded in fearmongering and pandering to his constituency with "tough talk" about sex offenders . . . it does not matter whether or not this type of treatment works, or whether it is legal or indeed ethical.

The United States has passed law after law in an attempt to prevent sex offenders from committing future crimes. In fact, in 2005 alone, lawmakers passed more than 100 sex offender laws, which was double the number passed in 2004. While one could argue that many of these laws infringe on the due process rights of sex offenders, lawmakers and the public are unconcerned with the individual liberties of "sexual predators" in their quest to reduce crime. A voice of reason, Nancy Sabin, the executive director of the Jacob Wetterling Foundation, recognizes that it is not as simple as passing one law after another:

> We keep getting sidetracked with issues like castration and pink license plates for sex offenders, as if they can't borrow or drive another car . . . Don't get me wrong, we need extreme vigilance for some. But these people are coming from us—society—and we have to stop the hemorrhage. We have to stop pretending that these people are coming from other planets.[162]

Terrible crimes against children have resulted in harsh laws against sexual offenses that do not help the struggle against sexual violence. Sexual violence and abuses pervade society, and turning our attentions to atypical dangers, such as stranger danger, does not make society safer. Instead, this shortsighted approach serves only to divert our attention from the structural elements in society that facilitate victimization of women and children.[163] Ours has become a society in which "risks that fall outside the predator template simply cannot figure into the public discourse. Because the risks must remain invisible, we are deflected from a sensible and effective fight against sexual violence."[164] We need a realistic evaluation of violence against women and children and realistic policies to address these concerns . . . policies that address the fact that violence usually comes from nonstrangers, those we know, those we love, not the "bogeymen" flashed on the evening news. Once we recognize typical sources of danger, we will be in a better position to protect society from violence on all fronts.

CHAPTER 4

# CASE STUDIES OF SELECT LAWS

This chapter will use case studies to examine four controversial issues in the area of sexual offending. First, the phenomenon of the hit NBC television show *To Catch a Predator* will be discussed, as will a tragic event that resulted from the airing of one of these episodes. In addition, residency restrictions and the effect of these highly restrictive laws on sexual offenders and their families will be detailed. The little-known law of civil commitment, or indefinite confinement, of offenders under the guise of treatment will be examined using the case of Leroy Hendricks, who challenged the constitutionality of this law. Finally, in 2008 the death penalty as applied to sexual offenses was decided in the courts, and this decision will be discussed. Each of these highly controversial controls on sexual offenders has very negative consequences, as will be seen through a variety of case studies.

## The Phenomenon of *To Catch a Predator*

In recent years, state and federal governments have begun to devote financial resources to the prevention of crimes against children committed on the Internet. Due to the recent attention to Internet sexual offenses, in 2008 MySpace and Facebook added significant safeguards to protect minor users from potential sexual offenders. These changes included a ban on use by those convicted of a prior sexual offense, limited searching ability by adults for users who are under age 18, and the creation of a task force developed to improve methods of verifying user identity information. In addition, these sites will also occasionally search and delete profiles of users violating their content rules. For example, in August 2008, MySpace deleted 146 profiles belonging to sexual offenders after comparing the profiles with the state's sex offender registry.[165] In addition, as of 2007, more than 59 state and local agencies are involved in Internet Crimes Against Children (ICAC) task forces nationwide; together they have made more than 10,000 arrests since 1998.[166]

In addition, there are laws that target offenders who have a history of using the Internet to access or target their victims. A law passed in New Jersey in 2007 bans sexual offenders who used the Internet in the commission of their crime from using the Internet for personal purposes, with an exemption for work required as a part of employment or in the search for employment. Monitoring takes place through the use of installed computer equipment, periodic computer scans, and polygraph examinations. Failure to comply could result in 18 months imprisonment and a $10,000 fine. This type of law is a relatively recent phenomenon, with similar legislation only in Florida and Nevada.[167] On January 1, 2009, Georgia became the first state to require sexual offenders to turn over not only their Internet address, but also their password![168] Because Internet monitoring is a relatively new area, if the past is any indication, the future will likely bring further restrictions for offenders.

Crimes against children on the Internet did not receive widespread media attention until *Dateline NBC* sponsored the series *To Catch a Predator*. In his book on the series, Chris Hansen, host of the show, describes the premise:

> If you had told me before our first *To Catch a Predator* investigation that (a) so many men would be willing to risk their careers, lives, and families to meet a young person for sex; (b) that so many people have apparently uncontrollable addictions and compulsions involving Internet chat rooms and porn sites; and (c) that these investigations, when broadcast, would resonate with our viewers as they have, I would have seriously doubted you. But that is exactly what is happening every day in chat rooms and social networking sites throughout the country. And when you consider that many of these cyber meeting places are populated with curious, boundary-pushing teens, it should surprise no one that the potential for a child to be approached by a predator is high.[169]

*Dateline* worked in conjunction with Perverted Justice, an organization that seeks to expose individuals who use the Internet to exploit children and teenagers. Agents from Perverted Justice posed as teens in chat rooms and engaged in graphic sexual conversations with adults. If the men wanted to meet the minor, arrangements were made for the man to arrive at a house where the Perverted Justice decoy and Chris Hansen were waiting, along with many hidden *Dateline* cameras. When the man arrived with the hopes of finding a young teenager for sexual activity, he was instead met by a television crew. Chris Hansen attempted to interview the individual about their motives. The question of the day: What were you thinking? For several seasons, American viewers were glued to their televisions as man after man arrived at the *Dateline* house only to begin a shaming ritual that likely ended in the demise of their career and family life. Because *Dateline* is a news program, permission was not required to show the faces of these individuals. So, even though they had not been convicted in a court of law, NBC was able to broadcast the identities of these men, with little regard for the impact this may have had on their lives or the lives of their families.

The "other" victims from this type of program are the family members of the alleged offenders. One woman wrote an e-mail to Chris Hansen:

> While I appreciate the fact that your program exposes and removes these vile beings from society, clearly saving potential child victims from these predators, I have yet to see any program on this subject recognize the other victims of this horrific crime . . . the unsuspecting spouses, children, family, and friends of these sick individuals. . . . But what of the lives of this man's grown children, who have to deal with the fact that their father is a sexual predator? Their pain is very real, too. I have seen it firsthand and it kills me to know their faith in those they are supposed to be able to look up to and whose trust has been ruined. To make matters worse, they have to suffer the embarrassment of having people find out. . . . they now go through their life wondering . . . who knows? Does he know? Does she know? Who is going to find out next about what my dad did? What about the way *their* lives have been affected? *We* are victims as well. We carry an unearned . . . undeserved stigma, which merely adds to the already painful and humiliating aftermath . . . for something *we did not do*. We too are punished, serving a sentence.[170]

As the public sits fascinated by the television, we give little thought to the wife or children at home or the parents of the offender, all of whom are humiliated. We also give little thought to the U.S. criminal justice system, which provides for the presumption of innocence until proven guilty. There are many ethical concerns with this program, but because most people despise sexual offenders, little regard is given to these considerations.

### Case Study: Dateline *Show Results in Death*

One of the stings involving Perverted Justice and *Dateline* occurred just outside of Dallas, Texas, in a little town called Murphy in 2006. It involved a decoy named "Luke," allegedly 13 years old, his parents divorced. Luke was purportedly dogsitting for some neighbors while they were away and therefore was alone in the house. He engaged in chat room conversation with a man named "Wil" who said he was a 19-year-old college student. After several days, Wil decided to talk to Luke on the phone. After Luke and Wil chatted, Perverted Justice was able to determine Wil's real identity: that of 56-year-old Bill Conradt, assistant district attorney in a neighboring Texas county. Upon realizing the identity of the man, "the Perverted Justice employee rubbed his hands together, clapped them, obviously energized by the news he was imparting. Chris Hansen's usual on-camera listening expression—lips tight, eyes slightly narrowed, just the hint of a furrow to his brow—did not change."[171]

As a prosecutor, Bill Conradt obviously knew the description of "online solicitation of a minor" in the Texas penal code (statute 33.021): "an adult offends when he 'communicates in a sexually explicit manner with a minor,' and defines 'minor' as anyone who represents himself or herself as being under the age of seventeen."[172] Despite being aware of the law and the potential penalties for violating it, over the course of two weeks, Bill wrote the following messages online to an individual he believed to be 13 years of age: "could I feel your cock; how thick are you; I want to feel your cock; maybe you can fuck me several times; has anyone sucked you; and just talking about this has me hard."[173] Eventually Conradt agreed to meet Luke at the decoy house but failed to appear. This is a glitch in the *Dateline* plan.

How do you lure a prosecutor to a decoy house? Inside the *Dateline* house was Jimmy Patterson, an off-duty detective hired by the show for protection, just in case any of the accused individuals became violent. He started to hear the Perverted Justice folks talk about Bill Conradt:

> He asked them to spell the surname. Sure enough. With a *t*. He knew a Bill Conradt. Had worked with him. Bill Conradt was the chief felony prosecutor of the county that included part of Detective Patterson's city. Bill Conradt had prosecuted people that Detective Patterson had arrested. Couldn't be the same Bill Conradt. . . . Something like this, somebody like this, you've gotta be extra careful. You're talking about law enforcement taking down law enforcement. You've gotta take extra precautions. But the way things had gone these last few days, what with the overzealous made-for-TV cops outside and the real TV people here inside, Detective Patterson wasn't at all sure that the necessary precautions would be taken. As the evening wore on, Detective Patterson learned that Bill Conradt had stopped responding to Dan Schrack's [posing as Luke] phone calls. He'd also stopped responding to the AOL instant messages that the Perverted Justice chat decoy was sending. The IMs were starting to read like semiliterate poems of longing and anxiety. . . . At a little after 9:00 P.M., Detective Patterson overheard Lynn Keller, the lead producer of *To Catch a Predator*, discussing . . . strategies they might employ to lure [Conradt] to Murphy. Detective Patterson was the only law-enforcement officer inside the decoy house, and at that moment, standing there listening to a couple of civilians devising ways to lure an assistant district attorney, he was beginning to feel very uncomfortable. He felt as if he was being made party to something he was not at all sure he wanted to be involved in. Finally he approached Keller, told her that as an officer with the Rowlett Police Department, he felt obligated to call his boss, the chief of police, and give him a heads-up regarding the whole matter brewing with Bill Conradt. Lynn Keller stopped him cold. "You're working for *Dateline* now," she said.[174]

Because Conradt had failed to respond to any further correspondence from the Perverted Justice decoy Luke and was not answering his telephone, *Dateline* decided the best course of action was to have the police secure both a search warrant and an arrest warrant for Conradt. The *Dateline* plan was to ambush Conradt when he left his house, and if an arrest warrant was ready, then the show could film his arrest and hopefully interview him as the scandal was occurring. The show pressured the small-town law enforcement for the warrants overnight. The agents were extremely overburdened with the sheer number of people showing up at the decoy house and the paperwork involved with all these arrests. Conradt had not shown up at the decoy house, had stopped conversation and online correspondence, and had deleted his MySpace page on which he impersonated a 19-year-old college student. For officers the pressure was high, but they succumbed and put together the warrants. The warrants were full of errors: the wrong city, the wrong county, the wrong date. But it was a warrant, and it was signed by a judge in the morning. The Murphy police plan was to go to Bill Conradt's house in the afternoon with the assistance of police from Terrell, the town in which Conradt resides. The *Dateline* crew had been sitting outside of the house for hours in the hopes of interviewing Conradt; however, he never appeared.

> When the cops arrive at Bill Conradt's door on Sunday afternoon, a dog starts barking somewhere inside the house.... Bill Conradt has shared his home with a mini-schnauzer named Lukas for the last several years.... A sergeant from the Terrell Police Department knocks on the door.... Along with the Terrell sergeant, a Terrell patrol officer and Murphy detective Snow Robertson are also at the door. Chief Myrick and Lieutenant Barber are about 30 feet away, hiding behind trees. Another man, a cameraman, is hiding behind a different tree, much closer to the door, evidently trying hard to stay out of the footage being recorded by the other NBC cameramen, perhaps for aesthetic reasons, perhaps because it is generally illegal for news cameras to be on private property without permission. Dateline's cast and crew outnumber the five cops here by a factor of two. One of their cameras captures the sergeant as he presses a door buzzer that has not worked in years. The Murphy detective then draws his gun and holds it in both hands, angling it down so it aims at a spot a foot or two in front of his feet. The sergeant knocks again on the door, which does not lead into the house but rather into a large open courtyard. He tries the doorknob. He presses the useless door buzzer. He waits. Eventually the cameraman stops filming.[175]

After confirmation that the arrest warrant arrived, police decided to call in the SWAT team. This decision was based on Chris Hansen's assertion that the morning newspaper had arrived while the television crew was watching Conradt's house, and while they had not seen him come out of the house, the paper was missing. This decision was widely criticized. A friend of Conradt's and fellow attorney refers to the decision to call in the SWAT team "the stupidest and most unnecessary thing that I have ever heard of in law enforcement. If they really wanted to do the right thing, they could have waited until Bill came out. Or they could have gone to the courthouse where he worked and arrested him. You know, he was not like John Dillinger. That was all for sensationalism."[176]

When *Dateline* aired the *To Catch a Predator* episode that included the case of Bill Conradt, the approach of the SWAT team is dramatic as it always is in television. In reality, however, the SWAT team trickled in and the goal of arrest proceeded once everyone had arrived ... that, of course, would not have been nearly as exciting to watch on television! The neighbors were out on their lawns, curious about what was going on. They knew Conradt as someone who was very private: they cannot remember anyone coming to visit him, and he struck most of them as friendly enough. The SWAT team entered the house through the backyard:

> The last SWAT officer through closes the gate behind him. SWAT's slow march resumes for a few more paces, delivering them past a coiled hose, past a lawn chair,

> past a grill, to a glass sliding door that leads into the house. One of the officers
> holds a black metal battering ram the size of a parking meter and is about to swing
> it. The leader of the team stops him, pulls out a device called a Halligan bar, and
> uses it to lever the door until the lock busts under the pressure and the door slides
> open. The SWAT team pushes through a floor-length curtain.... Eyes adjust and
> flashlights flare. [They yell]: Terrell Police? Search warrant![177]

Officers began to move through the downstairs rooms of the house looking for
Conradt. Through the living room, the kitchen, down a long hallway ...

> Up ahead, at the end of the hallway, an open door. Bill Conradt steps into
> view.... Today he's wearing one of his colored shirts. Black slacks, a colored shirt,
> the same shock of thick fright-white hair he's had since his thirties. His small
> mouth, his wide-set eyes ... Conradt is looking straight ahead. All he sees is Officer
> Todd Wiley and his men behind him.[178]

All the officers agreed that Bill Conradt next said something to the effect of
"I'm not going to hurt anyone!" But then his hands moved, something was
shining, and before anyone knew what had happened, Bill Conradt had placed
the muzzle of his handgun at his temple and fired the weapon.

> The camera settles on one of the SWAT team members standing outside the closed
> door of the ambulance after they load the body inside. A middle-aged man in slacks
> and a sport jacket walks haltingly into the frame. He approaches a cop.... He's ask-
> ing questions, though you can't hear what they are. The guy in the sport jacket is
> named Greg Shumpert. He's the assistant city attorney for Terrell, has known Bill
> Conradt for decades. A friend ... And soon he'll call other friends, mostly other
> lawyers, and the news will spread. And the questions that Greg Shumpert is asking,
> the initial questions of what the hell is going on here, will lead to other questions.
> Friends will question their memories of their friend. Could he have done what the
> police say he did? Those transcripts. The ghastly sordidness of it all. It's so hard to
> imagine a man who never tells a dirty joke having such a dirty mind. Some will con-
> clude that no, he couldn't have done it. Word will pass from friend to friend about a
> possible explanation. An excuse ... people, even smart people, invest themselves in
> explanations that provide them with the least painful world to live in. A world
> where their friends, their friend, the one who wears pressed white shirts and lives
> alone with his dog and always asks if there's anything he can do for you, doesn't,
> didn't, harbor unpleasant sexual fantasies. They'll try to dwell on the good things,
> recount his many kindnesses.... But they won't be able to stop wondering about his
> last hours. How long did he know what was coming? Did he see *Dateline*'s vans
> early in the morning, like so many of his neighbors did? Did he realize then? Or did
> he not realize until the police arrived? Or even until SWAT busted in? When did he
> know for sure? And when did he decide what he was going to do?[179]

After the dust had settled and further investigation of Bill Conradt's home took
place, it was revealed that there was no other evidence of sexual misconduct
than the chats with the Perverted Justice decoy. Police seized a mainstream

pornographic video but did not find any other illegal materials that would indicate that Conradt was a sexual offender or engaged in sexually predatory behavior online. In response to this disastrous investigation and its traumatic ending, Bill Conradt's family filed a $105 million lawsuit in 2007 against NBC. In June 2008, NBC settled the lawsuit with the family for an undisclosed amount, acknowledging, at least in part, their role in Conradt's suicide.[180]

What about the other men arrested in the Murphy, Texas, sting between Perverted Justice and *Dateline*? What happened to these men? After arrest, it is up to the district attorney's office to determine whether to present evidence to the grand jury. The grand jury then determines if there is sufficient evidence for trial or whether they will drop the case due to problems with evidence. Review of evidence for the 23 men arrested in Murphy was the responsibility of Doris Berry, one of the most experienced felony prosecutors in the office of more than 100 district attorneys. In each of the cases, Doris Berry ran into problems, ranging from problems with venue to illegal arrests. There are specific legal guidelines under which an arrest can be made without a warrant, and the Murphy Police Department failed to follow these guidelines; instead, they seemed to simply follow the wishes of the *Dateline* staff. It appeared as though "the Murphy Police Department was merely a player in the show and had no real law-enforcement position."[181] Because of the legal mangling of these cases by law enforcement, the district attorney's office could not pursue indictments for any of the 23 suspects arrested by the Murphy Police Department. Charged with no offense, these individuals and by extension their families were publicly shamed and humiliated, and in the eyes of the law had committed no crime for which they could be legally prosecuted. These actions run counter to the maxim "innocent until proven guilty," the basis of the U.S. criminal justice system.

## Residency Restrictions

Residency restrictions are another type of "banishment" applied to sex offenders as they limit where offenders are permitted to reside and essentially banish them from living, working, or visiting certain areas within a city or town. Since 2006, 18 states have passed such laws. For example, Maryland requires the state's parole commission to establish restrictions on where sex offenders may live, work, and visit. In Washington, legislation directs the Association of Washington Cities to develop statewide standards for determining residency restrictions on sex offenders. Illinois has the least restrictive laws, requiring a 500-foot distance from locations where children may be present, whereas California prohibits certain sex offenders who are on parole from residing within 1/4 mile of elementary schools and within 35 miles of a witness or victim.[182] Many states rushed to pass these laws, despite the fact that no empirical evidence exists to demonstrate that residency restrictions lower recidivism or increase public safety.

These laws have recently been challenged in the courts. For example, in New Jersey in July 2008, an appellate panel ruled that the state's Megan's Law was comprehensive enough to be the only law governing the restrictions placed on sexual offenders. Thus, the panel rejected municipal laws that placed residency restrictions

on sexual offenders in excess of those provided for in the Megan's Law legislation.[183] This ruling affects many municipalities in the state; these towns have
residency restrictions so strict that the entire town is off limits to those convicted
of a sexual offense. As a result of this ruling, many municipalities have repealed
their residency restrictions.[184] The repeal of banishment laws is applauded by
organizations such as the American Civil Liberties Union; however, Victims' Law
Centers and many victim's rights groups assert the importance of such laws and
are committed to appealing these rulings to the highest court. More than 30 states
currently have residency restriction legislation for sexual offenders who are on probation or parole that could be impacted by the ripple effect of this ruling. The case
study examines residency restriction in Georgia, the state with some of the harsh-
est laws geared toward the control of sexual offenders.

### Case Study: Georgia's Banishment Laws

Georgia has approximately 10,000 registered sexual offenders, and it is the state
with perhaps the most stringent laws in the nation. In November 2007 the
Georgia Supreme Court overturned the state residency law that banned registered
sexual offenders from residing within 1,000 feet of a school, playground, church,
school-bus stop, or any location where children might gather. In a unanimous
decision, the law was deemed unconstitutional because it placed a potentially
undue burden on individuals who may have been repeatedly uprooted to remain in
compliance with the law and because it effectively amounted to banishment. At the
root of this case was a convicted child molester who purchased a house with his
wife in 2003 that met the guidelines of the residency restriction law at the time. A
couple of years later, two day-care centers were built within the 1,000-foot buffer,
and the man was told by his probation officer that he must move or risk arrest for
being in violation of the residency restriction. The penalty for a violation is up to
10 years imprisonment. He sued the Department of Corrections because theoretically this scenario could have replayed itself over and over in different locales
throughout the state, so that he might never be able to find a permanent
residence.[185] While the stated goal of such legislation is public safety, Georgia's law
is particularly onerous in that it applies to even low-tier offenders. For example,
persons convicted of consensual sexual activity as high-school students (in an act
classified as statutory rape due to a difference in age) would be forced to register
as sexual offenders and comply with the state residency restrictions.

When created, the intent of this law was clearly stated by one of the sponsors
of the legislation, House Majority Leader Jerry Keen said, "he intended to make
its restrictions onerous enough that offenders will want to move to another
state."[186] This ruling, however, is a major step forward in reintegrating offenders
into the community after they have served their sentences and/or completed
their treatment programs. "In finding the residency restrictions unconstitutional,
the Georgia Supreme Court ruled that, by forcing a sex offender from his home,
the law violated his Fifth Amendment right to be safe from the government
'taking' his property."[187] Those who have been previously convicted are cautiously
optimistic about what this may mean for their future. "'It was outrageous—it was
ridiculous,' said Wendy Whitaker, 28, a registered sex offender whose case had

been used as an example by opponents of the law. When she had just turned 17 years old, Whitaker engaged in a single act of oral sex with a boy at school. The boy was 15 years old. 'The law didn't discriminate between a violent criminal and someone who made a mistake when they were a teenager,' she said. She and her husband have moved three times in the past year because of the law and have finally wound up in South Carolina because that state has no such residency regulations. 'I don't know that we'll go back,' she said. 'We're just getting settled again.'"[188] According to the ruling, "It is apparent that there is no place in Georgia where a registered sex offender can live without continually being at risk of being ejected." [189] In Georgia, this has changed. Perhaps other states will follow suit once they realize that changing this law will not result in an increase in sexual offending.

# Civil Commitment

Early sexual psychopath legislation of the 1930s and 1940s started to fall out of favor in the 1960s as the public became concerned with issues of due process and began to question the usefulness of current methods of treatment. In the 1990s, however, Earl Shriner's case revived the public's desire for severe and lengthy sentences. Recall that Earl Shriner had an extensive history of repeated child sex offenses and was released from prison after serving the full length of a fixed sentence for sexual assault. Before his release from prison, he reportedly expressed his continued desire to rape and torture children. However, attempts to commit him to a mental health facility were unsuccessful. Shortly after his release from prison, Shriner committed another violent sexual offense resulting in the death of a child. Within six months, the state of Washington had passed sweeping legislation to target sexual offenders. These laws were referred to as Sexually Violent Predator Laws or they were more commonly called "civil commitment." Similar laws were passed in many states; these laws take effect when an offender is about to be released from serving his prison term. As with earlier sexual psychopath laws, these laws are premised on the belief that "experts" can identify which offenders are likely to inflict future harm. The presumed goal is, therefore, to confine these individuals who are believed to be "mentally abnormal and dangerous sex offenders" and treat them until they are no longer a threat to society. The dilemma is that offenders are not necessarily offered treatment in prison but only on their release, making the primary purpose of such legislation incapacitation rather than therapeutic action. Perhaps the major problem with sexually violent predator or civil commitment laws is that "experts" capable of identifying offenders who are potentially dangerous are not nearly as effective at identifying when these same offenders are rehabilitated and no longer a threat to society. While offenders are incapacitated under civil commitment legislation on a fairly regular basis, they are very rarely "treated" and released.[190]

## Case Study: Double Jeopardy Isn't What It Seems

The law precludes punishing an individual twice for the same crime, in other words, double jeopardy. It appears, however, that an exception has been made for sexual offenders. Say, for example, that an offender has served 10 years in prison for his sexual offense. Six months prior to his release, the state petitions the court to have him civilly committed. If the court agrees (after a procedure that will be discussed below), the individual is then committed to a secure mental facility for "treatment" for an *indefinite* period of time. In layman's terms, this individual has served his sentence in prison and will now serve the remainder of his life in a mental facility! Everything about this appears to scream double jeopardy. However, in a key Supreme Court decision (*Kansas v. Hendricks*, 1997), sexual predator or civil commitment laws were ruled constitutional.

As of 2007, 20 states have sexually violent predator statutes: Arizona, California, Florida, Illinois, Iowa, Kansas, Massachusetts, Minnesota, Missouri, Nebraska, New Hampshire, New Jersey, New York, North Dakota, Pennsylvania, South Carolina, Texas, Virginia, Washington, and Wisconsin. Standards vary considerably by state regarding what qualifies an individual for civil commitment, but all of these standards involve some level of "dangerousness," a history of sexual offending, a "serious mental disorder," and "serious difficulty controlling" behavior. What does vary considerably is the language of the statute. For example: offenders in Minnesota must be "highly likely" to reoffend in order to be civilly committed, yet in Wisconsin the standard is "most likely to reoffend." The 1998 New Jersey Sexually Violent Predator Act is an example:

Effective August 1999, The New Jersey Sexually Violent Predator Act (SVPA) establishes an involuntary civil commitment procedure for a sexually violent predator, whom the bill defines as a person who: (1) has been convicted, adjudicated delinquent or found not guilty by reason of insanity for commission of a sexually violent offense, or has been charged with a sexually violent offense but found to be incompetent to stand trial; and (2) suffers from a mental abnormality or personality disorder that makes the person likely to engage in acts of sexual violence if not confined in a secure facility for control, care and treatment." "The Attorney General may initiate a court proceeding for involuntary commitment under this bill by submitting to the court a clinical certificate for a sexually violent predator, completed by a psychiatrist on the person's treatment team. . . . Upon receipt of these documents, the court shall immediately review them to determine whether there is probable cause to believe that the person is a sexually violent predator in need of involuntary commitment. If so, the court shall issue an order for a final hearing and temporarily authorize commitment to a secure facility designated for the custody, care and treatment of sexually violent predators. . . . The person's psychiatrist on the treatment team, who has examined the person no more than five calendar days prior to the court hearing, must testify to the clinical basis for the need for involuntary commitment as a sexually violent predator. Other treatment team members, relevant witnesses or next-of-kin are also permitted to testify. . . . At this hearing, and any subsequent review court hearing, the person has the following rights: The right to be represented by counsel or, if indigent, by appointed counsel; The right to be present at the court hearing unless the court determines that because of the person's conduct at the court hearing the proceeding cannot reasonably continue while the person is present; The right to present evidence; The right to cross-examine witnesses; and The right to a hearing in camera. The bill provides that if the court finds by clear and convincing evidence that the person is in need of involuntary commitment, it shall issue an order authorizing the involuntary commitment of the person to a facility designated for custody, care and treatment of sexually violent predators. Also, the court may order that the person be conditionally discharged in accordance with a plan to facilitate the person's adjustment and reintegration into the community, if the court finds that the person will not be likely to engage in acts of sexual violence because the person is amenable to and highly likely to comply with the plan. Additionally, the bill provides for annual court review hearings of the need for involuntary commitment as a sexually violent predator. The first hearing shall be conducted 12 months from the date of the first hearing, and subsequent hearings annually thereafter. In addition, at any time during involuntary commitment, if the person's treatment team determines that the person's mental condition has so changed that the person is not likely to engage in acts of sexual violence if released, the treatment team shall recommend that the Department of Human Services authorize the person to petition the court for discharge. Also, a person may petition the court for discharge without authorization from the department. In this case, the court shall review the petition to determine whether it is based on facts upon which a court could find that the person's condition had changed, or whether the petition is supported by a professional expert evaluation or report. If the petition fails to satisfy either of these requirements, the court shall deny the petition without a hearing.[191]

From state to state, the language of the statutes is highly subjective and open to interpretation.

While the New Jersey Sexually Violent Predator Act outlines the basic steps to commitment, not all state statutes outline this procedure clearly. Generally, however, the steps are fairly similar. The first stage of evaluation for civil commitment by a mental health professional usually involves a variety of processes completed by a psychiatrist. She (to distinguish from the offender) will gather outside information regarding the offender and his offenses from family and friends, gather previous treatment records and Department of Corrections records, and compile victim statements. She will create a background history, which will include a sexual history. This will involve any sexual deviations in which he has engaged or which he fantasizes about. A mental status examination is normally conducted to evaluate for mental disorders, paraphilic behaviors, or personality disorders, and a variety of psychological tests and other assessment tools are frequently used. In addition, a physical exam and standard medical examination are performed.[192] In many states, if the psychiatrist (on behalf of the Department of Corrections) determines that the offender meets the criterion for civil commitment, the case is referred to the Attorney General's Office. The decision to file a petition with the court is then left to the Office of the Attorney General. Should it be determined that a petition is going to be filed with the court, the offender is typically granted a variety of procedural protections that include counsel, the ability to procure expert witnesses, and the right to a jury hearing. The standard of proof in a civil commitment hearing is "beyond a reasonable doubt," the same standard that exists in a criminal trial. Should the offender be deemed a sexually violent predator, confinement is for an indeterminate length of time in order to "treat" the mental condition believed responsible for producing the sexual violence. Some state statutes provide a mandated period of reevaluation of the offender and his behaviors and propensities toward sexually violent behaviors once he has been committed, whereas other states do not provide for such reevaluation. The court/jury must rule the offender no longer poses a risk of sexual violence before he will be released to the community.[193] However, the number of individuals released after receiving a term of civil commitment is extremely low (as of January 2007, only 495 persons have been released, and 4,534 offenders are confined under this legislation).[194]

This case involved Leroy Hendricks who undoubtedly had a lengthy history of sexual offenses. His history included: indecent exposure (1955), lewdness against a child (1956), and several charges of sexual assault against children (1960, 1967, and 1984). Hendricks served time in prison for each of these offenses but was released after his sentence had terminated. In Kansas, there is a Habitual Criminal clause, which allows the state to petition the court to have an individual who has been convicted of three prior felonies designated as a habitual criminal. This designation dramatically increases the sentence on subsequent charges. In 1984, when Hendricks was charged with two counts of child molestation, the State of Kansas chose not to have him classified as a habitual criminal and instead permitted a plea agreement resulting in a sentence of 5 to 20 years.

As Hendricks was serving the tenth year of his sentence, the state petitioned the court to have him declared a sexually violent offender. Designation as a sexually violent offender would mean that he could be held indefinitely to "prevent" future sexual offenses. After a psychological evaluation, it was determined that Hendricks was clinically a pedophile, and at trial he was found "mentally abnormal," which is one requirement of the sexually violent persons legislation in Kansas. Hendricks contested the finding, and during the Supreme Court trial his lawyer argued that the statute was unconstitutional, violated the provision against double jeopardy, and provided for *ex post facto* (after the fact) punishment. The U.S. Supreme Court, however, in a 5 to 4 decision, disagreed. The Court stated:

> . . . a state statute providing for the involuntary civil commitment of sexually violent predators . . . does not violate the double jeopardy clause of the Federal Constitution's Fifth Amendment where, because the state did not enact the statute with punitive intent, the statute does not establish criminal proceedings, and involuntary commitment pursuant to the statute is not punitive; thus, for purposes of analysis under the double jeopardy clause, (1) initiation of commitment proceedings under the statute against a person upon his imminent release from prison after serving a sentence for the offenses which led to his being declared a violent sexual predator does not constitute a second prosecution, and (2) a person's involuntary detention under the statute does not violate the double jeopardy clause, even though that confinement follows a prison term.[195]

In essence, the Supreme Court justices permitted civil confinement because this legislation might protect society from dangerous persons whose violence was a product of a mental disorder.

*Kansas v. Hendricks* clearly emphasized the power of the state to protect the community over individual liberty. The Supreme Court in this case allowed statutes permitting the original offense that led to arrest to be a justification for continued confinement, even if the offense occurred 20 years prior and no treatment has occurred in 20 years. For some scholars, this is ethically problematic![196] Legally, however, this decision has been upheld since the1997 ruling: These laws are constitutional because they are civil proceedings, not a second criminal punishment. Civil commitment requires proof of "serious difficulty controlling behavior," and the condition must be one that the psychiatric community considers a "serious mental disorder."[197]

The goal of sexually violent predator/civil commitment legislation is to protect the public from offenders who are likely to reoffend because of a mental abnormality that predisposes them to sexual violence. This goal is admirable to a society that seeks to lower rates of victimization of women and children. This could be accomplished, however, without the appearance of a constitutional violation because, despite the ruling of the Supreme Court, sentencing an offender to prison for 3 or 4 years and then seeking an indefinite sentence of commitment under the guise of treatment for a "mental disorder" that causes "uncontrollable sexual desires" raises ethical issues. Widespread public support for civil commitment policies occurs only in situations in which the offender is perceived as receiving a lenient sentence for a serious sexual offense.[198] Society could send the same message to serious sexually violent offenders by changing the laws so that sexual offenses garnered a reasonably long sentence at the outset, similar to mandatory minimum sentencing policies, or "three strikes" laws. And some of these changes have been made, for example, in the Adam Walsh Act. It is ethically problematic to try and "predict" future behavior. While sex offenders are so despised and ostracized that they make for an easy first target, we should be wary because civil commitment laws could be applied to other types of offenders in the future.

Considering the practical side of civil commitment, there is the economic aspect. The financial investment in this legislation is enormous! For example, the cost of the average annual civil commitment program is $97,000 per offender, and at the beginning of 2007 there were 4,534 sexual offenders confined nationally under sexually violent predator legislation in eighteen states.[199] Despite the cost being so high, many of these facilities are too underfunded to offer treatment at all, or even to offer substandard levels of treatment with personnel who are not properly trained to treat sex offenders. Many programs that do offer treatment have not been empirically tested; therefore, the effectiveness of such programs are largely unknown. This begs the question: if you cannot empirically demonstrate the effectiveness of treatment programs, how do you determine who is "cured" and ready for release? Also problematic: many offenders committed do not attend treatment. "In California, three-quarters of civilly committed sex offenders do not attend therapy. Many say their lawyers tell them to avoid it because admission of past misdeeds during therapy could make getting out impossible or, worse, lead to new criminal charges."[200] This further reduces the likelihood of release. Some of these funds should be redirected to treatment of sexual offenders living *in* the community! For example, Minnesota spends approximately $20 million per year on civil commitment, but spends only $1.1 million for treatment of sexual offenders in the community and $2.1 million to treat sexual offenders who are in prison.[201] Most sexual offenders end up reintegrating and living within the community, so spending this huge amount of money for civil commitment compared to community treatment seems entirely disproportionate to community needs and safety prevention! Leroy Hendricks, the man who challenged the constitutionality of civil commitment and lost, continues to be confined in a secure mental facility in Kansas, more than 13 years after his prison term would have ended. He is 72 years old and has suffered a stroke. He spends most days confined to a wheelchair due to diabetes. It is unlikely he remains a public safety risk, though officials continue his confinement under sexually violent predator legislation. Civil commitment, however, is not the most severe punishment that has been considered by the criminal justice system for the control of sexual offenders.

## The Death Penalty Case Study

The death penalty has long been an issue of contention and controversy in the United States. One noteworthy case that prompted a consideration of the cruel and unusual nature of the death penalty occurred in Florida in 2006 when a lethal injection took 34 minutes to execute a condemned man. This is more than twice the anticipated length of the procedure. After a review of the procedures, the Florida Supreme Court ruled in November 2007 that the lethal injection procedure was acceptable. The first execution in Florida after this ruling was in July 2008. The condemned man, Mark Dean Schwab, had been convicted of kidnapping, raping, and murdering an 11-year-old boy named Junny Rios-Martinez in 1991. The murder of Rios-Martinez took place a mere month after Schwab was granted early release on a charge of raping a 13-year-old boy. As a result of Rios-Martinez's murder, Florida passed the Junny Rios-Martinez Act of 1992, which prohibits the early release of sexual offenders from prison and prohibits credit for good behavior for sexual offenders.[202]

The Rios-Martinez case involved the sexual assault and murder of a child, but can an offender be sentenced to die for a sexual offense that does not result in murder? U.S. Supreme Court rulings in 1976 and 1977 barred the death penalty for rape cases as unconstitutional. However, a handful of states such as Florida, Louisiana, Montana, Oklahoma, South Carolina, and Texas, passed laws permitting the death penalty for child rape. These states passed their laws under the guise that the Supreme Court decisions referred only to the sexual assault of adult women, not children. Even though these laws are on the books, a man has not been executed in the United States for a sexual offense in which the victim was not murdered since 1964. Did the Supreme Court justices bar execution for the rape of women *and* children? Could Louisiana execute a child sexual offender who did not murder his victim? This was the question before the court in 2008.

Patrick Kennedy had been on death row at Angola Prison in Louisiana since 2003, convicted of raping his 8-year-old stepdaughter. The prosecutor had argued: "In my opinion the rape of a child is more heinous and more hideous than a homicide.... It takes away their innocence, it takes away their childhood, it mutilates their spirit. It kills their soul. They're never the same after these things happen."[203] Conversely, an appellate attorney reminded the court: "When we look at what it means to be cruel and unusual, this is exactly the kind of thing that raises these serious concerns of the constitutionality of Mr. Kennedy's death sentence."[204] Is it cruel and unusual punishment to execute an individual who has not taken the life of his victim? Historically the death penalty has been reserved for murder, which made this case quite controversial. This case also had underlying racial elements. Patrick Kennedy is African American and resides in a southern state where racial discrimination has always been a consideration, even when the victim is also African American, which was the case in this particular scenario. "All fourteen rapists executed by Louisiana in the past 75 years were African American ... [and] nationwide from 1930 to 1964, nearly 90 percent of executed rapists were black."[205]

The court had decided. In June 2008, in a 5 to 4 ruling, the U.S. Supreme Court asserted that execution of child sexual offenders is unconstitutional and violates the Eighth Amendment's prohibition against cruel and unusual punishment. The justices stated, "we cannot sanction this result when the harm to the victim, though grave, cannot be quantified in the same way as the death of the victim."[206] The court further stated: "by in effect making the punishment for child rape and murder equivalent, a State that punishes child rape by death may remove a strong incentive for the rapist not to kill the victim. Assuming the offender behaves in a rational way, as one must to justify the penalty on grounds of deterrence, the penalty in some respects gives less protections, not more, to the victim, who is often the sole witness to the crime."[207] The Supreme Court thus concluded that the death penalty was not a proportional punishment for the crime of child rape.

Through case studies, this chapter has elaborated four controversial issues in the area of sexual offending: *Dateline*'s *To Catch a Predator*, residency restrictions, sexually violent predator laws, and the death penalty. All of them are serious controls on sexual offenders, and each can have very negative consequences. The shaming ritual and resulting humiliation of such programs as *To Catch a Predator* as well as residency restrictions make it extremely difficult for sexual offenders to exist in the community, as most offenders must do at the end of their prison sentence or during community management. If society seeks lower rates of victimization of women and children, we need to be cognizant of the factors that increase recidivism and work diligently on treatment and reintegration efforts. Those are the tools that will lead to increased public safety, not draconian banishment, shaming, civil commitment, or execution controls.

# PART III

# AN ANALYSIS OF CRIMES AND PUNISHMENTS

# CHAPTER 5

# "So-Called" Sex Crimes

Sexual activity is as varied as there are people. The sex acts we consider repugnant today have been around for thousands of years and at some point in history were considered acceptable, or at least tolerated. So why are so many people charged and convicted of victimless acts? Why does the government invade our bedrooms and punish us for consensual sexual activity? A host of factors, including religion, medicine, academia, and the media, combine to influence why Americans consider certain acts, although consensual and participated in by many, to be immoral and therefore illegal. This chapter reviews some of these victimless "crimes," including oral sex, homosexuality, prostitution, sadomasochism, statutory offenses, bestiality, polygamy, and certain forms of incest.

## Oral Sex

Oral sex, or mouth–genital sex, was a highly taboo form of sexual activity in American culture until the 1980s. Though the sexual revolution expanded the boundaries of sex, its influence was mostly in terms of the acceptance of premarital sex, having multiple sexual partners, and cohabiting versus marriage. Historically, oral sex was thought of as an activity engaged in by "bad girls" or prostitutes. However, oral sex, at least from a female-giver, male-recipient perspective, has been part of married sexual life for decades. Kinsey and his research team learned that between 20 and 46 percent of women and over 70 percent of men had received oral sex.[208] For some feminists, oral sex was the archetype of submissive sexual behaviors because the woman was seen as being on her knees servicing her male partner and receiving no pleasure of her own. But times have changed—or have they? Many young women now enjoy giving their male partners oral sex and find it sexually thrilling to hold such power over their partner's ability to orgasm. Moreover, many women are also the recipients of oral sex and are demanding it as part of their sexual relationships. So the taboo surrounding this behavior is slowly fading. But when we add in other factors, such as the race and age of the partners, it becomes glaringly evident that the law is light years behind understanding what Americans actually do in their bedrooms. The case study of Genarlow Wilson provides illustration.

### Case Study: Oral Sex and Race

Genarlow Wilson was an African American 17-year-old high school athlete in Georgia with a solid GPA. He was, from all accounts, a good friend and citizen who had never been in trouble with the law. On New Year's Eve, he attended a party where friends videotaped having sex with a 17-year-old female. Later in the evening, friends videotaped as a white 15-year-old female performed oral sex on him. He was subsequently charged with aggravated child molestation and rape. After a trial that garnered much media attention, a jury found him guilty of aggravated child molestation, acquitting him of rape. He was sentenced to 11 years. Ten years of this sentence was a mandatory sentence, and he received an additional year of probation.[209] Upon release, he was required to register as a sex offender for life. Wilson was convicted under the Child Protection Act of 1995, which raised the legal age of consent to 15 years. This law did not apply to oral sex, however, as this act was considered "aggravated child molestation" regardless of the age of the participants.[210] Though this law was intended to make it a misdemeanor for youth to engage in consensual sexual activities, its so-called "Romeo and Juliet" provision went into effect after Wilson's conviction. The provision states that no teenager prosecuted for consensual oral sex (provided the "victim" is at least 15 years old and the "offender" is no more than 3 years older) could receive more than a 12-month sentence and would not be required to register as a sex offender. Although Wilson's sentence was subsequently overturned on appeal, he had served almost three years in prison for this consensual sexual activity! This case raises serious questions about the American justice system. Was Wilson convicted because he was black and his female sex partner was white? Was he convicted because the jury found it distasteful that he videotaped sex acts with two females in one evening? Was Wilson convicted because oral sex is still regarded as obscene? Why did it take nearly three years for his sentence to be overturned despite the apparent growing public outrage over the conviction? The answers to these questions may never be known, but this case is certainly illustrative of an outrageous sentence for a minor crime.

## Homosexuality and Sodomy

The history of homosexuality is varied. In ancient Greece, men engaged in homosexual activities because women were considered inferior and men wanted to enjoy sex with equals. In some cultures, males were introduced to sex and sexuality through homosexual contacts. Historically, young men, often in their early teens, learned about sexual functioning by becoming involved with an older male. Such relationships were not considered abusive, but instructional and socially desirable. The history of female homosexuality is less well known, though we are aware that in Victorian times women were committed to mental institutions for participating in lesbian affairs. The church's stance against homosexuality strongly influenced the creation of sodomy and gross indecency laws in America. Homosexuals, defined under law as male, were regarded as child predators with violent and recurring urges to attack children. In response, sexual psychopath laws were created, affording the public some assurance of safety by allowing for the indefinite incarceration of convicted habitual offenders. Though homosexuality is no longer illegal, some acts associated with it are still criminalized in select states. Moreover, it has been de-listed as a mental disorder from the *Diagnostic and Statistical Manual* only recently. Three case studies illustrate the disparate treatment of homosexuality in the eyes of the law.

### Case Study: Matthew Limon

Matthew Limon lives in Kansas and had been diagnosed as having "borderline intellectual functioning" with "mild mental retardation."[211] He was a resident at a coed facility for developmentally delayed youth when one week after his eighteenth birthday he performed consensual oral sex on another male resident who was almost 15 years old at the time (3 years and 1 month younger than Limon). Limon was charged and convicted of criminal sodomy for the consensual act and was sentenced to 17 years and 2 months in prison. He was also sentenced to undergo 60 months of post-release supervision and register as a sex offender. All appeals have been denied. Limon's case is similar to that of Genarlow Wilson, except that Kansas law specifically excludes homosexual consensual sex between teenagers. Under Kansas's so-called "Romeo and Juliet Law," statutory rape offenses are considered less severe when they are engaged in by two consenting teenagers. However, the law reads: "(a) Unlawful voluntary sexual relations is engaging in voluntary: (1) sexual intercourse; (2) sodomy; or (3) lewd fondling or touching with a child who is 14 years of age or less than 4 years of age older than the child, and child and offender are the only parties involved and are members of the opposite sex."[212] Thus, because Limon is homosexual, he is subject to much harsher penalties—had his partner been female, he would have received a maximum sentence of 15 months. What was the court's reasoning behind upholding the verdict? The Kansas sodomy statute applies only to same-sex activity because there is already precedent for treating homosexuals differently under the law.[213] Justice Henry W. Green Jr., the judge presiding over the case, stated the following in his decision: "Throughout history, governments have extolled the virtues of procreation as a way to furnish new workers, soldiers, and other useful members of society. The survival of society requires a continuous replenishment of its members."[214] The judge continued:

> When a child is born from a relationship between a minor and a young adult, the minor is often unable to financially support the newborn child. In many cases, the minor is still a dependent. As a result, the financial burden to support the newborn child properly falls to the young adult. Obviously, the young adult cannot furnish adequate financial support for the newborn child while he or she is incarcerated. The legislature could well have concluded that incarcerating the young adult parent

for a long period would be counterproductive to the requirement that a parent has a duty to provide support to his or her minor child. On the other hand, same-sex relationships do not generally lead to unwanted pregnancies. As a result, the need to release the same-sex offender from incarceration is absent.[215]

This case illustrates clear discrimination based on sexual orientation under the law.

As a result of numerous cases involving homosexuals being charged and convicted of sex crimes, the Society for the Scientific Study of Sexuality, a nationally recognized body dedicated to the academic study of sexuality, developed a policy statement on sodomy laws. The statement reads:

> The decision of the Supreme Court to uphold Georgia's Sodomy Statute threatens sexual freedom of choice and intrudes into extremely intimate and private aspects of human life and personality. The Georgia Statute criminalized the acts of oral and anal sex occurring between consensual adults, whether married or not, in the privacy of the home transforming such common and noninjurious acts into felons, punishable by 20 years in prison.... Oral and anal sex is common sexual behavior and is not pathological whether engaged in with a member of the same or other gender. Freedom to express intimacy through such behavior is important to the psychological health of individuals and intimate relationships. The statute undermines public health goals for several reasons. First, it may inhibit the individuals from telling physicians about their sexual conduct or orientation. Second, it may interfere with health education efforts designed to encourage safer sexual practices. Third, because realistic fear of criminal punishment will inhibit accurate reporting of scientifically and medically necessary information, the statute may adversely affect scientific investigation directed toward containing and finding a cure for diseases such as AIDS. Because neither homosexuality nor oral and anal sex is pathological in and of itself, the State's imposition of criminal punishment for private, consenting sexual conduct only increases needless sex guilt, self-hatred, and homophobia.[216]

If such an ideological change began to influence laws nationwide, the attention of law enforcement would be focused on sexual offenses with a victim, as opposed to "victimless" sexual offenses.

### Case Study: Assaulted While Sleeping

In 2007, 33-year-old Glenn Murphy Jr. of Indiana, the elected chairperson of the Young Republican National Foundation, was accused of "criminal deviant conduct" after attempting to have oral sex with a sleeping man. After a night of drinking with the victim and the victim's sister, Murphy returned to the sister's home and fell asleep on the top bunk of a bed. The victim was asleep on the lower bunk. The victim reported to police that he awoke to Murphy performing oral sex on him. The victim physically removed Murphy from the house. Later that day, Murphy called the victim and informed him that he believed the act was consensual because the victim had caressed Murphy's hair after he moved from the top bunk to the floor. Apparently, this was not the first time that Murphy had performed oral sex on a sleeping man.[217] In 1998, an acquaintance had reported the same behavior but did not pursue charges. Murphy pleaded guilty and was sentenced to two years in prison and four years probation; it is likely that he will only serve one year in prison due to good behavior while incarcerated.

### Case Study: Public Sex

After receiving complaints about gay sex occurring at a public lookout area, police initiated an undercover investigation, which resulted in arrests of 24 men, aged 18 to 84 years. The local newspaper and news media published photos and personal information on all of the suspects, in some cases exposing their sexual orientation to family, friends, and co-workers for the first time. Two men pleaded guilty: a 65-year-old man was sentenced to 180 days in jail and a $500 fine, and a 69-year-old man was given the same sentence with 150 days suspended if he completed his 2 years probation without incident. Both men were required to register as sex offenders with the state.[218] Compare this to a young heterosexual couple from Manhattan, age 21 and 20 years, who had oral sex in the park while their 2-year-old child played nearby. Other parents at the park complained to police about the couple's behavior. The couple was charged with a misdemeanor and given a summons to appear in court for sentencing.[219] The maximum sentence the couple could receive was one year in jail.

Are African Americans treated differently than Caucasians when it comes to sex crime laws? Are the mentally challenged treated differently? Are homosexuals treated differently? If we look at these case studies, it certainly appears that minority groups, or those who do not conform to traditional notions of sexuality, are treated much more harshly under the law. But why? The answer is complicated and lies in history, religion, family background, and the political climate of the time, as well as other factors. In addition to the macro-factors (such as society and culture), some micro-factors are also relevant. The police officer who received the call about inappropriate behavior has discretion in deciding whether to charge the people involved, and the district attorney has discretion in deciding whether to proceed with charges. If defendants are charged, can they afford to hire a good lawyer who can get the charges dropped or reduced? The sexual attitudes and behaviors of the presiding judge or jury are also relevant. So many individual, cultural, and societal factors go into differential treatment of persons who come into contact with the criminal justice system for sexual offenses, but much of it can be traced to our beliefs about "normal" sexual behaviors.

## Prostitution

Prostitution is considered by some to be a victimless crime; however, there is great controversy over this issue, and both sides are very passionate about their position. On the one hand, some argue that prostitution is work, and as in any other type of employment, there are positive and negative experiences. This view holds that despite the mistaken belief that prostitution means drug-addicted women walking the street, street sex is an extremely small percentage of actual sex work. Many women and men now advertise on the Internet, are affiliated with escort services, or work out of clubs and bars. This perspective holds that many sex workers are not addicts but have freely chosen to participate in a line of work that pays significantly for female labor; therefore, they are not victims. Others argue that prostitutes are addicts, come from broken homes, and are often victims of childhood sexual abuse that has led them to "sell" their bodies as a continuation of a lifetime of sexual exploitation. Such women are considered both in need of help and of punishment for the crime and lawlessness they bring to city streets.[220] Male prostitution is rarely discussed.

At the heart of the issue of prostitution is how society views female sexuality, which has been repressed since the beginning of recorded history. Regardless of culture, country of origin or ethnicity, female sexuality has been deemed threatening to the social order, and thus men sought control over women's bodies. Historically, religion played a dominant role in society, often placing the blame for prostitution on women and their insatiable desire to attract and seduce men. This belief has placed extraordinary guilt on women for their sexual actions, which has resulted in a systemic suppression of female sexuality.[221] This suppression was further solidified in the Victorian era when men were given legal, moral, and political rights over the sexuality of women.[222] Marriage was the only socially acceptable outlet for women's sexuality and defined the woman as both a person and a sexual being.[223] Marriages of convenience and loveless marriages were common as women sought economic security in a society that refused them active involvement in the labor force. Women were often left with two options: marriage or prostitution.

As the women's liberation movement grew and economic conditions in America changed, forcing many women into the labor force as a result of World Wars I and II, the attitudes and behaviors of women were subsequently altered. These attitudes and behaviors shifted from conservatism in the 1930s through the 1960s, to more permissiveness in the 1960s through the 1980s, and then back to a more constrained view beginning in the 1990s through the 2000s. By the 2000s, young women waited longer for their first sexual encounter, increasingly used contraceptives consistently, and held more conservative attitudes about the acceptability of sex prior to marriage. In 2006, 23 percent of young people believed it was wrong to have premarital sex as compared to 10 percent in 1972.[224] Although sexual behaviors are strongly influenced by cultural gender norms, women's perceptions of their interpersonal relationships, gender roles, sexuality, and social status all impact sexual behavior. Consequently, despite women's increased sexual opportunities, many are restricted in their behavior by traditional gender role stereotypes (for example, many women minimize or lie about their number of sex partners). This restriction results in a lack of power in interpersonal relationships and an inability by many women to demand the use of safer sex practices. The result is that women often know what is expected of them sexually before they truly know who they are as sexual beings.[225]

Several themes emerge from reviewing the sexual attitudes and behaviors of women historically. Female sexuality is highly variable and is experienced differently based on race, educational level, religion, and socioeconomic status. While women may have received more social freedoms in general, sexual repression has continued into the present, albeit in different forms. Women are no longer controlled by their lack of access to contraceptives or legal abortions and no longer have to rely on men for economic subsistence. However, women are now dominated by the media and societal perceptions of ideal feminine beauty, perceptions that have driven many women to extraordinary lengths to meet the sexual ideals created by society. Young women are now engaging in oral sex more frequently than vaginal sex to ensure their status as desirable sexual beings while simultaneously remaining "chaste." Moreover, women have greater opportunities for choice sexually in terms of number of partners, activities, and venues; however, there are still adverse consequences for women who freely express themselves sexually. Labels of "slut" and "whore" still exist and continue to retain the stigma they did centuries ago. How does this relate to prostitution? Sex work remains a viable option for women interested in earning top dollar for performing behaviors they would normally conduct within the course of an intimate relationship. Although sex workers continue to be stigmatized as "whores," such labels are also used for women who are not sex workers but enjoy having intercourse with many partners. Why are men who frequent prostitutes rarely charged with crimes, while the women providing the services are often imprisoned and demeaned for their involvement?

### Case Study: The Hollywood Madame

Heidi Fleiss is a name synonymous with prostitution. In 1993, Fleiss was arrested after an undercover operation by state and federal law enforcement exposed her prostitution business in California. She was charged at the state level with pandering and at the federal level with tax evasion, conspiracy, and money laundering. In essence, she was charged with not reporting the earnings of her business. Fleiss pleaded guilty in 1997 for attempted pandering and was sentenced to 18 months in prison; though she was convicted on the other charges, the verdict was overturned on appeal. Fleiss was well known among the Hollywood elites, and the media speculated publicly as to the identity of many of her clients, among them the mega-rich: "These are the richest people on earth that I'm dealing with. Their conception of money is totally different than yours or mine. They'll pay $3 million a hand at blackjack and have five hands going."[226] The only confirmed client of Fleiss at the time was Charlie Sheen, who incidentally was not charged for his use of her services. Fleiss was released from prison in 1999. In an interview, she told CNN: "I took the oldest profession on earth and I did it better than anyone on earth. Alexander the Great conquered the world at 32. I conquered it at 22."[227] She went on to state: "I think it's unfair that men put laws on a woman's body. I think a woman has a right to choose with her own body. I mean, I don't think prostitution is a career . . . but maybe [it is] a little steppingstone?"[228]

What inevitability caused the attention of law enforcement was not likely the prostitution itself, as it remained invisible due to its occurrence inside the homes and social networking clubs of the rich: it was the money that drew the attention of the authorities. Fleiss was a woman making hundreds of thousands of dollars a month in tax-free earnings. She had taken control of a profession predominantly run by men for men. Despite the fact that she was supposedly providing services for judges, lawyers, and politicians, Fleiss remained the only person charged and convicted—none of her male clients were exposed, investigated, or served time in prison for their role in the business. Isn't this a double standard? Was Fleiss charged and convicted for being a dominant female in a male-dominated role? One thing is certain, Fleiss is not the archetype of a woman involved in prostitution, and she challenged the commonly held notions of both law enforcement and the general public as to who sex workers are and what they look like!

## Sadomasochism

Sadomasochism, or SM, is ultimately about the connection between love and pain in relationships. It is defined as "consensual, erotic interactive behaviors played out by partners deliberately assuming, for one, the dominant role, and for the other, the submissive role, where the role-playing forms the context for the activities, and where the behaviors can, but need not, include the use of physical and/or psychological pain to produce sexual arousal and satisfaction."[229] Contrary to popular belief, SM it is not about wanting to truly hurt another person, but aims to provide the partner with pleasure through the infliction of some pain and discomfort. All activities engaged in by partners are discussed thoroughly in advance to ensure that consent is given, and "safe" words exist so that the person in the submissive role can stop or decrease the stimulation at any time. But the courts do not necessarily regard SM as consensual. In 1980, a Massachusetts man was sentenced to 10 years in prison for hitting his partner with a riding crop as part of SM play.[230] The legal components are further complicated if the couple is homosexual or unmarried because they can then be forced to testify against their SM partner at trial.

Although SM itself is not illegal under American law, participants are subject to prosecution for assault. Prosecutions have mostly been of homosexuals, and gay SM clubs have been the main targets of enforcement. This is likely more a commentary on homosexuality than SM. Americans have taken their legal direction from Great Britain in this regard, with the landmark 1934 Donovan case in which a man strapped a 17-year-old young woman with her consent, but also for his sexual gratification. Donovan lost all of his appeals and was convicted of assault.[231] Years later in 1976, legal scholars sought to change the way the law handles SM cases by altering legal language to ensure that consensual activities could not be prosecuted. The advocacy failed, and convictions of practitioners of SM continued well into the 1990s. Practitioners is a word used deliberately because like statutory offenses, homosexuality, oral sex, and polygamy, SM is a consensual activity—a lifestyle choice—and one that continues to be the target of law enforcement and right-wing politicians. If I instruct my husband to spank me during sex, can that really be a crime? Should that be a crime? As one scholar concluded, SM exists in American culture because aggression is socially valued, unequal power between classes makes the illusion of its reversal highly erotic, and creativity in sexual activity is an asset.[232]

## Statutory Offenses

Statutory offenses involve sexual contact between a younger and older person. The age difference does not have to be great to result in a statutory sexual assault charge, and in fact, the difference in age can be as little as two years, depending on the state in which the parties are located. However, when we hear about statutory offenses, our first thought is often of intergenerational sex, usually an older male with a younger female. This often conjures up images of exploitation and abuse, but actually intergenerational sex is extremely common and has been common throughout history. Moreover, the alleged harms caused by such interactions are questionable. For homosexual men, intergenerational sex has traditionally been an introduction into how to perform sexually in a gay relationship. Likewise, for heterosexuals, such activity is often a learning activity in which an experienced older partner schools a younger mate in sexual technique. To understand the controversy surrounding statutory offenses, it is important to review the changing nature of puberty in our society.

Puberty is generally considered a time of significant upheaval for adolescents and their families. There is a great deal of media attention on the trials and tribulations of the teenage years, often with commentaries on how difficult, sexually active, and violent youth are becoming relative to previous generations. The question remains as to whether puberty has, in fact, changed significantly in the recent past. Most adolescent theorists and academics take a developmental approach when analyzing puberty. Biological (e.g., genetic), behavioral, and environmental (e.g., cultural, social, and psychological) elements are factored into discussions of puberty and its implications. Though puberty is primarily considered a biological event, it occurs within a social context,[233] and its reality is experienced differently depending on one's culture, religion, ethnicity, class, and family of origin. Therefore, age is not a reliable indicator of puberty because physical and emotional development can occur over extended periods when pubertal processes are under way.[234] Physiology, behavior, drug metabolism, motivation, emotion, and some aspects of cognitive development influence pubertal development.

In 1904, G. Stanley Hall defined adolescence for the first time and developed key themes that characterized the phases of puberty. Hall believed that adolescence must be analyzed from an interdisciplinary perspective because it includes so many elements.[235] Hall's work included the physiological patterns of growth (e.g., height, weight, proportion of parts), criminality and sexuality, treatment of adolescence as a phase in literary sources, perceptions and the senses, cognition, religion, and pedagogy. The result was a definition based on a biologically determined stage in the fixed cycle of development,[236] roughly occurring between 7 and 14 years of age. In the early 1900s, adolescence was considered the stage between childhood and adulthood in which individuals assumed increasingly adult roles and responsibilities, including those related to physicality, mental and emotional development, cognitive changes, and changes in social roles. There was ambiguity concerning the distinction between puberty and adolescence at this time. Adolescence was regarded as both social and physiological, whereas puberty was considered purely physical. During Victorian times, pubescence was believed to occur between 13 and 15 years of age, at which point changes in the body were especially evident.[237] During this time period, sexual exploitation of children was commonplace. Though childhood was considered to be a time free of sexualization, adults were constantly surveying youth and punishing them for their sexual curiosity and activity.[238] During puberty, the sexual experiences of females caused devaluation by family and peers, yet girls were also taught that they could withhold or use their sexuality as a commodity. Conversely, boys were taught that sex and sexual gratification were their natural rights.

Despite the rapid social change that occurred between the 1950s and 1970s, adolescence continued to be regarded as a predictable stage of life, the same for all groups.[239] During this time, adolescence became associated with images of dangerous and reckless behavior, and ungovernable teens in need of control. Media attention began to focus on the risk-taking behaviors of teens, such as drug and alcohol use, depression, and sexual "promiscuity." Society began to form a very clear understanding of what adolescence and puberty entailed and emphasized a longer transition period to adulthood. Puberty and adolescence continued to be merged concepts, and it was said to occur roughly between 10 and 19 years of age. The reasons for this change in age were predominantly economic. Society could no longer support unskilled labor in the numbers it had previously, so emphasis was placed on increased schooling or training for teenagers. Increasingly, structural (e.g., unemployment), peer-related (e.g., sex, drugs, and alcohol), and adult (e.g., drug dealers, pimps, and child molesters) factors came to shape the experience of adolescence in the 1950s through the 1970s.[240]

During the school years, sexual decision making and the exploration of emerging sexuality takes on prime importance.[241] This held special significance in the 1970s at the height of the sexual revolution. Many youth became initiated into partnered sexual activity and engaged in activities that would form the pattern of their subsequent behavior. Youth in high school viewed traditional heterosexual sex as their movement into adulthood, a definable moment in their lives that signified their maturity and ability to become adults. Moreover, the teen years became an important time in establishing personal boundaries and applying those boundaries to a variety of situations. The emergence of the sexual revolution further complicated the experience of adolescence. It brought unprecedented pressures to have a multitude of sexual experiences.[242] Virginity began to symbolize a variety of negative attributes, including a failure to be appropriately sexual, shunning by peers and members of the opposite sex, and a fear that inexperience equated with homosexuality.[243] Such historical and cultural changes are major determinants of the timing in which puberty is experienced. During the sexual revolution, courtship patterns and premarital sexual behavior changed, thereby lowering the age of awareness and experimentation. Adolescence became a time of learning to communicate about and negotiate sex while simultaneously acquiring basic sexual techniques to be transferred into adulthood.[244]

From the 1970s onward, adolescence has been regarded as a highly interactive stage of development. Despite the fact that menstrual and fertility growth becomes stable at approximately 14 years of age, the age range for adolescence has now extended into the twenties. Puberty is now linked to the capacity to perform sexually, but has little connection to actual sexual behavior.[245] In other words, sex is allowed in adolescence or puberty, but not for reproduction, as youth are not deemed to be socially or morally responsible enough for that type of commitment. The sexual behavior of youth has also changed throughout the years. The Internet now provides a source of information and entertainment for youth, relieving sexual anxiety previously dealt with through peer-to-peer interaction. A large majority of teens (98.9% of males and 73.5% of females) have viewed Internet pornography by the time they are 15 years old.[246] Moreover, as adolescents age, they view more pornographic materials. Currently, only 61 percent of high school graduates have reported having sex.[247] Puberty is a time of increased focus on the perceived behaviors and values of peers; consequently, initiation into sexual activity is directly related to the cohort in which a particular youth associates.

Several themes emerge when reviewing the history of puberty. Beliefs about adolescence tend to mirror the economic cycle. In times of economic downturn, such as in the early 1900s, adolescence was defined as being mostly biologically determined and progressing through predefined stages. This belief enabled society to terminate puberty early to ensure that there was an adequate workforce to staff factories and provide manual labor. In the economic prosperity of the post-war years, adolescence and puberty were extended to include the latter teen years. The reason for this extension was based on an enhanced educational system and society's increasing reliance on skilled labor. In recent years, adolescence and puberty have been pushed into the twenties, and youth are now expected to focus on educational attainment and socio-sexual development prior to leaving their family of origin. The relation of puberty to the economic cycle can also be extended to include the changing expectations and life trajectories of youth, as well as significant social movements that altered the culture of American society. Racial segregation, gay liberation, the women's movement, and the sexual revolution all occurred between the 1950s and 1970s when the length and age of onset of puberty were extended. Moreover, the age of puberty is correlated with sociocultural factors such as race, class, ethnicity, religion, and family of origin. Puberty is not a homogeneous stage in life, even though each person experiences similar physical and physiological changes. Puberty is experienced differently and at different times based on one's environment. The case study of Marcus Dixon relates these issues back to statutory offenses.

### Case Study: Marcus Dixon

Marcus Dixon was an African American 18-year-old high school senior in Georgia. He had consensual sex with his 15-year-old white girlfriend and was charged with rape and aggravated child molestation as a result. The young woman, despite claims to friends that the sex was consensual and that she was dating Marcus, testified in court that she was the victim of rape. The defense claimed that the charge stemmed from the fact that the young woman's father was a racist, and the girl believed her father would kill both her and Dixon if he discovered she was dating an African American. The jury acquitted Dixon of rape but found him guilty of aggravated child molestation, which carried a mandatory sentence of 10 years in prison. The case was overturned by the Supreme Court, which ruled that Dixon should have instead been charged and convicted of statutory rape, which carried a maximum sentence of one year in jail.[248]

Although this case has obvious racial implications, it also clearly relates to the perceptions that society has about the ability of teenagers to consent to sex. What are the real differences between a 15-year-old and an 18-year-old? The only difference rests in society's belief that at 18 years of age a person becomes an adult—at least in some respects. This is contrary to the push in some segments of American culture to extend adolescence into the twenties, and is related to the belief that adulthood is not reached until college is complete. Think back to when you lost your virginity—likely in your teens. Should you have been imprisoned for doing what biology and physiology prepared you—and drives you—to do?

## Bestiality and Zoophilia

Human–animal sexual contact is an issue that invokes great public attention. The cases heard about in the media are predominantly sensationalized accounts of "barn brothels" and animal torture. But is the media coverage accurate? How can the public ascertain the extent of human–animal sexual contact and its social, legal, moral, and economic implications? Human–animal sexual contact has occurred since early civilization. Archeologists have discovered carvings and paintings in prehistoric societies of human-animal sexual contact dating back between 15,000 to 20,000 years ago.[249] Zoophilia and bestiality have been depicted in fairy tales and myths for centuries, with the theme being that humans are attracted to animals because their needs are not being met in human society.[250] Only relatively recently in human history have such behaviors been condemned.[251]

The current taboo is a consequence of the Judeo-Christian belief that humans are superior and fundamentally different from all other species.[252] Sexual contact with animals is explicitly forbidden in the Old Testament, and early penalties in the United States included severe beatings and even death. This belief stems from the belief that an unbridgeable gulf separates humans from other animals. The world is organized hierarchically such that humans have absolute control over animals. However, research illustrates that humans and nonhumans are very similar physically; mammals have similar gynecological and pelvic structures and are not substantially morally different either.[253] Laws and social norms have changed over time to reflect the dramatic legal, political, scientific, and religious changes that have occurred in Western society. The concept of sin was replaced by the scientific concept of "perversity," and society shifted from social condemnation of "sinful" behavior to the creation of social institutions to diagnose and treat persons who were deemed perverse.[254]

Terms such as "zoophilia," "bestiality," "bestiosexuality," and "zooerasty" are used interchangeably by laypeople and the media to describe the sexual gratification that humans obtain by engaging in sexual contact with other species. However, the scientific community utilizes specific terminology when addressing human–animal sexual contact. In the early 1900s, Richard von Krafft-Ebing, a leading sexologist, distinguished between zoophilia and zooerasty. For Krafft-Ebing, zoophilia was defined as a desire to be close to and caress animals, but it did not necessarily involve an interest in animal genitalia.[255] Conversely, zooerasty was defined as an insurmountable yearning to have sexual intercourse with animals that was brought on by neuroses, an inability to have sex with humans, and general impulsivity.[256] The definition has not changed significantly over the years, except that the term zoophilia is now used to identify individuals who have an emotional and/or sexual attachment and/or attraction to animals.[257] Conversely, bestiality is generally used to refer to individuals who are only interested in a sexual outlet, not an emotional or other attachment to nonhuman animals. For Krafft-Ebing, having sex with animals did not necessarily result in a psychopathological condition; instead, it was the result of low morality, intense sexual desire, and a lack of opportunity to have sexual relations with human females.[258]

In the United States, it is estimated that approximately 27 million cats and 48 million dogs reside as pets in family homes, and research has shown that having an animal companion improves the physical and mental well-being of humans.[259] Yet society's attitudes toward nonhuman animals remain inconsistent. The legal response to animal abuse vacillates between absolute dominion over nonhuman animals, paternalism, and cooperation. Alfred Kinsey was the first scientist to gather data on the prevalence and frequency of human–animal sexual contact. Kinsey found that 6 percent of males and 3.6 percent of females had sexual contact with animals in their lifetime.[260] Research has demonstrated that the incidence, frequency, and significance of human–animal contacts decreases with age, and very few individuals have more than one such sexual encounter.[261] Because of the small number of people admitting to human–animal contacts, Kinsey's sample is too small to be statistically significant, which poses problems when attempting to generalize to the rest of the population. As well, recent scholars hypothesize that the prevalence rates are highly underestimated.[262] Human–animal sexual contact accounts for the smallest proportion of all human sexual activity, with only a fraction of 1 percent of all orgasms derived from this behavior. The most frequent contact occurs between adolescence and 20 years of age, yet most individuals who have engaged in human–animal sexual contact do so fewer than two times in their lives.[263] There is no comprehensive explanation, biological or psychological, that demands that sexual activity be confined to members of the same species. In fact, it appears that this type of sexual contact is most frequently a substitute for heterosexual sex, especially among rural males.[264]

Very little research has been conducted on human–animal sexual contact since Kinsey. Miletski conducted a study of self-identified "animal lovers." By using a questionnaire, she discovered that despite the significant taboos surrounding such acts, most participants were uninterested in changing their behavior. Reasons given for the intense interest in continuing with human–animal sexual contact included a desire to be true to themselves as individuals, because they enjoyed the sex and the relationship too much to stop, and because they had accepted their lifestyle choice despite society's stance against such behaviors.[265] The most common animal sexual partners tend to be male dogs, followed by female canines and male horses.[266] Further research has suggested that cats, cows, sheep, geese, goats, pigs, hens, and rabbits are also selected as sexual partners if they are available.[267] For women, most contact occurs with household pets, likely due to their proximity. Common sex acts include masturbating the animal, performing oral sex on the animal, submitting to anal or vaginal intercourse, having the animal perform oral sex, and general body contact.[268] The law enforcement response to human–animal sexual contact is varied between and within states.

Generally, there have been two opposing views in this debate: the scientific sexological perspective that human–animal sexual contact is a psychopathologic condition versus the view that men have sex with animals when they do not have access to human female partners. There is a tendency among professionals to ignore human–animal sexual contact when it emerges in a clinical setting and to deny the participation of women in the behavior. These two viewpoints demonstrate a fluctuation between moral and medical discourses. However, the medical perspective has begun to dominate, and human–animal sexual contact has been removed from the *Diagnostic and Statistical Manual IV*. Clinicians are now required to categorize the behavior as an "other disorder" or as a "sexual preference or paraphilia not otherwise specified." The reason for the change is the medical belief that human–animal sexual contact virtually never presents as a clinically significant problem in and of itself, but is generally accompanied by another disorder.

Opponents of the current laws suggest that in order for the laws to be valid practically and morally, there must be evidence that demonstrates the harm caused by zoophilia to society generally, and not necessarily just harm caused to the animal.[269] There is an underlying assumption that animals can consent to the activity so long as they willingly join in the behavior or their attempts at escape remain unhindered by humans. The willingness to participate or attempts at escape are deemed analogous to consent.[270] In addition, zoophiles and their supporters argue that it is unfair and inconsistent to assume that as people mature and transition into romantic relationships, it should preclude the comfort and security that was provided to them as children by their animal companions.[271] Zoophiles insist that sex is consensual and that they love their animals as others would love human companions.[272] Zoophiles go to great lengths to distinguish themselves from bestials, contending that they would never allow another person to have sexual contact with their animal companion, whereas persons considered bestials prostitute or use their animal companions, especially when human females are unavailable.[273]

On the other side of the spectrum are individuals who seek to keep zoophilia and bestiality illegal. They contend that nonhuman animals do not have the cognitive abilities to be able to consent to sex with those outside of their species. More important is the notion that nonhumans are not able to communicate regarding their sexual preferences and cannot fully comprehend the psychosocial significance of human sexuality. This is the same argument that is put forth to prohibit adult–child sexual contact as well as sexual contact between the mentally challenged and average-functioning individuals. Animals, including humans, use taxonomy as a way of making sense of their world. Thus, each species is capable of recognizing the mating signals of fellow members, but not of other species.[274] Nonhuman animals only mistake humans for sexual mates when it is imprinted at infancy; thus, proponents of the law argue that it is against the rules of nature to engage in cross-species sex. Research has illustrated that the main reasons expressed by humans for their participation in zoophilia include sexual expressiveness, sexual fantasy, no requirement to negotiate contact, no human social involvement, and limited economic and emotional involvement.[275] Proponents of the current law question the affection and attachment zoophiles claim to possess for their animal companions when their reasons for involvement are one-sided and stress a desire to move away from human social interaction.

To strengthen this point, proponents highlight the fact that many participants in zoophilia report experiencing childhood abuse of a physical, sexual, and/or emotional nature.[276] Research shows that zoophilia does not occur in isolation. The most common sexual and psychological issues that accompany zoophilic behavior are incestuous and nonincestuous female pedophilia, voyeurism, exhibitionism, and transvestitism.[277] Moreover, those who engage in zoophilia as youth often have poor relations with their families of origin, are isolated from peers, display aggressive behavior and indiscriminate object attachments, and groom and target animals as would-be sex offenders, yet they display no evidence of an ingrained sexual preference toward animals.[278] Importantly, engaging in zoophilia disengages individuals from full participation in human communities and prevents others from incorporating zoophiles into human society. People who engage in zoophilia have removed themselves from the cultural and moral community.[279]

The debate over the appropriateness of human–animal sexual contact goes beyond the sexual components and underpins the way in which nonhuman animals are treated in American society. Currently, there is confusion over how nonhuman animals should be treated socially and legally. Some argue that nonhuman animals should be given equal protection under the law and afforded the same protections as children and the mentally challenged. Others argue that nonhumans are under the absolute domain of humans and should not be afforded any legal protection. If nonhuman animals were given equal recognition under the law, it would no longer be acceptable to use animals for food or research testing. Moreover, the issue of consent is key for both sides of this debate, with one side believing that consent can be freely given and the other equating nonhumans animals with children in relation to their cognitive functioning and ability to consent. Proponents of zoophilia also argue that even if the activity is coerced, it is not an argument against legalizing or decriminalizing the behavior, just like the fact that rape exists is not an argument against "normal" sexual activity between adults. The most important consideration is that it is not acceptable to engage in behavior that is abusive, coercive, or otherwise nonconsensual. Nonhuman animals are not capable under current law and social conditions of freely giving themselves sexually to humans. Nonhuman animals are legally considered property, as African American slaves or women have been in the recent past, and society cannot permit sexual relations between unequal partners in which one partner holds power over the life and well-being of the other.

## Polygamy

Polygamy made national headlines in 2008 when the government entered a polygamist compound and removed 439 children, claiming that massive sexual abuse was occurring. This move reignited the debate about the permissibility of multiple marriages and how polygamy affects young girls and women. Many see the issue not as one of religious freedom, but as an example of sexual indoctrination or the existence of "sex cults." This was one of the largest child abuse investigations in American history and cost taxpayers $12.4 million.[280] The state claimed that 91 families in the compound had a possible connection to underage marriages. Child abuse investigators reported that 12 girls, between the ages of 12 and 15 years, were sexually victimized at the compound with the explicit knowledge and approval of their parents.[281] Ultimately, most of the children were returned to their parents when the Texas Supreme Court ruled that child protection workers had overstepped their authority by removing all of the children, regardless of whether they were at imminent risk of abuse.[282]

Polygamy, the practice of a man taking multiple wives, has existed for thousands of years. Often reserved for the wealthy due to the cost of obtaining and sustaining multiple brides, it continues to be common throughout parts of Africa and the Middle East. Polygamy is different from polyandry in which a woman takes multiple husbands. Polyandry is significantly rarer, likely a result of women's devalued position in society and the attention almost all societies focus on tracing lineage through the male.

### Case Study: Polygamy in Utah

Tom Green of Utah was convicted of bigamy and failure to provide support for his children and was subsequently sentenced to 5 years in prison.[283] Green was the first man in 50 years to be charged with bigamy in Utah. The husband of five wives and father of 29 children, Green lived in a remote compound with other polygamist Mormons on the border of Nevada. When he was arrested, the prosecution was also contemplating charging Green with child rape for marrying a 13-year-old girl, who subsequently bore him seven children.[284] After preparing their case, the state charged Green with child rape for marrying Linda Kunz Green in 1986. Green was convicted and received a sentence of five years to life—the lightest possible sentence for such a charge.[285] The judge rejected the arguments of the defense, claiming the statute of limitations had expired on the child rape charge and that intercourse did not occur within the boundaries of Utah, but during a Mexican honeymoon.[286] The judge ruled that although the victim remained devoted to her husband and contended that no harm was caused, the situation was grave and could not be taken lightly: "Clearly there is a pattern with children, involvement with young girls, and that's an aggravating circumstance."[287] At trial, Green acknowledged his wrongdoing by stating: "I recognise, under the law, she was not capable of consenting to marriage. . . . I accept full responsibility. I never have blamed my victim."[288]

# Swinging

Swinging is a phenomenon that came to public attention in the 1970s. It occurs when married couples have consensual sex with people other than their partners in the same room, as a group, or separately. Swingers refer to their activity as a "lifestyle" or an open marriage. The definitive book on open marriage defines it as:

> ... a non-manipulative relationship between man and woman. Neither is the object of total validation for the other's inadequacies or frustrations. Open marriage is a relationship of peers in which there is no need for dominance and submission, for commandeered restrictions, or stifling possessiveness. The woman is not the caretaker, the man is not the dictator. Because their relationship is based on mutual liking and trust, each one has enough psychic space, which is to say mental and emotional freedom, to become an individual. Being individuals, both the woman and the man are free to develop and expand into the outside world. Each has the opportunity for growth and new experiences.... Therefore their union thrives on change and new experiences.... Even falling in love with the other can become a cyclically recurring event. As each becomes more attractive to the other by means of their individual growth and their developing knowledge of one another, their union grows in strength, constantly revitalized, constantly expanding.[289]

Many Americans would regard this lifestyle as distasteful but hardly criminal. However, there have been incidents in which the police have investigated swingers and attempted to charge them with prostitution or running a bawdy house, or have tried to close down swinging clubs because they pose a "health risk" due to the potential transmission of HIV/AIDS. In 1998, Phoenix banned swingers' clubs due to the nuisance they caused and the HIV/AIDS risk. There is no law in the United States specifically prohibiting swinging, but states draft laws based on general nuisance behaviors. It is worthy to note that members of the "lifestyle" as a rule do not have unprotected sex with anyone other than their primary partner as there is a clear distinction between sex and love. Thus, the outlawing of swinging clubs has more to do with moral outrage than with actual public health considerations.

## Incest

Incest is having sexual contact with a person related by either blood or marriage. There are varying degrees of incest: father–daughter, mother–son, sibling, stepparent–stepchild, cousins, and aunts/uncles–nephews/nieces, among others. Incest has been taboo since biblical times, with the Bible specifically outlining relatives with whom it is and is not acceptable to have intercourse. However, in biblical times, it was expected that brothers would marry their deceased sibling's wife to ensure that the bloodline continued (termed "levirate marriage"). Incest became a topic of national debate when Woody Allen went public with his relationship with his adopted daughter, whom he subsequently married. Questions emerged about whether incest laws are keeping pace with the rapid rate of social change. With a dramatic increase in blended families and more people opting for adoption, should incest laws apply to non–blood-related individuals? What about a stepparent who has sex with a stepchild? The law is struggling to deal with these issues, as there are many interrelated factors.

What if the stepparent entered the household when the stepchild was older? What age should be placed on such relations, or should a stepchild be deemed unable to consent to sex regardless of age? These are all challenging questions, especially for a society that is continually altering the definition of adolescence and its notions of acceptable sexuality.

### Case Study: Sex with a Stepdaughter

Paul Lowe of Ohio was charged with sexual battery for having a consensual sexual relationship with his 22-year-old stepdaughter, who was the biological daughter of his wife. Lowe argued that under the law "stepchild" should apply only to persons under the age of legal consent, and not to a stepchild who is of the age of majority. Under Ohio law, incest is defined as having sexual contact with a natural or adopted child, or when the offender is a stepparent, guardian, custodian, or fulfilling a similarly parental role. Lowe pleaded no contest and was sentenced to 120 days in jail and 3 years probation. He appealed his conviction but was denied.[290]

What do all of the "so-called sex crimes" discussed in this chapter have in common? The obvious answer is that they are all consensual. Unlike the traditional notion of a sex crime, all participants in these activities consciously chose to participate in the sexual act. This raises the question: why would the government find it necessary to intervene in the bedrooms of its citizens? As garnered from the case studies, this is extremely complex and involves both macro-and micro-considerations. Macro-factors include race, gender, age, sexual orientation, socioeconomic status, and political affiliation. Micro-factors include the political, religious, and sexual attitudes of the investigating officers, prosecutors, and judges, local bylaws, the participants involved, and access to adequate legal representation. According to Kinsey's research from the 1940s and 1950s, virtually all Americans have participated in sexual activities that are illegal. Remember that a sex crime does not necessarily involve the use of force or lack of consent—crimes are not necessarily stranger rapes or child assaults. What activities have you engaged in that could result in a sex crimes charge or conviction? Perhaps you had oral sex as a teenager or a homosexual experience? Perhaps you hit or bit your partner in a moment of passion? Should these activities result in imprisonment and registration as a sexual offender? Participation in consensual prostitution with an adult prostitute in the state of Alabama results in *lifetime* registration as a sexual offender if convicted![291] Most citizens would deem this excessive. When are we going to demand that the government focus on governing and get Big Brother out of our bedrooms?

# Chapter 6

# Sexually Explicit Materials

Sexually explicit materials (SEM), also known pejoratively as pornography, generally elicit one of two responses: it is harmless to watch and is actually beneficial for couples, or it is offensive and degrading to women. It is unlikely that either side of the debate would be willing to shift their position regardless of the evidence presented because the use of SEM is deeply influenced by religion, ethics, gender, family of origin, and socioeconomic background. In the 1970s and 1980s, following on the coattails of the sexual revolution, Americans became acutely concerned with the impact of SEM on the public and its relationship to sexual violence. Commissions were formed with the media covering proceedings in sensational detail. Americans became polarized over the debate, a situation which remains today as SEM proliferates as a result of the ever-expanding power of the Internet. This chapter will examine the history of SEM and then look in detail at adult and child SEM to ascertain what, if any, harm is caused by reading, viewing, or creating sexual materials.

Throughout this chapter, the term sexually explicit materials (SEM) will be used to describe all forms of media containing depictions of graphic sexual activity. Using SEM eliminates the negative connotations most often associated with the word pornography. Governments and religious leaders have used the word pornography to describe materials they consider to be degrading, immoral, and evil. The public reaction is frequently one of shame and guilt as often an individual is both interested in—and on some level offended by—the various types of pornographic materials available.

Sexually explicit materials have a long and colorful history, beginning in antiquity with the depiction of intergenerational sex. As noted previously, intergenerational sex between males was considered highly desirable, and many city-states actually regarded it a dereliction of duty if its older male citizens did not "adopt" male youth.[292] In fact, the older male was held responsible for the behavior of his young protégé. The reason for the large amount of writing on homosexual intergenerational sex is because the male sex was regarded as superior, and beauty was personified and idealized in boys and youth. Sex with youth was considered the most important form of education for young males and was not regarded as harmful but as mutually beneficial and culturally valid.[293] Thus, men enjoyed reading about the crushes and relationships of others. In this sense, SEM was reserved for the wealthy and highly educated as they were the only people capable of reading, and these materials reinforced cultural mores and the social hierarchy.

Fast forward to a more recent point in history, and SEM provides an opportunity for people to share their sexual fantasies pictorially or in writing. These fantasies are often derived from unsatisfied sexual desires or "real life" that has proved to be boring. The impulses expressed vary according to age, sex, the character of the person involved, and the conditions of their life. SEM becomes a way for people to have a sexual outlet for desires that are not being met or that the person did not want met in reality. It becomes a critical method for allowing people who are otherwise inhibited to express sexual urges that cannot be acted upon. Thus, as social restrictions increased and became more rigid, the use of SEM also increased.[294] As noted by two historians on the topic:

> When the discussion on "immoral literature" at intervals flames up, and it is claimed that pornography inflames "baser" passions, then it is just as right to claim that it releases and removes many "lower" passions which otherwise might break out and materialize as crimes against society. And to talk in our time about stopping the spreading of pornographic literature is quite absurd as long as newspapers, the tabloid press, full of attempts to outdo competitors in "realistic" and cunningly detailed accounts of sadistic murders, and similar sexual manifestations daily come into the hands of children.[295]

Thus, SEM has become a challenge against the status quo for viewers or readers—a way to continue to express interest in various forms of sexual activity, despite the fact that having these interests runs counter to government regulation and/or religious conviction.

It could be argued that modern America is actually desexed in comparison to the nineteenth century. In Victorian times, almost everything remotely sexual elicited a harsh moral and religious reaction; most of the codes of conduct created by the government and Christianity were impossible and inconvenient to live by. Thus, people turned to SEM to challenge these codes of conduct. Currently, everything is related to sex: advertisers use sex to sell virtually every product, and society is inundated with sexual images and connotations on a daily basis. This has created a desensitization by Americans to most sexual things, which helps to explain the strong reaction against certain forms of SEM, such as those containing children or youth. With such a laissez-faire attitude toward sexuality, it becomes increasingly necessary to have some clear, commonly agreed-upon boundaries—areas in which society can focus on policing sex and sexuality. Currently, this means that images, contrived or real, containing children and youth, and other materials of this sort have been deemed obscene by local or state authorities.

## Adult Sexually Explicit Materials

Sexually explicit materials for adults have come in a variety of forms, including comics, still pictures, silent films, magazines, feature movies, and short vignettes. Regardless of the form, SEM has been overwhelming designed by men for men's sexual gratification. Even with the shift to feature-length movies in the 1970s, which contained plots and character development, SEM continued to objectify women for the pleasure of men.[296] This is a major concern of many feminists who regard any form of male-created SEM as offensive. The debate on adult SEM came to a head in the 1970s and 1980s when commissions were created to investigate whether SEM caused social harm and what, if any, recommendations could be implemented by federal and state governments and various law enforcement agencies.

There are two types of SEM that are not protected under the First Amendment: obscenity and sexually explicit materials involving children. Obscenity continues to be one of the most controversial and vaguely defined legal concepts in the United States. The Supreme Court and the lower courts have struggled with the issue for decades. In an infamous ruling, Justice Potter Stewart in the case of *Jacobellis v. Ohio*, stated, "I know it when I see it."[297] And Justice Hugo Black stated in his ruling in *Mishkin v. State of New York*, "I wish once more to express my objections to saddling this Court with the irksome and inevitably unpopular and unwholesome task of finally deciding by a case-by-case, sight-by-sight personal judgment of the members of this Court what pornography (whatever that means) is too hard core for people to see or read."[298] This legal and public confusion over obscenity forms the backdrop for political commissions on the subject. The following case study will discuss the debate between SEM and violence.

### Case Study: SEM and Violence Link? The Meese Commission

The inexpensive availability of the VCR dramatically changed the nature of the adult entertainment industry in America. Prior to the popularity of this technology, SEM was only available to the rich who could afford projectors and the high cost of SEM films. By the early 1980s, SEM accounted for an estimated 34 percent of all movie rentals![299] Moreover, the advent of the sexual revolution made it hip to go to movie theatres to view SEM. This was especially evident with the marketing of *Deep Throat*, which completely changed the way Americans regarded SEM films. With a newfound attitude of freedom in America, sex began to permeate popular culture with movies like *Porky's, Caddy Shack, Sixteen Candles, Risky Business*, and *Meatballs*—all of which were rife with scenes of adolescent sexual initiation.[300] In 1970, the president initiated a commission on "pornography" to ascertain if it was a cause of sexual violence. The commission operated in secrecy, and the public fully expected the findings to recommend that SEM be banned or at minimum outlawed in many of its forms. Surprisingly, this commission found that SEM does not cause any social harm and is not a source of sexual violence.

Many sectors of society, especially right-wing religious groups and feminists, were extremely disappointed in the commission's findings and sought to have the issue reopened for public debate. This debate did not occur until Ronald Reagan was elected president. Anti-SEM crusaders lobbied the White House heavily, and finally during Reagan's second administration, a second commission was formed called the Meese Commission. This commission was under the general direction of Attorney General Edwin Meese. From the outset, the commission was suspect to many because it was known that Meese believed that the Supreme Court should not force states to abide by the Bill of Rights or provide a Miranda warning to accused persons. He said, "Miranda only helps guilty defendants. Most innocent people are glad to talk to the police."[301] Moreover, in a press conference announcing the establishment of the commission, Meese stated that "the content of pornography has radically changed [since 1970], with more and more emphasis upon extreme violence. . . . [The commission] has not come to their task with minds made up. Their job is to approach the issues objectively. . . . In any recommendation the commission makes, it will carefully balance the need to control the distribution of pornography with the need to protect very carefully First Amendment freedoms."[302]

Unlike the first commission, the Meese Commission was to be held publicly, and the public was to have access to all of its correspondence and reports. The commission received $500,000 and one year to report on a "solution" to SEM. From June 1985 through January 1986, the commission held two-day hearings in Washington, D.C., Chicago, Houston, Los Angeles, Miami, and New York City. The purpose of the Meese Commission was to clearly establish a connection between SEM and child and female rape.[303] Obviously, the mandate of the commission was extremely one-sided, as were the commission members who came overwhelmingly from Republican organizations. Moreover, many argued that Reagan was trying to find a scapegoat for violence against women and children, instead of addressing the structural factors leading to their abuse. Critics argued that it was contradictory to establish a commission to investigate sexual violence while simultaneously withdrawing funding from women's shelters across the nation.[304] Despite this fact, many feminists supported the commission and its work.

From the outset there were concerns with the commission and how it operated. The chair attempted to pass sweeping anti-SEM measures without hearing any testimony as to its dangerousness. Proposals included:

- Increased enforcement of existing obscenity laws;
- Increased cooperation between all levels of law enforcement and the Internal Revenue Service;
- Computerized national database of distributors;
- Development and implementation of forfeiture statutes;
- Development of statutes making the hiring of people for commercial sex an unfair labor practice;
- Prohibiting the transmission of obscene materials on television and over the phone;

- Use of pandering laws against SEM producers;
- Requirement to have health inspectors investigate adult bookstores for violations;
- Prohibiting the employment of persons under the age of 21 in any sex-related business; and
- Defining vibrators and dildos as obscene.[305]

Though this was recommended as a position prior to the commencement of the hearing, the commission withheld ruling on these proposals until after the public hearings were completed. Moreover, the commission scheduled witnesses to discuss how their childhood sexual abuse could be blamed on "pornography," with most witnesses coming from organizations closely associated with Nancy Reagan's anti-drug campaign.[306] Fewer than one-quarter of all witnesses called were pro-SEM, including Annie Sprinkle, a SEM actor who stated:

> Over the years I've seen pornography help a lot of people, and on occasion I've seen it hurt people. Being in pornography has really helped me, and perhaps in some ways it might have hurt me. I've been exploited by pornography, but mostly I exploited pornography, and it paid my bills for many years. Porn pays well, but it could pay better. Some people say porn makes people want to go out and rape. I suppose it's possible that pornography may have somehow inspired some already very sick person to commit a rape, but millions of people have watched porn movies and never raped anyone. If a tree falls down and kills someone, do we cut down the whole forest? If people get hurt in car accidents, do we get rid of all cars? (Cars are far, far more dangerous than porn could ever be). While making pornography, I have on occasion felt exploited or used, but mostly I have felt very free and joyful. I've had porn make me look and feel like a mindless bimbo, piece-of-meat sex object, and I've had pornography make me look and feel more beautiful, glamorous, and sexy than I ever would have dreamed possible. Some of the pornography I've made is pretty awful schlock, and some of the pornography I've made is very creative, interesting, wonderful stuff that I'm very proud of and that has even been educational and helpful to others. On occasion I have questioned if some of my work in pornography might have somehow hurt the women's movement, and if it did I would be very sad. But I honestly feel like a freedom fighter who is contributing something wonderful to women's liberation and sexual education, and that makes me very happy. I believe that people have the right to buy, sell, see, and make pornography if they want to, and for better or for worse, I will continue to express myself with sexually explicit images, creating what I like to create, doing what I like to do. There is no other side to this coin.[307]

Added to the list of anti-SEM witnesses was a long line of law enforcement personnel who sought to "prove" a link between organized crime and SEM in hopes the commission would recommend mandatory minimum sentences and heavy fines, and establish a broader definition of what could be prosecuted.

On the other side of the debate were lawyers and researchers claiming that SEM was not harmful and should not be restricted because restriction was a violation of the First Amendment. One researcher who conducted a study of incarcerated sexual offenders shared his research findings, which indicated clearly that persons convicted of sex crimes had no unusual interest in SEM and in fact were less interested in such materials than "normal" men.[308] Alan Dershowitz, a law professor at Harvard University, was also clear that there was no evidence to suggest a linkage between sexual violence and SEM and argued that the commission had no choice but to side with civil libertarians. As quoted in *United States of America vs. Sex*:

> "There is no basis for concluding that even a significant proportion of rapists or other sexual criminals have been exposed to pornography," he exclaimed. Dershowitz treated the commission like a first-year law class. "Let's assume that every rapist in America in 1984 was exposed to *Playboy* and *Penthouse*," he lectured. "We would still have to determine what proportion of their readers went out and committed rape. Even if we were to assume that each rape was committed by a different person, certainly not the case, approximately 99.97 percent of readers did not commit rapes."[309]

Other pro-SEM witnesses included Rev. Dr. Ted McIlvenna and Dr. Loretta Haroian from the Institute for Advanced Study of Human Sexuality. These witnesses testified about their knowledge of "the industry":

> In the past several decades of the scientific study of human sexuality there has evolved a body of information readily available to those in the field of sexology. These statistics demonstrate the fact that we live in a society which does not wish to directly confront a natural (God-given, if you will) instinct and source of creative art, fantasy, and pleasure. Nonetheless, it exists, in all variations, documented for thousands of years in all languages, cultures, and forms. Everything from T-shirts to cave art, from the Bible to Picasso, from a Betty Grable pinup over a World War II locker to an AIDS statistic. And it will continue as long as men and women are born and grow up healthy. It is an undeniable aspect of our nature. If we refuse to look at it, we can be made to feel shame, resentment, restriction, and disgust—all of the emotions which follow ignorance and confusion. Twenty years ago, what we are calling the pornography industry was characterized as being run by morally, legally, and economically marginal entrepreneurs. Today, while there still are some who might be regarded this way, the majority are mainstream American business people. . . . If there is anything we have learned, it is that there is no organized industry. The FBI often refers to the people involved in the production and distribution of sexually explicit material as organized crime. It has been our observation that they are, in truth, a large number of individual producers and distributors all trying to make a buck off a ready market. The people in the so-called "industry" are neither any better nor any worse than any other group of people. Most of them love their children and grandchildren, a few don't. Most of them pay their taxes, a few don't. Most are law-abiding citizens who vote, pay their bills on time, and are no different in private areas of their lives than any other person. . . . Our involvement with the so-called industry began when we were asked to evaluate evidence and testify on behalf of the defense in a trial in the late sixties. Initially it was sometimes not

possible to testify because we had no documented research data. In the ensuing years, we have gathered much data and have served as expert witnesses in many trials, trained other witnesses, and provided statistics and information to courts all over the country. We have had an opportunity to study the laws, consider the data, survey the population, weigh the statistics, and speak with the defendants and the offended. . . . In the last few years we have seen a considerable shift in the boundaries of law enforcement, the prosecutorial conduct, and judicial attitude in obscenity trials. Quite frankly, we are alarmed and frightened by what we have observed. The distributors of explicit sexual materials are sitting ducks for an easy bust, a quick headline, or the polishing of political aspirations. It has become a parlor game for the FBI and other law enforcement officers.[310]

Ultimately, the Meese Commission concurred with civil libertarians. To the surprise of the public and the White House, it was concluded that SEM was generally not harmful to society. However, it did attempt to define "pornography" as material that "is predominantly sexually explicit and intended primarily for the purpose of sexual arousal. . . . Whether some or all of what qualifies as pornographic under this definition should be prohibited, or even condemned, is not a question that should be answered under the guise of definition."[311] However, if the government had decided to adopt this definition, virtually anything related to human sexuality, including educational materials, would be deemed "pornographic" and possibly subject to prohibition or restriction.

To pacify the right-wing contingent of the commission and its supporters, the commission developed a classification system of sexually explicit material. This classification system was to be adopted by law enforcement when determining prosecutions for SEM. The four classes included:

- Class 1 contained sexually violent materials and was found to be immoral, unethical, and an offense against nature;
- Class 2 was deemed nonviolent but contained content that demonstrated degradation, submission, domination, or humiliation, and was found to be unethical and immoral and an offense against human dignity;
- Class 3 contained sex without violence, degradation, dominance, humiliation, or submission, and was found to be predominantly not negative; and
- Class 4 was nonprovocative nudity and was found to cause no harm.[312]

Importantly, the terms violence, submission, sexual activity, and virtually all others used in the classification scheme remained undefined by the commission. Class 4 was put in to satisfy nudists who believed they would be subject to penalty for their lifestyle without adequate recognition that nudity exists without sex. Thus, after more than 15 years of debate, it was ultimately concluded that there is no causal linkage between SEM and sexual violence or the subjugation of women. In fact, the commission had no choice but to vote in this manner. Even the researcher they hired to review and summarize existing studies on the link between SEM and violence reported that: "No evidence currently exists that actually links fantasies with specific sexual offenses; the relationship at this point remains inference."[313] In exchange for the researcher's work, the commission issued a gag order so her findings would not be included in the final report. The commission decided to include a caveat in the final report about the role of academia and stated: "The commission has examined social and behavioral science research in recognition of the role it plays in determining legal standards and social policy. This role, while notable, is not, nor should it be, the sole basis for developing standards or policy."[314] In other words, although a link between sex and violence could not be established, the commission did not want to preclude the development of social policy and laws based on the misguided notion that SEM causes sexual violence. The Society for the Scientific Study of Sexuality responded with this statement to the findings of the Meese Commission:

> The Society for the Scientific Study of Sexuality disputes the scientific accuracy of the conclusion of the Attorney General's Commission on Pornography that "some forms of sexually explicit materials bear a causal relationship . . . to sexual violence." The evidence for a direct causal link between exposure to sexually explicit materials, pornography, or violent pornography to consequences such as sexual violence, sexual coercion, or rape is incomplete and inadequate. Thus, it is premature to draw conclusions about the conditions under which socially harmful or helpful effects might

---

**What Do You Think?**

For decades, sexologists have been using SEM as part of their treatment plans for individuals and couples experiencing sexual concerns. Different forms of media are used in counseling to help normalize various types of sexual activity as well as to provide visual instruction of different sexual techniques. SEM is also used as part of Sexual Attitudes Restructuring (SAR) seminars, which form part of the curriculum for student sexologists, and is also used as an instructional tool with other groups such as therapists, sex offenders, and law enforcement officers. SAR is used to help people identify their sexual discriminations and to assist them in working through their negative attitudes.

Research has demonstrated that the use of SEM in therapy may help the client to overcome a whole host of issues, including problems with sexual functioning, improving communication, reducing shame, providing permission to be sexual, providing education about various activities, and treating specific sexual concerns.[315] In surveys of sexuality workshop participants, 90 percent felt that incorporating SEM was both useful and enjoyable, as well as helpful to increase understanding about the ways that people relate to each other sexually.[316]

The following scenario is an example of using SEM in counseling: John is 17 years old and has been charged and convicted of sexual assault for molesting a 12-year-old boy. John is very confused about his sexuality and is afraid he may be gay. John thinks that gay sex is dirty, evil, and aggressive, and does not believe that gay men can be loving toward each other. As part of his treatment program, John's sexologist counselor has him and his family view a variety of SEM (e.g., videos, pieces of literature, photos) of gay male sexual activity with an emphasis on the relational components. The sexologist then works with John and his family to educate them about what a healthy sexual relationship entails and that gay men are capable of such loving relationships. Do you think SEM should form part of sexual counseling?

occur. Additional scientific research should be federally funded in order to create a scientific basis for formulating effective social policy. The report of the Commission on Pornography threatens the freedom of inquiry of sexual scientists because it falsely claims scientific proof for the conclusion that exposure to pornography harms humans. This, research on the effects of pornography could be prohibited by any University ethical review board or human subjects committee that erroneously accepts the conclusions of the Commission as factual. This restriction would be due to the existing Federal Code which prohibits exposure of human subjects to risk of known harms as a consequence of participating in scientific research.[317]

### Case Study: Transporting SEM

On November 15, 2007, John Stagliano, owner of Evil Angels Production, was charged with seven counts of transporting and distributing adult sexually explicit materials, including the films *Milk Nymphos, Storm Squirters 2, Target Practice*, and *Fetish Fantasy Chapter 5*.[318] The government claimed Stagliano sold the films over the Internet and transported them from California to Washington, D.C., thus violating federal obscenity laws. If convicted, Stagliano faced up to $7 million in fines in addition to prison time. It is unclear why the government focused their efforts on Stagliano. The adult entertainment industry transports materials across state lines regularly, including in the processing of online orders for private citizens. What this may illustrate is an enhanced effort by law enforcement to target large distributors in the hopes of discouraging others from participating in the adult SEM business. It was not long ago in American history that individuals, as well as businesses, were charged for mailing sexual aids across the country. In many cases, these charges and convictions did not withstand court challenges, but it often caused serious financial difficulties for the individuals and small business owners involved. Do we want to live in a country where the government decides what books we can read, the movies we can watch, and the Web sites we can visit? America's war on sex may be heading in that direction.

### Case Study: Distribution of SEM

Paul F. Little was sentenced to 3 years and 10 months in prison by a federal judge for distributing SEM "over the Internet and through the mail."[319] All of the films indicated in the indictment involved consenting adults and were sent only to adults who purchased them online. Little was a resident of California who was charged in Florida because the government contended he violated obscenity standards in Florida. The only reason the government was able to pursue federal charges against Little was because the servers for his Web site were physically located in Florida as opposed to California and some of the films were mailed to Florida residents. This case was pursued as part of Attorney General Alberto Gonzales's "war on sex." In 2005, Gonzales publicly announced that adult pornography prosecutions were his department's top priority. The Little case focused on films containing scenes of sadomasochism that the government

**Did You Know?**

Sexological treatment is the only form of treatment that has resulted in zero recidivism for juvenile sex offenders. A cornerstone of this treatment is Sexual Attitudes Restructuring (SAR) and the use of SEM. The purpose is to establish respect for oneself and others and to fully understand the concept of consent. Topics addressed in the SAR sex offender treatment include sexual orientation, offending behaviors, communication, establishing boundaries, and sexual self-esteem. William Seabloom, a sexologist and reverend, was the first to conduct research on this form of treatment, which focused on providing sexual education to teen offenders and their family members and sought to challenge sexual stereotypes and misconceptions. Treatment consisted of large and small groups sharing reactions to various topics and SEM over a 2-day, 16-hour experience.[322] After this portion of therapy was completed, bi-monthly 27-hour group therapy marathons and bi-annual family education/sexual awareness seminars occurred.[323] Seabloom followed 122 youth sex offenders and more than 400 family members between 14 and 24 years and discovered that recidivism was zero for individuals who completed the program.[324] This illustrated that sexological treatment garnered better results than all other forms of psychotherapy, surgery, and pharmacotherapy combined. In an interview with a journalist, Seabloom asked an interesting question: "But, one might ask if the state chooses to ignore the facts, to abandon proven treatment methods, and to ignore the evidence, based on solid data available for years, that sex offenders are treatable, isn't the state then choosing to be complicit in criminal sexual behavior?"[325]

contended were both obscene and pornographic. Little's unsuccessful defense involved ironically the same argument used by the federal government to claim that torture was not occurring within the prisons at Guantanamo Bay, Cuba. In that case, the federal government argued that subjecting detainees to severe pain and violent treatment was not illegal, degrading, or humiliating. The result was a redefinition of "torture" to exclude all acts that fall short of "pain accompanying serious physical injury, such as organ failure, impairment of bodily function, or even death."[320] This includes acts such as pouring scalding water or acids on prisoners. Yet the court ruled in the Little case that sadistic conduct was anything that intended to be degrading and/or humiliating.[321] Put another way, the government allows sadistic behavior to occur legally in prisons with foreign detainees, but not between consenting American adults for the purposes of sexual pleasure!

## Case Study: Sexually Explicit Materials on the Internet

The Communications Decency Act (CDA) came into effect in 1996 as part of the Telecommunications Reform Act. It was the intent of the CDA to manage sexually explicit images on the Internet, and the law made it an offense to send "indecent" materials to others via the Internet.[326] The American Civil Liberties Union filed a lawsuit against the government, claiming the law placed restrictions on the Internet that other communications media did not have to contend with. In 1997, the Supreme Court voted unanimously that the law violated the First Amendment. The Court based its decision on the fact that an individual has free choice to enter sites that contain sexually explicit materials—much like phoning a sex line. This decision also left the door open to allowing the government to create zones on the Internet, which would have the effect of separating adult content from general content or children's content. Moreover, the case ruled only on pornography, which is protected under the First Amendment, and not obscenity, which has no constitutional guarantee.[327] In 1973, the Supreme Court defined obscenity when hearing arguments in *Miller v. California*. Obscenity was defined as containing three elements: (1) the average person using contemporary moral standards finds the material to appeal to prurient interests, (2) the material describes or depicts "offensive" sexual conduct as defined by state law, and (3) on a whole the work lacks serious artistic, political, or scientific value.[328] Basically, this meant that while nudity alone could not be defined as obscene, communities were entitled to define their own moral standards, unencumbered by the government. Chief Justice Warren Burger of the Supreme Court contended, "To require a State to structure obscenity proceedings around evidence of a national community standard would be an exercise in futility. . . . Nothing in the First Amendment requires that a jury must consider hypothetical and unascertainable 'national standards' when attempting to determine whether certain materials are obscene as a matter of fact. It is neither realistic nor constitutionally sound to read the First Amendment as requiring that people of Maine or Mississippi accept public depiction of conduct found tolerable in Las Vegas or New York City."[329]

In 2005, the FBI stated that cracking down on "deviant pornography" on the Internet was a top priority. After increasing public concerns over the content available online, the federal government responded with harsh new regulations on what it perceived to be a growing threat to decency.[330] As opposed to previous crackdowns, the FBI focused its efforts on consensual sexual activity between adults and created the Anti-Obscenity Squad to put together criminal cases against those sites considered to be legally obscene. The Miller case would be used as the test to define obscene materials. This move by the federal government was especially controversial as it shifted monies away from child pornography investigations and came at a time when budgets were constrained.

### Case Study: Internet Sex in the Classroom

In 2004 in Norwich, Connecticut, Julie Amero, a substitute teacher, was charged with four felony pornography counts for what the state considered her malicious intent to allow pornographic pop-ups to display on her computer and then allow students to view those images. Amero eventually agreed to plead guilty to a misdemeanor disorderly conduct charge and surrender her teaching credentials, but only after four years locked in a legal battle with the state. The case elicited great controversy because state computer forensic experts mistakenly testified that Amero purposefully allowed and displayed the pop-ups. Computer security experts from around the country heard about Amero's case and contacted the defense attorney, agreeing to voluntarily testify on her behalf. Due to overwhelming support from the computer industry, Amero's conviction was overturned in what the court ruled was a conviction based on "erroneous" and "false information" by state experts. It was discovered that the state had never conducted a forensic examination of the hard drive and instead relied on the limited computer experience of one of its detectives as key evidence. Independent computer experts stated that the problem stemmed from the school system's failure to routinely update its software. This failure then permitted spyware to become attached to the computer, thus encouraging pop-ups.[331] Despite the overturned conviction and a lesser plea by Amero, the state is adamant that she is guilty of felony pornography charges and continues to examine its options for retrial.

## Child Sexually Explicit Materials

Despite popular belief, child SEM is not common. In fact, it began as a cottage industry in which private creators would trade their personal collections with other interested parties. Even with the advent of the Internet, child SEM has not experienced an explosion. In fact, according to conservative research, most child SEM currently involves photos, magazines, and video—not the Internet.[332] Even the Meese Commission's experts noted that no child SEM is readily being sold, and as a retired FBI agent stated, "The laws against child porn could not be better. It never constituted more than 1 percent of the total market, but still gets 99 percent of the attention."[333] According to the National Center for Exploited and Missing Children, about eight million child sexually explicit images have been discovered on the Internet since 2002.[334] Compare this to the tens of billions of images available on the Internet, and it becomes clear that child SEM is not nearly as significant as the media contends. So why is there so much panic from the media and politicians about children being abused and exploited online and in the movies?

It was only in 1982 that the U.S. Supreme Court created a special child "pornography" category of constitutional inquiry and removed such materials from the protection of the First Amendment. This shift was based on a belief that child SEM was a direct cause of child sexual abuse and the hope that child abuse could be resolved through the creation of legislation.[335] Obviously, this notion has proven false over the past two decades as child abuse is as prevalent as in the past. Legislation has only reinforced the stereotypes of what offenders and victims look like according to law enforcement and the public. Offenders matching the stereotypes are more likely to be charged and convicted. The stereotypes include: a low-functioning male who did not know his behavior was wrong, a "dirty old man" who turned to children because of a lack of adult sexual partners, a sexually frustrated male who cannot relate to adult women, a sexually obsessed male, a stranger, and someone with a psychiatric disorder.[336]

In *Ginsberg v. New York*, the court found that the constitutional rights of minors to read or watch materials of all kinds, including sexual materials, are significantly narrower than for adults. The court reasoned that parents should have an interest in rearing their children as they see fit, including limiting access to SEM, and that the state has an independent interest to ensure the well-being of minors.[337] This was reiterated in the 1998 Child Online Protection Act, which imposed criminal and civil liabilities on offenders. Criminal liability included a fine of up to $50,000 and 6 months in jail, and civil liability included up to $50,000 in damages for knowingly placing content online that is "harmful" to minors. Harmful was defined as:

> [A]ny ... matter of any kind that is obscene or that—(A) the average person, applying contemporary community standards, would find, taking the material as a whole and with respect to minors, is designed to appeal to, or is designed to pander to, the prurient interest; (B) depicts, describes, or represents, in a manner patently offensive with respect to minors, an actual or simulated sexual act or sexual contact, an actual or simulated normal or perverted sexual act, or a lewd exhibition of the genitals or post-pubescent female breast; and (C) taken as a whole, lacks serious literary, artistic, political, or scientific value for minors.[338]

A 1990 court ruling in *Osborne v. Ohio* claimed that prosecution for viewing child SEM does not result in punishing the thoughts and fantasies of Americans, but stated rather that "Ohio has enacted ... [the law] ... in order to protect the victims of child pornography; it hopes to destroy the market for exploitative use of children."[339] However, despite the supposed threat caused by child SEM, persons caught with such images often receive much lighter sentences than persons charged with actual abuse of children.[340] This is significant when compared to the original purpose of child SEM legislation, which was to stop the abuse of children. At some point, lawmakers realized that child SEM does not directly cause child abuse, or at least is not a major factor in the abuse of children. That being said, Americans are not yet ready to recognize the sexual rights and freedoms of children. As sexologist E. J. Haeberle stated:

> Children should have the same right to sexual information and sexual activity as adults, and they should not be forced into stereotypical sex roles. This means not only that children would have to be told about contraception, abortion, and venereal disease, but also that they would have to be given access to all "adult" books, magazines, films, and stage shows including those that are called "pornographic." It further means that children could choose their sexual partners freely (including adult partners), as long as they observed the same decorum as everyone else. "Child molestation" and incest would therefore no longer be crimes unless they involved unwilling children. (Needless to say, at the same time, the right and ability of children to refuse sexual advances would have to be strengthened). Finally, all sexual discrimination between children would have to cease.[341]

### Case Study: What Is Child Pornography?

The Free Speech Coalition, a California Trade Association representing creators and distributors of sexually explicit materials, sought to challenge the 1982 Supreme Court decision of *New York v. Ferber* in reference to the definition

**Did You Know?**

The vast majority of sexually explicit materials (SEM) containing children were generally created from one of two sources: (1) magazines celebrating the nudist lifestyle, mostly from European countries, and (2) still pictures taken of children, alone or in pairs, engaging in various forms of sexual activity, mostly from South American countries and taken by American "tourists" in the 1960s and 1970s.[342] The former were legitimate magazines that were used by individuals who already had sexual proclivities toward children. These magazines were used in much the same way that adolescent boys use the lingerie sections of retail catalogs as masturbatory tools. The latter were created for the sole purpose of providing sexual gratification to the viewer and often the (overwhelmingly) young boys were paid for their time and efforts. If we look at this through a sexual anthropological lens, it is necessary to consider the cultures of South American countries in the 1960s and 1970s. Paying young boys to demonstrate their sexual experiments for the camera may not have been that significant. Perhaps the boys were only allowing behaviors to be caught on film that they would have done anyway. Or maybe these boys were forced into posing for pictures and were traumatized as a result. The point is that unless we know the context in which the pictures were taken, it is difficult to ascertain whether harm was caused in the creation of the materials, and this greatly affects what, if any, punishment should be meted out to the creators, distributors, and viewers.

of child pornography. The coalition also challenged the 1996 Child Pornography Protection Act (CPPA). The case centered around what is termed "virtual" child pornography—materials that seem to depict children, but actually are adults or computerized images. The CPPA defined child pornography as any visual image that appears to be of a minor engaging in sexual activity or merely suggests that minors are involved in sex. The law carried a penalty of up to 15 years imprisonment for distribution and up to 5 years imprisonment for possession.[343] The government's position was that such materials could harm real children by allowing them to be seduced by child offenders who would be interested in engaging in the activities that they viewed. The opposition stated that the law went too far in defining what is considered child pornography and is based on the faulty notion that all sexual materials depicting children are evil or harmful. In a six to three ruling, the Supreme Court sided with the plaintiffs, and in 2002, the Child Pornography Protection Act (1996) was struck down as unconstitutional.[344] However, Congress redrafted the law in 2003, and it has since withstood a Supreme Court challenge. In 2008, the Court ruled that child pornography exists if the person viewing it believes it to be real or if the person distributing the materials attempts to convince potential buyers that it is real.[345]

For example, Dwight Whorley of Iowa received 20 years in prison for possessing 20 cartoon pictures depicting children being forced to have sex with adults. The cartoons were Japanese animation, made illegal in the United States in 2003. Whorley also had in his possession some digital images of children in various types of sexual conduct and e-mails that described the sexual abuse of children by their parents.

Whorley appealed his conviction, but it was upheld by the court.[346] Compare this case with an Arizona teacher who was convicted of possessing 20 images of child pornography. In Arizona, possession of sexually explicit images of children results in a mandatory 10-year prison sentence. The teacher, previously in good standing, was sentenced to 200 years in prison.[347]

In Ohio, a 15-year-old high school student faced felony child pornography charges after taking a nude photo of herself and sending it to classmates. The charges included possession of criminal tools and the illegal use of a minor in sexually explicit material. If convicted, the teen could receive a sentence varying from probation to several years in prison, and could be forced to register as a sex offender. In addition, the classmates who received the pictures could also face charges of possession of child pornography. As the county prosecutor stated, "There's a totally false perception among juveniles that there is no risk to this. That picture, once taken and sent, gives anyone who receives it the ability to do anything with it, forever. If a picture of you found its way onto the Internet, that's going to haunt you, potentially forever."[348]

This case raises an obvious question: what is the harm if the minor took and distributed the picture of herself? The answer lies in an American culture that is utterly confused about how to handle adolescent sexuality. The laws are designed to deal with situations in which adults victimize young people. But what if the young person is a willing participant? What if the young person is exploring their sexual identity and seeks out sexual contact with others? As historians note:

> Maturity is accompanied by feelings of power, and it is both human and reasonable that a young woman is tempted to take advantage of the desire which she is able to rouse in the male. Let us be sure not to forget that the male has abused his power through all those centuries during which he reigned. She has more or less had only one weapon against him, and when she sense[s] that [it works], she strikes. Today this can lead to the mature man being seduced by a girl "under age". . . . As in all tragedy, this case is pushed to extremes, but the Lolita phenomenon and young men's corresponding seduction of older homosexual men are good examples of the misfortunes which obsolete laws create. How is the judge to give everyone his due when the law is distorted?[349]

The debate over SEM will continue for many years to come, despite strong evidence indicating that it is unconnected to sexual violence. SEM has a long history as a tool to fight government and religious oppression—it is a way to release sexual tension while not participating in the actual sex act. The value of SEM in therapy has been proven as well, and sexologists have been incorporating it into treatment of sexual dysfunction for decades. The "war on pornography" has more to do with society's desire to control the sexuality of its members than any supposed harms caused by its use. For persons who have offended sexually, SEM is generally unrelated to their offensive behavior, but it can be extremely beneficial as part of treatment. It may be time for society to re-evaluate its position on SEM and how we define obscene materials.

# CHAPTER 7

# NONCONSENSUAL OFFENSES

A nonconsensual sexual offense occurs when one party has not agreed to participate in the sexual activity that takes place. Examples to be discussed are voyeurism, exhibitionism, and sexual assault and rape. Voyeurism and exhibitionism are examples of offenses that do not involve physical contact between perpetrator and victim; this type of sexual offense is therefore considered less serious by the criminal justice system and medical professionals. Sexual assault and rape are contact offenses and can involve a wide range of contact between the perpetrator and his/her victims, as well as a wide range of degrees of force. Sexual assaults and rape offenses are taken more seriously by medical professionals and the criminal justice system; however, barriers to the prosecution of these offenses remain.

In each of these types of offenses, the issue of consent is essential because it transforms an act from one that is offensive and criminal to one that is perfectly acceptable and legal. Consent, however, is not simple and straightforward. Can consent be conveyed nonverbally as two parties are engaged in sexual activity? Does consent even need to be conveyed verbally? That is, does an individual have to give verbal consent to a sexual activity in order for consent to occur, or can consent be implied by the actions between two parties? Is there a difference between force and lack of consent? Can a nonconsensual activity occur without the use of force? These are just some of the complications that arise when one party indicates that a nonconsensual offense has occurred, and the other party indicates that a consensual act has occurred. Legally, in order for a crime to occur, the act must be nonconsensual, but the perpetrator must also have *intended* for the act to be nonconsensual. In other words, the perpetrator must have been aware that the victim's consent was lacking. The problem is that we live in a society in which consent to sex (and indeed rejection) is most often nonverbal . . . which can sometimes lead to the miscommunication of signals. In cases such as these, it is up to criminal justice system personnel (either police, prosecutors, or sometimes jurors) to determine if consent was indeed lacking. The elements of voyeurism, exhibitionism, and sexual assault and rape will be detailed in this chapter and will be illustrated with the use of case studies.

## Voyeurism

Voyeurism involves the sexual arousal of an individual from secretly observing other parties involved in private activities such as disrobing or engaging in sexual acts. The aroused individual often masturbates to these activities. Known commonly as "peeping," voyeurism was a hot topic among the psychiatric and psychological communities in the 1950s, 1960s, and 1970s, and appeared in the first and second *Diagnostic and Statistical Manual of Mental Disorders* as a personality disorder. It was believed during this period that:

> ... voyeurs are fixated on experiences that aroused their castration anxiety, either primal scenes or the sight of adult genitals. The patient attempts to deny the justification of his fright by repeating the frightening scenes with certain alterations, for the purpose of achieving a belated mastery ... these conditions then represent either a repetition of a condition present in an important childhood experience, or more often a denial of these very conditions or of their dangerous nature.[350]

For an example using a real patient, the following is provided:

> ... the case study of a middle-aged male "voyeur" who rented a room in a bordello. Rather than engaging in a sexual contact himself, the man 'obtained gratification' by looking through a peephole into an adjoining room where another man and a woman had intercourse. The voyeur would begin to cry as the activities progress, a response ... to the man's intense feelings of anxiety and his desire that the woman next door leave her partner and come to comfort him. Subsequently, the voyeur would masturbate and would then leave the bordello feeling calm and relaxed, only to return to repeat the scenario the very next day.[351]

According to psychoanalysts then, the voyeur was someone who passed through life compulsively viewing sexual organs and sexual activities in an attempt to deflect from an emptiness in the self.[352] Though the field of psychiatry may have been concerned with voyeurism between 1950 and 1970, publicly this issue received minimal attention (although, to be clear, voyeurism has long been considered illegal). One of the few popular (though nonsexual) references of the time was in the 1954 film *Rear Window* in which the main character turned to voyeurism when he became wheelchair-bound after breaking his leg. The entire film was dedicated to his obsession with watching his neighbors through his courtyard window.

In the 1980s, definitions began to change. The American Psychological Association's *Diagnostic and Statistical Manual of Mental Disorders*[353] defines a paraphilia as any sexual disorder that involves recurrent and intense sexually arousing fantasies, urges, or behaviors that involve atypical activities or targets.

These urges and fantasies must exist for a period of at least 6 months and result in some sort of disruption in functioning for the individual in question. Examples of paraphilias include masochism, in which an individual is aroused by his own suffering; sadism, in which a person is aroused by the suffering of others; or pedophilia, in which a person is sexually aroused by prepubescent children. Voyeurism was now classified as a paraphilia, a recurrent and intense sexual fantasy, urge, or behavior, as opposed to a personality disorder. But how many people actually engage in this behavior?

In a 1996 Swedish study of adults between the ages of 18 and 60, it was revealed that 7.7 percent of individuals reported sexual arousal from voyeuristic behavior.[354] In this study, voyeurism was more likely to occur in men with psychological difficulties, involvement in drug or alcohol use, and greater interest in frequent sexual activity as well as greater participation in a variety of sexual activities, including the use of sexually explicit materials. These individuals were also more likely to have engaged in other "less mainstream" sexual behaviors, such as sadomasochism or cross-dressing.[355] Studies conducted using populations of sexual offenders reveal that those who have paraphilias such as exhibitionism and voyeurism are more likely to start offending at a younger age and may have more victims over the span of their offending,[356] and they may be more likely to recidivate.[357] In addition, studies reveal that paraphilias are much more likely to occur together than they are to occur singularly in an individual. In a study of 581 men voluntarily seeking evaluation or treatment for a sexual paraphilia, researchers revealed that exhibitionism and voyeurism occurred up to 150 times more frequently than indicated in official police arrest records.[358] Sixty-three percent of men in this study who were diagnosed with voyeurism also self-reported involvement with exhibitionism.[359]

Perhaps the analysis of sexual voyeuristic behavior is complicated in that we have become a voyeuristic society. As a society, we increasingly watch reality television shows such as *Survivor, Big Brother, Temptation Island,* and *The Bachelor,* which allow us to act as voyeurs into the lives of others. For example, *Temptation Island* was a Fox show that sent four seemingly committed couples to an island in Belize to test their loyalty to one another when they were tempted with the seductions of attractive singles. The couples were placed on opposite sides of the tropical island and the "goal" of the singles was to liaison with the contestants. Viewers watched weekly from home as the events unfolded but were also given access online to a 24-hour live action site to fulfill their inner voyeur. The Internet allows us to log on to Web sites such as *ucanwatch.com* or *voyeurnation.com,* to name only two of many, that allow us to watch a person carrying on the daily business of their lives. Web sites exist that permit us to watch people showering, engaging in sexual activities, or simply performing routine activities, permitting us all, at any moment, to participate legally in voyeurism if we choose. In addition, Web servers exist to "trade" in pictures of a voyeuristic nature, for example, photos taken of women in various stages of undress from a distance, photos taken of individuals in public places who are unaware that the picture is being taken, pictures of sexual acts, pictures of bathroom activities, photographs of dressing room situations, sunbathing, or pictures of incest.[360] While some circumstances in which voyeurism occurs are clearly illegal, the line between "normal voyeurism" (i.e., *Temptation Island* or *Survivor*) and "deviant voyeurism" (i.e., illegal peeping) has become increasingly blurred in recent years. In the 1950s, voyeurism was denoted by psychiatrists as an "obsession to see," but today many of us have that obsession to see, so psychiatrists now call voyeurism a "deviant obsession to see," which often is merely deviant because the person being observed has not consented to being observed. This distinction is what makes voyeurism a nonconsensual sexual offense.

Laws in the United States vary by state for voyeurism offenses, but generally they are weak because voyeurism is a noncontact sexual offense and is therefore taken less seriously by the criminal justice system than a contact offense such as rape. Many states have what are commonly referred to as "Peeping Tom" laws; some are misdemeanors, some are felonies, some require the offender to use a camera or video device in order for a crime to be committed, whereas others consider peeping a crime in and of itself. Sentences are typically light and involve a fine, probation, or for repeat offenses, a maximum of one year in jail. If the victim is a child, however, more serious charges may be attached, making the sentence longer.

In 2004, the Federal Video Voyeurism Prevention Act was passed, which prohibits recording or disseminating photographs or video of an individual's "private areas" without their consent if that individual had a reasonable expectation of privacy, whether the person was in a private or public place. Violation of this law may result in a fine and/or up to one year imprisonment. This is a federal law, however, and therefore does not apply to each state individually. Two case studies, one in Louisiana and one in Oregon, follow. They illustrate the dramatically different approaches that can be taken by states to the crime of voyeurism.

### Case Study: 56 Years for Taping!

In December 2006, a Louisiana Second Circuit State Appeals Court ruled on the appeal of a video voyeur who was sentenced to 56 years in prison for using a wireless camera to record his 18-year-old stepdaughter. In 2005, defendant James Boudreaux was living in a mobile home with his son and his 18-year-old stepdaughter. Boudreaux installed a wireless camera in the bedroom of his stepdaughter to record her dressing and undressing over a period of approximately four months. According to court records, "Other tapes allegedly showed some of the victim's young female friends partially or completely naked, and one tape purportedly depicted [the] defendant masturbating while holding a pair of the victim's underpants up to his face."[361] His stepdaughter found out about the camera and confronted Boudreaux. He said that it was his home and therefore he could film whatever he wanted to film. Shortly thereafter, the stepdaughter was kicked out of the home. She sought the assistance of the sheriff to retrieve her belongings and mentioned the videos, at which point a warrant was secured, Boudreaux's home was searched, and he was arrested.

Once the search was complete and law enforcement had viewed the videos, it was revealed that seven women had been taped in various stages of nudity over the four-month period. Boudreaux was apologetic about the situation, which he blamed on an addiction to drugs and alcohol. His adult criminal record had seven prior offenses, none of them sexual in nature, and six of them involved issues related to drugs or alcohol (such as possession or driving while intoxicated). While some states have lax laws for video voyeurism, Louisiana was not one of these states, due to an earlier high-profile case involving Susan Wilson that was turned into a made-for-television movie. Wilson's situation involved a neighbor who unknowingly planted a camera in her home, and at the time there was no law to deal with such circumstances. Public outcry resulted, and Louisiana's "video voyeurism" law resulted. This law prohibits any nonconsensual "observing, viewing, photographing, filming, or videotaping . . . any portion of the female breast below the top of the areola or of any portion of the pubic hair, anus, cleft of the buttocks, vulva or genitals." The possible penalty is up to 5 years imprisonment. James Boudreaux decided to plead guilty to 14 counts of video voyeurism, and he was sentenced to 4 years of hard labor for each count, to be served consecutively, for a total of 56 years in prison. Once released, he would be required to register as a sex offender. To put this into perspective "the average total incarceration time imposed by state courts for murder is 18 years; rape is 8 years; and robbery is about 6.5 years."[362]

Due to its severity, Boudreaux appealed his sentence as excessive, and in December 2006 the appeals court of Louisiana agreed and sent the case back to the trial judge for resentencing. The following is an excerpt from the ruling of the appeals court:

Defendant was 42 years old at the time of sentencing. His criminal history consists primarily of drug- and alcohol-related offenses. In fact, his conviction in 1984 of bringing marijuana into a correctional facility occurred while he was serving time on the weekends for DWI. Defendant's last violent offense was a conviction for simple battery in 1990, which arose out of an argument with his sister. Any sentence for video voyeurism under La. R.S. 14:283B(3) must be served without benefit of parole, probation or suspension of sentence. As a practical matter, 14 four-year terms without benefit of parole to be served consecutively is a life sentence. Even as a second felony offender, defendant would have been subject to a fixed term. Although defendant's video voyeurism does not involve any physical contact or violence, it is nonetheless a reprehensible violation of a personal nature. At 18 years old, the victim may not legally have been a minor, but she was a young and callow girl. Defendant perpetrated the crime against someone he had essentially raised as a daughter. According to the victim, her mother and defendant began dating when she was 8 years old and married when she was 11. After the parties separated in April of 2003, the victim lived with her mother for approximately four months, then moved in with defendant. She lived with defendant and defendant's son until June 2005, when defendant ordered her to leave. The experience has had, and undoubtedly will continue to have, a significant effect on the victim. However, defendant's activities all formed a part of a single scheme or plan, something that the trial court did not adequately address at sentencing. While it is within the trial court's discretion to impose sentences consecutively in an appropriate "scheme or plan" case, in the instant matter, the imposition of a 56-year term without parole is out of proportion to the offense and appears to impose a purposeless and needless infliction of pain and suffering. . . . For the reasons set forth above, defendant's sentence is vacated, and the matter is remanded to the trial court for resentencing.[363]

The initial sentence exemplifies the contempt with which sexual offenders are held in society. Although no updates regarding this case could be located in time for the publication of this work, it is hoped that the trial court will determine a sentence that is more reasonable given the offense committed.

### Case Study: Treat the Peeper

In Oregon, voyeurism is not considered a sexual offense, so 31-year-old Jeremy Peter Goulet, convicted of voyeurism in June 2008 was not pleased with the variety of conditions attached to his sentence. The judge told Goulet that he had "violated a cherished societal boundary: the ability to retreat behind closed doors and feel safe. . . . Personal privacy is one of the most important and sacred things we as individuals have. . . . This is an act that is highly inappropriate. It is life altering to the victim. It's wrong. . . . And it's got to stop."[364] Goulet was convicted in California of voyeurism eight years prior and had admitted to "hundreds" of acts of voyeurism in recent years, most frequently watching women shower, although he also admitted to taking videos with his cell phone of women in various stages of undress.

The particular offense for which he was convicted involved watching a 22-year-old woman in the shower. The woman's boyfriend, Danny, saw Goulet before he vanished and saw him again several days later in the courtyard near the apartment building. At that time, he chased him down and advised him to stay away from his girlfriend. A few weeks later, the boyfriend saw Goulet for a third time near the building and confronted him. Bystanders called the police. While Goulet was charged with several felonies and attempted murder (because of the confrontation and the fact that he was in possession of a gun), jurors only found him guilty of illegal possession of a weapon and invasion of personal privacy. Goulet was sentenced to three years probation, with the terms to include sex offender treatment, random computer searches and random cell-phone camera searches, random polygraph testing regarding recent behaviors, and a curfew. Goulet chose not to appeal the sentence.[365]

# Exhibitionism

Exhibitionism is perhaps most commonly referred to as "flashing." Exhibitionists are sexually aroused by the exposure of their genitals, usually to an unsuspecting stranger who views the act as inappropriate. This paraphilia, or recurrent and intense sexual fantasy, urge, or behavior, may also involve a desire to be watched by others, typically in the act of masturbation. Generally speaking, the exhibitionist seeks no further sexual contact with the stranger involved. The definition of what constitutes exhibitionism or indecent exposure has changed throughout history; what is considered indecent at one historical moment in time is considered perfectly acceptable at another. Take, for example, the bathing suits worn by women prior to World War I. By today's standards, these bathing suits were composed of enough material to constitute an evening dress. Pre-World War I society would have been appalled at the scant bathing suits women wear today!

Female exhibitionists are very rare, perhaps because there are outlets for women to expose themselves legally should they choose to do so, such as employment in a strip club.[366] According to the American Psychological Association's *Diagnostic and Statistical Manual of Mental Disorders*[367] as well as other scholarly references,[368] exhibitionism may be rooted in feelings of anger, shame, or inadequacy, and often the exhibitionist act is to elicit a reaction, any reaction, from an individual. The exhibitionist experiences intense sexual desire when discovered as revealed in this case study:

> ... Mr. K goes to the park on his lunch hour and finds a shady grove. He unzips his pants, exposes himself, and begins to masturbate. Soon, a group of women walk nearby, but instead of hiding himself from them, he moves forward. He wants them to see his genitals so he can experience their reaction. In this exact moment he is gratified. The women's expressions of shock, disgust, and fear provoke the greatest sexual excitement he can experience. Later in the day, however, he is ashamed of himself and disgusted by his behavior. He vows not to do it again. He succeeds for 3 or 4 days in avoiding the park at lunch but eventually returns to repeat the scenario time and again.[369]

His feelings of inadequacy and shame are translated into a compulsive need to "prove" himself and his virility to others, which unfortunately only further develops his feelings of shame, inadequacy, and anger. These feelings are often found in all areas of the exhibitionist's life. For example, Mr. K is described in this way by his therapist:

> ... he blames his exhibitionism on stress and identifies work and intimate relationships as the particular areas to be addressed.... At work, he has an intense need for approval and feels easily slighted. He has a great deal of difficulty coping with negative reactions from others or with any perceived criticisms. He also struggles with feeling unacknowledged, and feels angry that he works harder and longer than his colleagues, with insufficient reward or recognition. When he does receive praise, his pleasure in it is short-lived as if the experience cannot be retained for prolonged or future gratification.... Like his work, romantic relationships have fallen short of satisfying his need for emotional stimulation.[370]

Most psychologists and psychiatrists believe that the sexual arousal of exhibitionism comes from the fear elicited in the women and/or children who are the targets of the exposure and that it is motivated by feelings of emptiness and powerlessness.[371]

A 1996 Swedish study of a general population of adults between the ages of 18 and 60 revealed that 3.1 percent of the population reported sexual arousal from exhibitionism.[372] This behavior was more likely to occur among men with psychological difficulties; those who were involved with drug or alcohol use; those with a greater interest in sexual activity as well as greater participation in sexual activities, including the use of sexually explicit materials; and individuals who were more likely to have engaged in other sexual behaviors, such as sado-masochism or cross-dressing.[373] As mentioned in the discussion on voyeurism, in a study of 581 men voluntarily seeking evaluation or treatment for a sexual paraphilia, researchers revealed that exhibitionism (and voyeurism) occurred up to 150 times more frequently than indicated in official police arrest records,[374] and 46 percent of men diagnosed with exhibitionism were also involved with sexual abuse of girls under the age of majority who were unrelated to them.[375] The relatively scant amount of research that has been conducted on exhibition-ism shows high recidivism rates, a high frequency of exposing behavior, and a low success rate for treatment when compared to other types of sexual offenses.[376]

Laws in the United States vary by state for exhibitionism and usually fall under public lewdness or indecent exposure statutes, but they are generally weak because this is a noncontact sexual offense similar to voyeurism. Many states prohibit this type of behavior, and in most statutes, this offense is a mis-demeanor. Sentences are typically light and involve a fine, probation, or for repeat offenses, a maximum of one year in jail. A few states, such as Louisiana and Vermont, provide for more severe penalties. Currently, there is no federal indecent exposure legislation, though there is a move to create one, which would also mean that individuals convicted of this offense would be added to the grow-ing list of persons required to register with the national sex offender registry. Several short case studies to illustrate the dramatically different approaches that can be taken by state when dealing with the crime of exhibitionism follow.

### Case Study: Career Exhibitionism Taken Seriously in California

A 52-year-old man in San Francisco, California, was sentenced to 13 years and 4 months in state prison on five felony charges of indecent exposure. Kenneth Ray Burton pleaded no contest after he allegedly exposed himself and began masturbating in front of a woman on a commuter train. The prosecutor's office sought a lengthy sentence for Burton because he had two prior sexual convic-tions for indecent exposure as well as a previous conviction for sexual assault. Chief Deputy District Attorney Steve Wagstaffe, in seeking the long sentence, said: "Our concern was, Are we being too lenient? Are we adequately protecting the public? . . . We have a person here who has done this for many, many years. And with all likelihood, he will be doing it again."[377] The defendant faced a max-imum term of 25 years to life imprisonment for the five felony offenses.

### Case Study: Career Exhibitionism Taken Less Seriously in Hawaii

In 2005, a 38-year-old former administrator for a substance abuse treatment program pleaded guilty to three misdemeanor counts of fourth-degree sexual assault involving indecent exposure. The charges stemmed from three separate events in which Francis Kim exposed himself to various women in a parking lot and masturbated during these encounters. Each offense carried the possibility of one year in prison, and prosecutors in the case requested that Kim be sentenced to the maximum penalty to be served consecutively. The judge asserted that Kim's offenses were "too serious and recurring" to grant probation and treatment alone, and that "there must be just punishment and society must be protected, specifically women of this community.... This behavior must be stopped."[378] The judge also acknowledged the defendant's need for treatment and his history of productivity to the community as a counselor and administrator at a premier substance abuse treatment program in Hawaii. The prosecutor objected to leniency in sentencing as Kim had a history of sexual offenses and a history of failure to comply with treatment that was ordered by the court. In 1990, Kim served 30 days in jail for indecent exposure to two adult women; in 1993, he was sentenced to treatment and probation for indecent exposure to two prepubescent girls. Each of these incidents also involved Kim masturbating. During the 1993 incident, he failed to comply with the treatment order and was sentenced to 60 days in jail. On the 2005 charges in question, Kim was sentenced to 6 months in jail as well as 6 months probation and treatment. It has been reported that "after pleading guilty ... Kim told a probation officer that he had exposed himself to around 200 victims in the past 20 years."[379]

### Case Study: Therapy Instead of Prison for Career Exhibitionist in North Carolina

A 33-year-old man in Raleigh, North Carolina, has pleaded guilty to indecent exposure in order to seek treatment and avoid prison on his ninth conviction. This ninth offense involved exposing himself to a group of female preteen cheerleaders between the ages of 5 and 10. "The mother of one girl became suspicious, walked to his car, and saw Joseph Michael Hilliard exposed and masturbating. He covered up and drove away. The mother called [the] police, and they stopped him soon after and he confessed."[380] He was on probation at the time for an indecent exposure conviction. This current offense was the first charged as a felony (due to a recent law change in 2005), and while he could have received a sentence of up to 10 months, he instead agreed to plead to 3 years of probation, participation in sex offender therapy, and registration as a sexual offender. Hilliard's arrest record dates to a 1999 charge of indecent exposure that was later dismissed. In 2001, he was sentenced to probation on two misdemeanor counts of indecent exposure, he was charged several times for indecent exposure in 2002, and in 2006 he again received probation for a misdemeanor indecent exposure offense. Nothing in his history or his arrest records indicate violence or that he has ever attempted to touch a victim, making attorneys on both sides willing to consider treatment for Hilliard. The defendant's attorney said: "He's never been convicted of any felony or any violent offense ever.... Hilliard will have to attend therapy while on probation, something that might not have happened in prison.... The prison system doesn't have a lot of resources for those sort of things."[381] The prosecutor also said: "[T]he waiting lists to get into the prison system's therapy program are lengthy.... [I] want to ensure Hilliard would get treatment and would have to register as a sex offender. He'll be monitored by probation officers as well."[382]

## Sexual Assault and Rape

Though both voyeurism and exhibitionism are noncontact sexual offenses, in sexual assault and rape there is physical contact between the perpetrator and the victim. Definitions of sexual assault and rape have changed throughout time, but they have always reflected male superiority in society, and historically these offenses were not taken seriously by the criminal justice system. Women were stereotyped as manipulative and seductive, and it was believed that a woman would "cry rape" to explain away a variety of other situations, including pregnancy, premarital sexual contact, or for the purpose of revenge. As well, often during a rape trial a judge informed the jury that rape was an allegation easily made but difficult for a man to defend. Testimony was permitted regarding a woman's prior sexual contact and behavior in order to impeach her credibility. This obviously worked against the successful prosecution of men accused of sexual assault or rape and deterred women from reporting rape because they did not want to deal with the emotional and mental ordeal associated with a trial. In the 1970s, women's and feminist groups worked successfully to reform rape laws, and many changes resulted.

Society once thought of rape as a crime of sexual passion and frustration, and one rape law reform involved changing the term "rape" to "sexual assault" or "sexual battery" in order to highlight the violent nature of the offense. This change in definition also broadened the crime from a traditional focus on sexual intercourse to other types of sexual violation that occurred without consent but did not necessarily involve penetration. Also, the category of individuals that can be held accountable for sexual assault offenses has broadened to include persons of either sex in most states, as well as spouses who were historically exempt. Until recently, men were permitted to have intercourse with their wife at their whim without regard to consent by the wife. The wife's consent was not required: legally it was not possible for a man to "rape" his wife. Women's groups wanted the criminal justice system and society generally to understand that rape could occur in a variety of situations, involve a diverse array of individuals, and did not necessarily conform to the stereotypes that had historically pervaded societal views. As such, reformers sought to expand the list of potential sex crimes to include incest offenders, acquaintance rape, marital rape, rape that did not involve serious physical harm, and assailants who did not fit the traditional stereotype of a rapist.[383]

Another significant change was the removal of the legal requirement that the victim physically resist as much as possible and potentially put herself at increased risk of harm by angering the perpetrator. This reflected a change of focus to the behavior of the offender. A major legal advancement was the passage of rape shield laws that placed restrictions on questioning a rape victim about her prior sexual encounters. By 1999, these laws had been passed in 49 states. Although this reform dramatically limits questioning the victim regarding her sexual history in order to prove she consented to sexual activity, it still permits questions regarding her sexual history to challenge her credibility.[384] Therefore, while these laws are a major step forward in protecting the victim at trial, there is room for defense counsel to bring in a victim's sexual history.

Unlike historic rape trials, the judge is no longer permitted to give cautionary instructions to the jury. As well, a defense of "mistaken age" has been eliminated so that men can no longer "claim" they "thought" the victim was "of legal age." It remains to be seen whether, in light of online chat rooms and social networking sites, this aspect of the law will be challenged. After all, when you are chatting with someone on *myspace.com*, is there any possible way for you to know how old they truly are? Moreover, it is problematic that the mistaken age defense is no longer permissible despite the fact that American culture strongly encourages young girls to adorn themselves with makeup and clothing that makes them look sexually attractive and much older than their chronological age to men and boys who are then expected to control their sexual impulses.

The most recent legal change, which will be elaborated in a case study, permits a woman to withdraw consent to sex in a handful of states *after* initial consent to sex has been given. If, in such a scenario, the man continues with sexual intercourse, he can be charged with rape. For example, Illinois was the first state to enact such legislation. Conversely, in other states, once a woman consents to intercourse, she cannot then withdraw consent and allege rape. Legal reforms can be very complicated in nature and are not federal in scope; therefore, they vary dramatically by state. Questions of consent, as posed at the beginning of this chapter, are paramount to sexual assault and rape because consent or lack of consent can transform an act from one that is criminal to one that is mutually acceptable. The following case studies will address how issues of consent have been handled first on a college campus and second in the law.

### Case Study: Sex Contracts

Research suggests that rape and sexual assault on college campuses are even higher than among the general female population,[385] with many studies reporting that between 15 and 20 percent of female college students have experienced forced sexual intercourse.[386] When male college students are asked about their involvement with forced sexual activity, between 5 and 15 percent admit to forcing sexual intercourse, and between 15 and 25 percent admit to sexually aggressive behaviors.[387] A national study of college men conducted in 1987 revealed that one in twelve admitted to the commission of an act that met the legal definition of rape. Significantly, 84 percent of those men did not believe their actions were illegal.[388] In a study of college men a decade later, almost 9 percent admitted to either raping or attempting to rape a woman.[389] While there are a variety of risk factors involved in sexual aggression, such as male sex-role socialization, alcohol abuse, personality traits, and child abuse and neglect,[390] there are also issues of consent to consider. It was this issue of consent that Antioch College was trying to "solve" with its Sexual Offense Prevention Policy.

Sexual violence was challenged in 1991 on the campus of Antioch College in Ohio by a group called the Womyn of Antioch. This group worked to create a "campus culture of positive, consensual sexuality . . . that is about empowerment, changing our rape culture, and healing."[391] The solution was the creation of a Sexual Offense Prevention Policy (SOPP) that required *verbal* consent at *each and every* stage of a sexual encounter. They recognized the variation between their standards and those of the legal system but sought to create a "consensual standard" at the college. According to the Sexual Offense Prevention Policy at Antioch College:

... Consent is defined as the act of willingly and verbally agreeing to engage in spe-cific sexual conduct. The following are clarifying points: Consent is required each and every time there is sexual activity; All parties must have a clear and accurate understanding of the sexual activity; The person(s) who initiate(s) the sexual activ-ity is responsible for asking for consent; The person(s) who are asked are responsi-ble for verbally responding; Each new level of sexual activity requires consent; Use of agreed upon forms of communication such as gestures or safe words is accept-able, but must be discussed and verbally agreed to by all parties before sexual activ-ity occurs; Consent is required regardless of the parties' relationship, prior sexual history, or current activity (e.g., grinding on the dance floor is not consent for fur-ther sexual activity); At any and all times when consent is withdrawn or not ver-bally agreed to, the sexual activity must stop immediately; Silence is not consent; Body movements and nonverbal responses such as moans are not consent; A person cannot give consent while sleeping; All parties must have unimpaired judgment (examples that may cause impairment include but are not limited to alcohol, drugs, mental health conditions, physical health conditions); All parties must use safe sex practices; All parties must disclose personal risk factors and any known STIs. Indi-viduals are responsible for maintaining awareness of their sexual health. These requirements for consent do not restrict with whom the sexual activity may occur, the type of sexual activity that occurs, the props/toys/tools that are used, the num-ber of persons involved, the gender(s) or gender expressions of persons involved.[392]

This policy at Antioch College applied to all students, faculty, and staff, as well as visitors. Antioch College closed for financial reasons in 2008, so this policy is no longer in effect. When this policy first came to the attention of the media in 1993, it created national controversy. The idea behind the policy was to reduce sexual assault and rape on campus, but the notion of a verbal agreement to each and every stage of sexual activity seemed ridiculous to much of the American public. The president of Antioch College said of the public's reaction:

I believe it's not just sex that has created the reaction, but the Antioch requirement that students talk about sex! Talking about it with someone whom you desire; get-ting consent before having sex; having to think about [the] sexual act that you are about to do; communicating with a partner about your interests.[393]

This begs the question, do men and women generally misread sexual cues and need to verbally indicate consent at each stage of a sexual encounter? Was Antioch's policy sound? A study conducted after Antioch's policy was enacted analyzed the communication of sexual consent between men and women and found minimal gender differences, indicating that miscommunication of sexual cues is not a likely explanation for rape. Both women and men are likely to convey consent to sexual intercourse nonverbally, and both seem to read these cues effectively.[394] Thus, while the Sexual Offense Prevention Policy at Antioch College may have been a reasonable idea to curb sexual assault and rape on campus, it likely would have accomplished little in terms of reaching these objectives on campus. It may, however, have served to increase respect for autonomy between sexual partners as each party would be forced to consider the clear indications of consent of another.

### Case Study: The 5-Second Rule

In a ruling in Maryland in 2008 (*State v. Baby*) the Court of Appeals ruled that after initially giving her consent to sexual intercourse, a woman may then withdraw her consent *after* penetration has begun. If the man continues intercourse through force or threat of force, this may constitute rape. The incident in question occurred in 2003 and involved Maouloud Baby who was with his friend "Mike" and "J. L.," the female in question. The three were on their way to a party together when they stopped and parked. J. L. got into the backseat with the two men and engaged in sexual contact (no intercourse) with both men. Baby briefly left the car, and Mike attempted to penetrate J. L. but was not successful. When Baby returned to the car, Baby asked if he could have sex with J. L., and she agreed on the condition that he stop if she asked him to stop. He agreed to this condition.

J. L. testified at trial that as she and Baby had sex she experienced pain and told him to stop, but he continued irrespective of her request. She tried to push him away while objecting verbally to the sexual activity and was able to push him off her several seconds later. At this point, J. L. testified that she returned with the two men to the restaurant at which she had initially picked them up. In contrast, Baby testified at trial that he tried to penetrate J. L. after she consented to have sex with him but that he was not able to do so and did not try to penetrate her a second time.[395]

After testimony was heard at trial and the jury began to deliberate, the jurors submitted a note to the judge requesting an answer to the following: "If a female consents to sex initially and, during the course of the sex act to which she consented, for whatever reason, she changes her mind and the man continues until climax, does the result constitute rape?"[396] While the jury was waiting on a response, they followed with a simpler version of the same question: "If at any time the woman says stop, is that rape?"[397] The judge responded by saying: "This is a question that you as a jury must decide. I have given [you] the legal definition of rape, which includes the definition of consent."[398] The jury deliberated and found Baby guilty of first-degree rape.

This issue of withdrawal of consent, however, is one that is very contentious and varies considerably by state. Historically, issues of consent have been paramount in rape trials but have never directly dealt with post-penetration withdrawal of consent. Only recently has this issue been legally challenged. The Supreme Court of North Carolina (*State v. Way*) in 1979 ruled that withdrawal of consent after penetration does not constitute rape, whereas the Supreme Judicial Court of Maine in 1985 (*State v. Robinson*) ruled that withdrawal of consent after penetration does constitute rape. States such as Maine support this position by suggesting that once consent is revoked, threat of force or force is used to continue the act of penetration, thereby making it equivalent to rape. Critics refer to this with a derogatory tone as the "5-second rule" because it begs the question: how long must the perpetrator continue penetration before it is considered rape? 1 second, 2 seconds, 5 seconds, 10 seconds, 1 minute? Maryland's rape ruling adds that state to the list of only a handful of states that punishes penetration that persists after the withdrawal of consent. The remaining states all believe that once consent is given to sexual intercourse, the act must be finished! For a few progressive states, however, an individual may withdraw consent, and if penetration continues by force or threat of force, this may constitute rape.[399]

CHAPTER 8

# SEPARATING FACT FROM FICTION

Many legislative endeavors have resulted from policymakers falling victim to fictitious information about sexual offenders. Because the media is the source of "reality" for much of the public, society generally has difficulty separating fact from fiction when it comes to sexual offenses and offenders. The purpose of this chapter is to dispel several common myths and answer some outstanding questions in the area of sexual offending. The questions to be addressed in this chapter include: Are strangers the greatest source of danger? Do sex offenders keep reoffending and therefore pose a great risk to community safety if they are not indefinitely confined? Does community notification and registration increase community safety? Do residency restrictions increase community safety? And, finally, does treatment work to lower the recidivism of sexual offenders?

## Are Strangers the Most Dangerous?

Although the public's greatest fear is from stranger danger, and laws have been passed in response to high-profile stranger sexual assault and murder cases, this is not where the greatest risk of sexual victimization comes from by an overwhelming margin. Government data collected in the National Incident Based Reporting System between 1991 and 1996 revealed that 33 percent of sexual assaults reported to law enforcement involved victims age 12 through 17 years, and 34 percent of reported sexual assaults involved victims under the age of 12 years.[400] Of those sexually victimized under the age of 6 years, 97 percent were victimized by a family member.[401] In 65 percent of cases of adult sexual assault, the offender was known to the victim.[402] Especially in the case of child sexual victimization, it is important to create treatment programs and pass legislation that protects children from nonstrangers because overwhelmingly, persons known to them are their victimizers.

## Do Sex Offenders Keep Re-offending?

Recidivism involves the measurement of whether or not an individual commits another offense. Research varies dramatically in this regard, typically because of the way the study is designed. Simply stated, if researchers use different measurement time frames or ask different questions, they will naturally receive different responses. For example, if researchers measure recidivism over a period of a year, they will get a much lower rate of re-offense than if they measures recidivism over a period of 10 years. Also, a researcher may measure recidivism as a new sexual offense (which would translate to relatively low rates of recidivism), or a researcher may measure recidivism as *any* new offense, even minor offenses such as parole violations (which would obviously translate to a much higher rate of recidivism). To complicate matters even further, how can researchers measure who has reoffended? Does the researcher rely on whether or not the person was rearrested? Does the person have to be convicted? Or can the researcher merely interview previously convicted offenders, and if they admit to committing another offense, count this as recidivism? All of these questions and many others impact how a researcher "measures" or "counts" recidivism and therefore impacts how high the recidivism rate appears in a study. To complicate matters further, sexual offending is very underreported, whether as a first or second offense.

Also, regardless of what academic studies reveal, the general public believes that sexual offenders have a very high re-offense rate! A questionnaire was distributed in Florida six months after Jessica Lunsford and Sarah Lunde were murdered inquiring about public perceptions regarding sexual offenders. The cases were big news and therefore were likely fresh in the minds of participants in the study. Those involved estimated the sexual offender rate of re-offense at approximately 75 percent and ranked this group of criminals as the most likely to reoffend.[403] Do the views in this study represent fact or fiction?

A study conducted in 2000 involving a group of sexual offenders on probation for almost 5 years found a re-arrest rate of 35 percent for nonsexual offenses and a 5.6 percent re-arrest rate for sexual offenses.[404] A government study with a 3-year follow-up period found a re-arrest rate for nonsexual offenses of 43 percent and a re-arrest rate for sexual offenses of 5 percent.[405] Some studies have found slightly higher rates of sexual recidivism, ranging from 9 percent[406] to 12 percent.[407] These rates are significantly lower than anticipated by the general public and much lower than for many other offenses (especially drug offenses). Research has demonstrated that not all types of sexual offenders have similar rates of recidivism and that various aspects in an offender's history can affect his likelihood of reoffending. For example, offenders who have been sexually victimized during childhood have higher rates of recidivism.[408] The highest rate of recidivism is found among sexual offenders whose victims are adult women (approximately 40 percent),[409] whereas heterosexual sexual offenders who have victimized a child within their family have the lowest rates of recidivism (approximately 3 percent). An important variable that influences recidivism is treatment. Major statistical analysis of 43 studies in Canada, the United States, and Great Britain found that re-offense rates over a 4-year period were approximately 12 percent for treated offenders and 17 percent for untreated offenders.[410]

A study conducted in Washington State provides an interesting case study with which to examine recidivism because it involves the most serious sexual offenders. Washington State has a sexually violent predator (SVP) law, and just prior to an inmate's release from prison, the Department of Corrections can petition to have the individual indefinitely confined under the SVP statute. For individuals who meet the requirements, the Attorney General's Office determines whether to file a petition to seek to have the offender committed. This study involved a 6-year follow-up period of 135 sexual offenders who met the requirements under the state's sexually violent predator legislation, but for whom the Attorney General's Office decided not to file a petition. For this reason, the individual was released from prison at the end of his sentence. The study measured the re-offense rate of these serious sexual offenders. Of the 135 men released, 23 percent were convicted of a new sex-related felony within the 6-year follow-up period; of these recidivists, only 29 percent had participated in a treatment program in prison. Ten percent of the men were convicted of a new non–sex-related felony offense, and 19 percent were convicted for failure to register as a sexual offender. This study revealed the significance of age in reoffending: the youngest age group at release was at the highest risk of reoffending. Also, none of the offenders who were over 50 years old committed a sexual offense during the 6-year follow-up period.[411] It is clear from the research monitoring offenders' re-offense rates that the longer an individual remains in the community offense-free, the less likely it is that they are going to reoffend.[412] In addition, sexual recidivism can be reduced by community-based treatment, intensive supervision programs, broad-based community notification for Tier 3 offenders,[413] and the reduction of transience. Simply releasing sexual offenders into the community after serving a sentence without proper reintegration skills is setting them up for failure and sexual reoffending, which means putting the community at risk of victimization.

## Does Community Notification and Registration Increase Community Safety?

As a brief reminder, community notification is commonly referred to as Megan's Law and requires sex offenders (often even juvenile sex offenders) to register with law enforcement, and in many states it requires officials to notify communities when a sex offender of a certain tier moves into the neighborhood. In 2006, the Adam Walsh Act was signed into law. This law organized sexual offenders into three tiers and created SORNA, which requires sex offenders to register their whereabouts regularly with law enforcement or face felony charges. The registration of sexual offenders with law enforcement is not the part of the legislation that is controversial; it is the public notification aspect. Who has the right to be notified of an offender's whereabouts after he has served his time in prison? How "dangerous" must he be for the community to be notified? Why are communities notified when a sexual offender moves in next door, but not a murderer, or someone who has been convicted of drunk driving, or someone who has been convicted of selling drugs to children? Wide discrepancy exists from state to state regarding who has the right to know, and the 10 states that use a tier classification system for offenders have a more "objective" system of notification than the states that do not use a tier classification system. Varying degrees of information about the offender are available to the public, and this information is delivered by varied methods. Some states require citizens to search out information on their own via Web sites or registration lists and therefore afford the offender more privacy. Other states are extremely broad and make privacy and community reintegration very difficult for the offender by releasing his information in the media, via door-to-door distribution, or in letters to residents.

The community overwhelmingly views these laws as integral to the protection of children from sexual victimization. A study in Washington revealed that 63 percent of public residents surveyed believed these laws encourage released offenders to abide by the law, and 78 percent felt safer knowing the whereabouts of sexual offenders. These laws are supported, even though 84 percent of the people in this study felt notification laws make reintegration into the community more difficult for sexual offenders.[414] Shortly after the murder of Jessica Lunsford and Sarah Lunde in Florida, a study revealed that 95 percent of those surveyed felt the public should be given the name and shown a photo of sexual offenders, and 85 percent believed that a home address should also be provided. Almost 76 percent supported this policy for all sexual offenders, regardless of the seriousness of the offense.[415] Interestingly, although 83 percent of participants believed that community notification was effective in reducing sexual violence, 73 percent at least partially agreed that they would support this policy even without scientific evidence demonstrating that it reduced sexual abuse.[416] In essence, these policies have widespread public appeal even if the public recognizes that the policies may impede the reintegration of offenders into the community and even if there is no "proof" that they will make communities safer. Could this be simply an extension of the offender's punishment that the public views as necessary retribution, even if it is not effective?

Offenders are obviously not eager to abide by these laws and have challenged the constitutionality of community notification laws in two U.S. Supreme Court cases. In the first case, the question dealt with the Fifth Amendment double jeopardy clause and whether registration and notification laws constitute a second punishment. In the second case, the question dealt with whether the law constituted cruel and unusual punishment by posting the photos of offenders online. In both cases, however, the Court ruled that registration and community notification laws are constitutional despite the recognized harm that results for the individual. In one case, U.S. Supreme Court Justice Clarence Thomas elucidated the potential harms to offenders:

> Widespread dissemination of offenders' names, photographs, addresses, and criminal history serves not only to inform the public but also to humiliate and ostracize the convicts. It thus bears some resemblance to shaming punishments that were used earlier in our history to disable offenders from living normally in the community. While the [majority of] the State's explanation that the Act simply makes public information available in a new way, the scheme does much more. Its point, after all, is to send a message that probably would not otherwise be heard, by selecting some conviction information out of its corpus of penal records and broadcasting it with a warning. Selection makes a statement, one that affects common reputation and sometimes carries harsher consequences, such as exclusion from jobs or housing, harassment, and physical harm.[417]

Since 2003, state courts have upheld these laws, and the U.S. Supreme Court has refused to hear any further cases addressing the constitutionality of sexual offender legislation.

The courts have permitted these laws, the public feels safer with these laws, but do these laws actually work to lower the re-offense rate of sexual offenders in the community? Has our knowledge of where offenders live and what they have done made society safer? From the offender's perspective, the answer is mixed. In interviews with sexual offenders, 75 percent revealed that community notification and registration laws would not deter them from committing another offense.[418] Another study interviewed 239 sexual offenders in Connecticut and Indiana. In this study, almost 75 percent of participants admitted that they were more motivated to stay offense-free to "prove something" to family, friends, or the public. Additionally, about 33 percent believed that neighborhoods were safer because of these laws. Approximately 67 percent believed that being watched by neighbors had no influence on the likelihood that they would reoffend.[419]

So if you ask an offender if community notification works, the answer is unclear; but what does the research reveal about the relationship between community notification laws and recidivism rates? A variety of studies beginning in the early 1990s and continuing to 2008 have found no significant reduction in sexual recidivism rates against either children or adult women due to community notification laws.[420] Another study using more advanced statistics and data from Washington and Wisconsin, both with tiered systems of risk management for sex offenders, found some reduction in sexual recidivism from this legislation.[421] More recently, a study in Minnesota of only Tier 3 offenders found that broad community notification was effective in significantly reducing sexual recidivism over an 8-year follow-up period. These high-risk offenders were also involved in intensive supervision (ISR), however, so it was not entirely clear whether community notification or constant supervision lowered the recidivism rate.[422] What is unclear from the research that has been conducted is the true effect of the law on recidivism because the law is never the only factor in an offender's life. The offender may also be part of an intensive supervision program, but if he is not, he is usually part of a community treatment program. Either of these may reduce reoffending, and an offender's "good behavior" may have nothing at all to do with the community notification and registration laws (as many studies indicate).

If these laws do not necessarily work to lower reoffending, what impact does this legislation have on the offender? Years of research in the field of criminology has revealed that the factors that encourage continued desistance from offending include integration or reintegration into the community, management of individual stress, and establishment of a stable lifestyle. To do this, the offender must locate himself in a community with supportive friends and/or family, find a stable place of employment and residence, and develop appropriate social relationships. Broad-based community notification policies can hinder all aspects of reintegration for an offender trying to reestablish a life because neighbors and neighborhood organizations are informed of his past before he gets a chance to begin his reintegration process. Once a community finds out a sex offender is moving in, regardless of his offense, he is at a decreased likelihood of forming friendships; will have greater difficulty finding employment, which is often the linchpin of successful community reintegration; will experience difficulty locating housing; and will likely experience decreased feelings of societal attachment. One former offender said: "Community notification can be a real problem for sex offenders. . . . These are the things that can set a sex offender off and make him offend again."[423]

Offenders are also subject to harassment by community members who may not have all the facts of the case and may react simply out of fear. A handful of vigilante cases across the United States have come to the attention of law enforcement, although studies suggest that about 25 percent of offenders are victimized by some sort of vigilante justice.[424] An additional 40 percent of offenders worry about being the victim of harassment.[425] One offender indicated: "There are a lot of nuts out there so you got to be real careful. That's why a lot of ex-offenders don't register because they don't want people to know who they are and come kill them or burn down their house or something."[426] As a result of harassment or the fear of harassment, some offenders relocate and decide not to register with law enforcement to avoid stigma and harassment in their new location. This burdens law enforcement in that they are forced to look for offenders who have absconded. In interviews with 239 sexual offenders released in Connecticut and Indiana, a significant number of the offenders felt stressed, avoided various activities as a result of community notification, felt isolated, felt decreased hope regarding the future, or feared for their safety. In this same study, 10 percent of participants had experienced a physical assault or injury that they attributed to community notification. In addition, about 20 percent of offenders indicated loss of employment due to notification.[427]

Community notification and registration is geared toward stranger offenders; community notification of family offenders would potentially reveal the victim's identity as well as the offender's identity. While the public may feel safer, these laws are not protecting society from the most common type of sexual victimization—the known offender. There is no scientific evidence to suggest that these laws significantly reduce recidivism rates for Tier 1 or Tier 2 sexual offenders, but there is evidence that these laws make community reintegration of offenders in Tier 1 and Tier 2 more difficult. If the goal is to protect the public from the truly dangerous sexual offenders, registries and notifications must focus on the most dangerous offenders and not overwhelm the public with notification of offenders in the neighborhood who are no real threat. For both the safety of the public and to increase reintegration for offenders, policies should be geared toward the most potentially dangerous offenders.[428]

To improve the way these laws are implemented, Human Rights Watch offered a variety of useful suggestions in a report written in 2007. The first is to make the law reasonably narrow in scope and not apply it to all tiers of sexual offenders. Applying such a law too broadly renders it useless in terms of community feelings of safety and security and prevention of sexual abuses. The law that is very broad is not useful for community safety because every offender for even minor sexual offenses is required to register, and community members and law enforcement are less able to "keep track" of high-risk, more violent offenders. In addition, periodic reevaluation of an offender's risk should occur to determine whether their registration is still necessary for the safety of the public. Second, Human Rights Watch advocates a reasonable length of time for the enforcement of these laws, which would be determined by the offender's likelihood of continued harm to the community. As of 2007, 17 states had lifetime registration! This is the case, even though statistics indicate the longer offenders remains offense-free, the less likely they are to re-offend. Realistically, lifetime registration is unnecessary for an overwhelming number of offenders. Human Rights Watch also suggests that the United States follow the lead of countries such as Canada that limit access to registries to law enforcement only. This would limit many of the negative public consequences for sex offender reintegration yet allow law enforcement to monitor dangerous offenders. Finally, offenders should be able to challenge their inclusion on the registry and present evidence of rehabilitation through treatment, a significant amount of time offense-free, or a significant change in one's life situation.[429] This would allow ex-offenders to work toward a positive goal as well as community safety, rather than working merely to survive the negative consequences of current community notification and registration guidelines.

## Do Residency Restrictions Increase Community Safety?

Another method used to control sexual offenders is the use of residency restrictions that place limits on where an individual can live, work, or visit. In 2006, 18 states passed such restrictions, despite the lack of empirical research to demonstrate that they lower recidivism or make communities safer. From the offender's perspective, these restrictions do not act as a deterrent against future offending. One offender suggested that these laws "serve no purpose but to give some people the illusion of safety."[430] For other offenders, such regulations lack logic: "I couldn't live in an adult mobile home park because a church was 880 feet away and had a children's class that met once a week. I was forced to move to a motel where right next door to my room was a family with three children—but it qualified under the rule."[431]

These laws are not statewide and vary by jurisdiction. In many jurisdictions across the country, all tiers of sex offenders are subject to residency restrictions, and these laws may extend indefinitely (and therefore theoretically past the time an offender is required to register as a sexual offender). Currently, residency restrictions have the unintended consequence of overwhelming a select group of communities with sexual offenders because these regulations severely limit where offenders can live in a specific jurisdiction. For example, in one trailer park in St. Petersburg, Florida, 95 of the 200 residents are convicted sexual offenders, leading some to refer to the park as a "Paradise for Sex Offenders."[432] The benefits for the offenders are obvious: the park is a place to live and begin their process of reintegration without risk of violating a residency restriction. The unintended consequence is that the neighbors in such a community become uncomfortable with so many ex-offenders around, and inevitably their property values are lowered. In addition, from a therapeutic perspective, placing convicted sex offenders together for extended periods of time where they are very likely to associate with each other (which is usually a parole violation) could possibly increase the likelihood of recidivating.

When they leave prison, offenders are required to register an address with law enforcement; however, residency restriction, combined with the unwillingness of landlords to rent to ex-offenders, makes finding a place to live very difficult, leaving many of the individuals homeless and in an enormous catch-22. Without an address, an ex-offender faces imprisonment. While New York is progressive and provides emergency shelter to ex-sex offenders, other states leave homeless sex offenders in violation to fend for themselves. Some states allow offenders to register an inexact address such as a highway mile marker, a post-office box, or to list something similar to "near a bike path," "behind a cemetery," in the "woods behind Wal-Mart,"[433] or "under a bridge." In other states however, an exact address is required, and if homeless shelters are out of the question, finding a place to live can become problematic, as described by a former sex offender:

> I was homeless—I went to two homeless shelters—told them the truth—I was a registered sex offender—I could not stay. No one helps sex offenders, I was told. The third shelter I went to—I did not tell them. I was allowed to stay. November 2002 I was to register again—my birthday. If I told them I lived at a shelter—I would be thrown out—if I stayed on the streets I would not have a [sic] address to give—violation. So I registered under my old address—the empty house, which was too close to a school. Someone called the police—told them I did not live at that address anymore—I was locked up, March 2003. I was given a 10-year sentence for failure to register as a sex offender.[434]

Homelessness is a huge problem for the population of men released from prison on sexual offense convictions. Not only does lack of a permanent address make law enforcement's task more difficult, but transience increases the likelihood of recidivism. In 2007, *USA Today* reviewed the registry of sex offenders in each state and interviewed officials in 45 states that were willing to cooperate. The analysis showed some startling results: "Two-thirds of the states allow convicted sex offenders, including violent predators, to register as homeless or list a shelter or inexact location as long as they stay in touch with police. . . . At least a dozen states list hundreds of sex offenders without specific addresses. California registered 2,716 as "transient." Washington State listed 564 as homeless, but the number is probably much higher. . . . Arkansas, Connecticut, Florida, Illinois, Maine, and other states say the number of homeless sex offenders is rising."[435] The system clearly is broken, and no state has figured out how to deal with the problem. In Illinois, officials recognize that homeless offenders do not usually stay at a shelter for a year and therefore prefer to have the offender report weekly to law enforcement rather than register an address he likely will not keep for a month. Other states have more restrictive policies: "Some states keep sex offenders locked up until they find housing. In Michigan, they are less likely to get parole than murderers. In Georgia, sex offenders can be arrested for being homeless."[436] When it is difficult for an ex-offender to find housing and employment in their attempt to reintegrate into society, another arrest for being homeless is likely not going to help the situation. According to the director of the Justice Department's office for tracking sexual offenders: "Homeless sex offenders are not necessarily more dangerous than those with housing. . . . The people you need to be worried about most are the ones who aren't registering at all."[437]

It is important to remember that residency restriction laws only restrict where offenders sleep, not their movements or more general interactions with potential victims. An alternative to this type of law would be the creation of "child safe zones" where offenders would be prohibited from entry under any circumstance. These zones would prohibit any offender who has violated a child under the age of 14 years, regardless of whether that child was a stranger or a nonstranger. In a press release, the Iowa County Attorneys Association said: "Residency restrictions were intended to reduce sex crimes against children by strangers who seek access to children at the covered locations. Those crimes are tragic, but very rare. In fact, 80 to 90 percent of sex crimes against children are committed by a relative or acquaintance who has some prior"[438] offense. The creation of "child safe zones" would protect children from all types of offenders, strangers and nonstrangers.

In society's zeal to persecute sexual offenders, little thought is given to how these regulations may impact their families. Residency restrictions prohibit ex-offenders from residing in many areas where they would want to locate their families. This can interfere with community reintegration and may prevent an offender from living with supportive family members (this would also include parents, for example, who live too close to a school, day care, etc., and therefore their son cannot reside with them after his release from prison). These restrictions add another stressor to the life of an ex-offender as elaborated by a male convicted of sexually assaulting an adult female:

You can't imagine everything these people [speaking of the criminal justice system] ask you to do. It is just too much. I mean, I understand about punishment to society and everything, but I think all this stuff they ask of a guy might just backfire on 'em. Just for the fact it doesn't take a whole lot to go back to where you've been. It's harder to keep focused on where you're going than where you've been. And I think all this stuff they ask from you, the registration, all these appointments, all this money, the therapy, it just goes on and on. I sometimes do think it could be so much you just give up trying.[439]

Another offender suggests that all the laws and regulations are "overkill and it has the potential to push people to that point where they reoffend."[440] Community management of ex-offenders has to be about balancing community safety from the risk of dangerous offenders and permitting the lower-risk offenders to successfully reintegrate back into society. These individuals have served their sentence (often in full) to society and are now trying to re-establish some sense of normalcy in their life. No other type of offender, not drug dealers and not murderers, are punished after serving their sentence to the extent that sexual offenders are. Patterns of recidivism illustrate that restricting where an ex-offender resides does not prevent future sexual offenses. Instead it is an enormous drain on law enforcement because it encourages transience and forces law enforcement to chase absconding offenders. If the goal is community protection and safety, some courts are starting to realize that residency restriction laws are not the way to go.

## Does Treatment Work?

Unlike the perception of the general public, not one scientifically sound research study has concluded that sex offenders are incurable and have an insatiable desire to commit more offenses.[441] As indicated previously, studies repeatedly demonstrate that sex offenders have reasonably low rates of recidivism, and rates of reoffending decrease when an individual participates in either institutional or community-based treatment.[442]

Treatment design has traditionally been based on a one-size-fits-all approach. Currently, three broad treatment options, surgery, psychotherapy, and pharmacotherapy, are used for sexual offenders. First, surgical treatment of offenders involves chemical or surgical castration, and studies of the effectiveness of this type of treatment are contradictory, with the general consensus being that this type of treatment is ineffective.[443] Second, psychotherapy is the most common type of treatment and refers to virtually any type of talk therapy. Psychotherapy can be divided into four categories: sexological, polygraph, plethysmography, and cognitive behavioral therapies. Sexological treatment is a form of intensive therapy that seeks to help offenders realize their full sexual potential within society's legal limits. It teaches respect for oneself and others, stresses the importance of consent, and challenges the offending behaviors. Although this type of treatment is not used frequently due to lack of government funding, a follow-up of 122 juvenile participants over a period of at least 14 years revealed a recidivism rate of zero.[444] This extremely successful result points to the potential of using an education-based approach and involving the family members of the offender in treatment.[445] The polygraph is included in a discussion of psychotherapy as it may be incorporated into this form of treatment because it is often mandated to offenders on probation or parole. A polygraph is almost always accompanied by talk therapy. Limited research has been conducted on its effectiveness as part of a treatment model for sex offenders. A recent five-year study demonstrated that there was no difference in sexual recidivism rates between offenders who were polygraphed versus those who were not.[446] Penile plethysmography is also used with psychotherapy. It is an instrument that measures changes in the circumference of the penis when a male is exposed to various types of sexually explicit material. Changes in penis size are recorded, and computer software illustrates the degree of arousal the male is experiencing for each sexually explicit image. Treatment accompanying penile plethysmography may include some form of aversion therapy; if the male becomes aroused at "deviant" sexual materials, he receives an electric shock or is subjected to a foul odor to help redirect his arousal to more appropriate images. Studies regarding the effectiveness of the device are contradictory with most research suggesting that this method of treatment is ineffective. The final form of psychotherapy is cognitive behavioral therapy (CBT), whose overarching principle is that thoughts cause feelings and behaviors. Thoughts can be changed, and people can change their behavior, regardless of the situations they encounter. CBT grew out of behavior modification techniques, wherein behaviors and reactions to certain stimuli are altered through positive and/or negative reinforcement or punishment. CBT focuses on changing the sexual fantasies of offenders and identifying and eliminating the beliefs that justify their sexual offending. Other forms of CBT incorporate relapse prevention, which examines the factors that potentially cause offending behavior and identify ways that an offender can avoid or address those factors in a positive manner. One offender describes his response to cognitive behavioral therapy:

"Fred" is a convicted sex offender from the Champlain Valley. He admits he sexually molested a young girl and said he knew it was wrong while it was happening. The Champlain Valley man said he "felt guilty immediately afterward, but at the time I really couldn't control it. Arousal is a very powerful thing." He turned himself in and was eventually sent to jail. When he was released, he went to counseling. There he says he learned why he manipulated, controlled and abused the 9-year-old girl. Fred underwent group therapy, individual therapy, and polygraphs routinely to make sure he wasn't reoffending. In regards to therapy, Fred had this to say: "It's not easy. But it shouldn't be. What we have done is extremely devastating to our victims." Fred explained that he started having negative thoughts about children when he was very young but didn't act on them until he became addicted to Internet pornography. He said he groomed his victim and told her it was their "little secret." When he realized the abuse was escalating, he turned himself in. Fred said there is no cure for sex offenders; there are only tools that they can use to control and manage their thoughts. Fred believes he was once a danger to society, but not anymore. He said counseling turned his life around. "For the first time, I started learning how to control things and what to look for. And for the first time I felt there was hope that I could change."[447]

Another offender describes a similar situation:

"Joe," a convicted sex offender from the Champlain Valley who had sex with a young teenager . . . served time in jail and has completed counseling. Some days "all I can do is wish I never caused the pain in the first place," Joe said. "If I never put her in this spot, she wouldn't have to deal with it. That's the bottom line." But Joe knows "the people out there could care less the pain that I'm in." Joe's not sure if there's a cure for sex offenders, but he is sure that some can be rehabilitated. He said he's living proof. Joe spent 2-1/2 years in counseling. "I wanted to get better. I want to know why I hurt this person. I want to be a good person. I was a good person before and to this day believe I'm still a good person, with a bad mark now," Joe said. Through group and individual therapy, Joe said he learned how to control urges and how to extinguish any negative thoughts quickly. He said he couldn't graduate without a safety plan that he carries with him every hour of every day. It contains the people to call and places to go if he feels himself going down the wrong path. "I can't change what I did. It is what it is. What I can change is understanding it and controlling it."[448]

Some of the dynamic, or changeable, risk factors of offending include "deviant" sexual arousal, sexual preoccupation, pervasive anger or hostility, emotional management difficulties, impulsivity, cognitive distortions, and intimacy deficits.[449] Relapse prevention treatment is very popular among government officials and law enforcement and is advantageous because it tends to be a more positive approach to treatment by focusing on how an offender can improve his life. Because cognitive behavioral therapies can involve so many approaches to treatment, research on its effectiveness has been mixed, with some approaches working better than others.

Pharmacotherapy is the third type of treatment used with sexual offenders and involves the use of drugs to treat the symptoms of offending. In some instances, this treatment is mandated by the court as part of sentencing. Two types of medications are typically used in this form of treatment: antiandrogens and psychotropic drugs. Antiandrogens work to decrease the normal production of testosterone and are therefore believed to decrease both sexual desire and the ability to sustain an erection.[450] Psychotropic drugs are used to control conditions that mental health professionals believe are associated with sexual offending, such as obsessive compulsive disorder or manic depression. Recidivism for pharmacotherapy patients while on the drugs varies widely depending on the study, with the average at about 6 percent. Also, the effects of treatment are reversible within one to two months after termination of the medication.[451]

Studies illustrate that treatment can keep recidivism rates low for sexual offenders; however, the effects of other variables, such as social networks, employment, the response of the criminal justice system, and socioeconomic status, are not fully understood. Almost every study has demonstrated that sexual offenders recidivate less often than non-sex offenders, but they cannot explain why this is the case. This is a major gap in the scientific literature and has serious repercussions for the development of treatment programs. Treatment programs must focus on both sex (the biological aspects) and sexuality (the sociocultural aspects). Sex remains a highly taboo subject that many people, including treatment professionals, avoid discussing. The literature on treatment illustrates clearly that issues of sex and sexuality lack consideration in current treatments, making developing effective treatment methods challenging for professionals. Existing cognitive behavioral treatments work to lower the risk of reoffending, but there is much room for improvement and positive treatments. So, yes, treatment does work for sexual offenders, but they vary in effectiveness.

Many legislative endeavors have resulted from policymakers falling victim to this fiction regarding sexual offenders: "once a sex offender, always a sex offender." For too long this belief has guided the actions of law enforcement professionals in charging offenders, developing presentence reports, giving sentences in court, and naming conditions for probation and parole.[452] Because the media is the source of "reality" for many citizens, society has experienced much difficulty separating fact from fiction when it comes to sexual offenses and offenders. The purpose of this chapter is to dispel several common myths about sexual offending. The truth is much more complicated than the message that can be conveyed in a 60-second news headline, and citizens should not rely on such sound bites to inform them about issues as important as community safety and policies to protect women and children from victimization.

# NOTES

## Chapter 1: Religion, Medicine, and Social Science

1. Palmer & Haffner 2007.
2. Ibid.
3. Morrison 2008.
4. Ibid.
5. Ibid.
6. Ibid: 14–15.
7. Ibid: 33–34.
8. Chenier 2003.
9. Ibid.
10. Petrunik 1994.
11. Cowburn 2005.
12. Ibid.
13. Petrunik 1994.
14. Cowburn 2005.
15. Krafft-Ebing 1922.
16. Freud 1962.
17. Ibid: 26.
18. Meyenburg & Sigusch 1977.
19. Haeberle 1983.
20. Lewandowski 1984/85.
21. Krafft-Ebing 1922.
22. Ibid.
23. Ibid.
24. Bullough 1998.
25. Ibid.
26. Kinsey, Pomeroy, Martin, & Gebhard 1953: 8.
27. Kinsey, Pomeroy, Martin, & Gebhard 1953.

28. Ibid.

29. Bullough 1998.

30. Gebhard, Gagnon, Pomeroy, & Christenson 1967.

31. Ibid: 2.

32. Sutherland 1939.

33. Hirschi 1969.

34. Ibid.

35. Ibid.

36. Gottfredson & Hirschi 1990.

37. Cleary 2004; Zimring, Piquero, & Jennings 2007.

38. Simon 1997.

39. Simon & Zgoba 2006.

40. Scully 1994: 159.

41. Ibid.

42. Haas & Haas 1990; Meloy 2006; Pithers 1990; Quinsey & Earls 1990; Warren, Reboussin, & Hazelwood 1998.

43. Haas & Haas 1990.

44. Warren, Reboussin, & Hazelwood 1998.

45. Wakeling, Webster, Moulden, & Marshall 2007.

46. Meloy 2006: 82.

47. Ibid: 81–82.

48. Kinsey, Pomeroy, Martin, & Gebhard 1948.

49. Kinsey, Pomeroy, Martin, & Gebhard 1953.

50. McIlvenna 2007.

51. McIlvenna 2007.

52. Ibid 2007.

53. Ibid 2007.

54. Brecher 2000.

55. Davenport 1977.

56. Kinsey, Pomeroy, Martin, & Gebhard 1948; Kinsey, Pomeroy, Martin, & Gebhard 1953.

57. Weeks 1986.

58. Ibid.

59. Simon 2000: 277.

## Chapter 2: How Many Sex Offenders Are There?

60. Human Rights Watch 2007.

61. Estrich 1995.

62. Briere 1989.

63. Murray 2000.

64. ACYF 2007.

65. Ibid.

66. OJJDP 2001.

67. BJS 2000.

68. Ibid.

69. Snyder 2000.

70. BJS 2000.

71. UCR 2007.

72. Ibid.

73. Ibid.

74. BJS 2006.

75. Ibid.

76. Ibid.

77. Ibid.

78. Ibid.

79. Ibid.

80. BJS 2005.

81. BJS 2006; Holmes & Holmes 2009.

82. Texas Office of the Attorney General 2001.

83. Deirmenjian 1999; Quayle, Vaughn, & Taylor 2006.

84. BJS 2006.

85. Finkelhor 1984.

86. Travin, Cullen, & Protter 1990.

87. Denov 2004.

88. Mayer 1992: 49–50.

89. Fehrenbach & Monastersky 1988; Lewis & Stanley 2000; Travin, Cullen, & Protter 1990.

90. Grayston & DeLuca 1999.

91. Ferguson & Meehan 2005.

92. Vandiver & Walker 2002.

93. Idaho Statutes 2003 11 § 18-6101.

94. Idaho Statutes 2003 11 § 18-6108.

95. UCR 2007.

96. Epps 1999.

97. NAPN 1993.

98. Ibid.

99. Ibid.

100. Juvenile Sex Offender Laws Struck Down—For Now 2008.

101. UCR 2007.

102. Ibid.

103. Ibid.

104. BJS 1997.

105. Ibid.

106. Petrosino & Petrosino 1999.

107. BJS 1997.

108. Ibid.

109. Ibid.

110. Ibid.

111. Ibid.

112. Sentencing Guidelines Commission 2004.

113. Ibid.

114. Ibid.

115. Lucken & Bales 2008.

### Chapter 3: Creating Laws to Deal with Sex Offenders

116. Benedict 1992; Carringella-MacDonald 1998; Dowler 2006.

117. Kitzinger 2007: 128.

118. Jewkes 2004.

119. Muraskin & Domash 2007.

120. Potter & Kappeler 2000: 38.

121. Cohen 1972: 9.

122. Dowler 2002: 12.

123. Kitzinger 2007.

124. Lieb, Quinsey, & Berliner 1998: 11.

125. Zilney & Zilney 2008.

126. Hacker & Frym 1955.

127. Petrunik 1994.

128. Ibid.

129. Ibid.

130. Lucken & Latina 2002.

131. Wertham 1938: 847.

132. Jenkins 1998.

133. Harris 1946: 4.

134. The Unknown Sex Fiend 1950.

135. Ibid.

136. Group for the Advancement of Psychiatry 1977.

137. California Welfare and Institute Code § 5501 1955.

138. Burick 1968.

139. Cole 2000: 299.

140. Ploscowe 1960: 223.

141. Jenkins 1998.

142. As quoted in Sutherland 1950: 146 (original source unknown).

143. Reinhardt and Fisher 1949: 734.

144. Sutherland 1950: 142.

145. La Fond 2000.

146. Sutherland 1950: 142.

147. Corrigan 2006.

148. Zonana, Bonnie, & Hoge 2003:132.

149. La Fond 2000: 159.

150. The Jacob Wetterling Crimes Against Children and Sexually Violent Offender Registration Program, 42 U.S.C. § 14071(a)(3)(E)(2001).

151. *In re G.B* 1996; *In re R.F.* 1998.

152. Pallone 2003.

153. Human Rights Watch 2007: 47.

154. Ten-Year Old's Crime Tests Limits of Megan's Law 2001.

155. Ibid.

156. As cited in Human Rights Watch 2007: 47.

157. Department of Justice 2005.

158. Drifter Killed Adam Walsh in 1981 2008.

159. Miller 2003.

160. State of Louisiana 2008.

161. Ibid.

162. Janus 2003: 1.

163. Janus 2003.

164. Ibid: 144.

## Chapter 4: Case Studies of Select Laws

165. MySpace Deletes 146 Profiles of NE Sex Offenders 2008.

166. DOJ 2007.

167. No Internet for Some Sex Offenders in New Jersey 2007.

168. Sex Offenders Must Hand Over Online Passwords 2008.

169. Hansen 2007: 11.

170. Ibid: 93–94.

171. Tonight on *Dateline* this Man Will Die 2008.

172. Ibid.

173. Ibid.

174. Ibid.

175. Ibid.

176. Ibid.

177. Ibid.

178. Ibid.

179. Ibid.

180. Ibid.

181. Ibid.

182. Levenson & Cotter 2005b.

183. Sex Offenders Can Have More Freedom, Court Rules 2008.

184. Eatontown to Repeal its Sex Offender Law 2008.

185. *Mann v. Georgia Dept, of Corrections* 2007.

186. Georgia Court Rejects Law on Sex Offenders 2007.

187. Ibid.

188. Ibid.

189. Ibid.

190. Doubts Rise as States Hold Sex Offenders After Prison 2007.

191. SENATE, No. 895, L.1998, c. 71.

192. Lacoursiere 2003.

193. Ibid.

194. WSIPP 2007b.

195. *Kansas v. Hendricks*, 521 U.S. 346 1997.

196. Cornwell 2003.

197. *Kansas v. Crane* 2002.

198. Carlsmith, Monahan, & Evans 2007.

199. WSIPP 2007b.

200. Doubts Rise as States Hold Sex Offenders After Prison 2007.

201. Janus 2003.

202. Florida Executes Child Killer 2008.

203. Rape a Child, Pay with Your Life, Louisiana Argues 2008.

204. Ibid.

205. Ibid.

206. *Kennedy v. Louisiana* 2008.

207. Ibid.

## Chapter 5: "So-Called" Sex Crimes

208. Kinsey, Pomeroy, Martin, & Gebhard 1948; Kinsey, Pomeroy, Martin, & Gebhard 1953.

209. Why is Genarlow Wilson in Prison? 2007.

210. Towery 2007.

211. Kansas v. Limon: Case Background 2005.

212. Ibid. (emphasis added)

213. The Other Matthew 2007.

214. Defying U.S. Supreme Court, Kansas Court Upholds 17-Year Prison Sentence of Bisexual Teenager 2004.

215. Ibid.

216. Society for the Scientific Study of Sexuality 1987: 284.

217. Young GOP Leader Accused in Gay Sex Crime 2007.

218. Two Men Plead Guilty to Sexual Misconduct at Overlook 2008.

219. Couple Busted in X-Rated Antics at Riverside Park 2006.

220. Bernstein & Schaffner 2004.

221. Wolf 1991.

222. Bean 2002.

223. Greer 1999.

224. Sawhill 2006.

225. Wolf 1997.

226. Then and Now: Heidi Fleiss 2005.

227. Ibid.

228. Ibid.

229. Moser & Madeson 1996: 33.

230. Moser & Madeson 1996.

231. Thompson 1994.

232. Weinberg 1995.

233. Graber and Sontag 2006.

234. Dorn, Dahl, Woodward, & Biro 2006.

235. Shanahan, Erickson, & Bauer 2005.

236. Connell 2005.

237. Haroian 1994.

238. Ibid.

239. Raby 2002.

240. Ibid.

241. Michels, Kropp, Eyre, & Halpern-Felsher 2005.

242. Sarrel & Sarrel 1979.

243. Ibid.

244. Ibid.; Haroian 1986.

245. Graber and Sontag 2006.

246. Wallmyr & Welin 2006.

247. Sieving, Eisenberg, Pettingell, and Skay 2006.

248. Marcus Dixon Rape Conviction Reversed 2004.

249. Peretti & Rowan 1982.

250. Frost 1991.

251. Ibid.

252. Levy 2003.

253. Ibid.

254. Rydstrom 2000.

255. Ibid.

256. Ibid.; Krafft-Ebing 1922.

257. Miletski 2001.

258. Krafft-Ebing 1922.

259. Frost 1991.

260. Kinsey, Pomeroy, Martin, & Gebhard 1953; Kinsey, Pomeroy, Martin, & Gebhard 1948.

261. Miletski 2001.

262. Duffield, Hassiotis, & Vizard 1998.

263. Kinsey, Pomeroy, & Martin 1948.

264. Ibid.

265. Miletski 2001.

266. Ibid.

267. Peretti & Rowan 1982.

268. Miletski 2001; Peretti & Rowan 1982; Kinsey, Pomeroy, Martin, & Gebhard 1953.

269. Levy 2003.

270. Ibid.

271. Frost 1991.

272. Smith 2005.

273. Ibid.; Rydstrom 2000.

274. Doniger 2004.

275. Peretti & Rowan 1982.

276. Miletski 2001.

277. Duffield, Hassiotis, & Vizard 1998.

278. Ibid.

279. Ibid.

280. Texas Officials: FLDS Raid About Child Abuse, Not Religion 2008.

281. Ibid.

282. Ibid.

283. Polygamist Guilty of Child Rape 2002.

284. U.S. Polygamist Gets Five Years 2001.

285. Polygamist Jailed for Child Rape 2002.

286. Polygamist Guilty of Child Rape 2002.

287. Polygamist Jailed for Child Rape 2002.

288. Ibid.

289. O'Neill & O'Neill 1973: 39–40.

290. *State of Ohio v. Lowe* 2007.

291. Human Rights Watch 2007.

## Chapter 6: Sexually Explicit Materials

292. Brunsendorff & Henningsen 1961.

293. Ibid.

294. Ibid.

295. Ibid.: 428.

296. Williams 1989.

297. Hudson 2008.

298. Ibid.

299. Noble & Nadler 1986.

300. Ibid.

301. Califia 1986.

302. Ibid.

303. Noble & Nadler 1986.

304. Ibid.

305. Califia 1986.

306. Noble & Nadler 1986.

307. Sprinkle 1986.

308. Noble & Nadler 1986.

309. Ibid.: 110.

310. McIlvenna & Haroian 2001: 6–7.

311. Califia 1986.

312. Noble & Nadler 1986.

313. Califia 1986.

314. Ibid.

315. Robinson, Manthei, Scheltema, Rich, & Koznar 1999.

316. Society for the Scientific Study of Sexuality 1987: 284–285.

317. Robinson, Manthei, Scheltema, Rich, & Koznar 1999.

318. *United States of America v. John Stagliano, John Stagliano Inc. and Evil Angel Productions Inc.* 2007.

319. Porn Producer Invokes the Bush/Yoo Defense—Uunsuccessfully 2008.

320. Ibid.

321. Ibid.

322. Seabloom 1983.

323. Tokheim 2005.

324. Seabloom, Seabloom, Seabloom, Barron, & Hendrickson 2003.

325. Tokheim 2005.

326. Hogg 1999.

327. Ibid.

328. Ibid.

329. Hudson 2008.

330. Paul 2005.

331. Green 2008.

332. Hall & Hall 2007.

333. Califia 1986.

334. Sher & Carey 2007.

335. Adler 2001.

336. Sanghara & Wilson 2006.

337. Wheatland 2005.

338. Ibid.: 378.

339. Hudson 2008.

340. Sher & Carey 2007.

341. Haeberle 1983: 462.

342. This information is gathered from an extensive review of federally confiscated child SEM images in 2007 by Dr. Laura Zilney.

343. Mauro 2001.

344. *Ashcroft v. Free Speech Coalition* 2008.

345. Greenhouse 2007.

346. O'Dell 2008.

347. Zahorsky 2008.

348. Michels 2008.

349. Brunsendorff & Henningsen 1961: 584–585.

## Chapter 7: Nonconsensual Offenses

350. Fenichel 1945: 347–348.

351. Metzi 2004a: 415.

352. Metzi 2004a.

353. APA 1994.

354. Langstrom & Seto 2006.

355. Ibid.

356. Dunsieth, Nelson, Brusman-Lovins, Holcomb, Beckman, Welge, Roby, Taylor, Soutullo, & McElroy 2004.

357. Hanson & Morton-Bourgon 2004.

358. Abel, Becker, Cunningham-Rathner, Mittelman, & Rouleau 1988.

359. Ibid.

360. Holmes, Tewksbury, & Holmes 2004.

361. Wireless Voyeur Appeals 56-Year Term 2007.

362. Ibid.

363. Ibid.

364. Judge Tells Peeping Tom That Privacy is Sacred 2008.

365. Ibid.

366. Marshall, Laws, & Barbaree 1990.

367. APA 1994.

368. Piemont 2007.

369. Ibid: 80.

370. Ibid.

371. Piemont 2007.

372. Langstrom & Seto 2006.

373. Ibid.

374. Abel, Becker, Cunningham-Rathner, Mittelman, & Rouleau 1988.

375. Ibid.

376. Firestone, Kingston, Wexler, & Bradford 2006.

377. Career Flasher Sentenced to 13 Years for Indecent Exposure 2007.

378. Admitted Flasher Sentenced 2005.

379. Ibid.

380. Nine-Time Flasher Avoids Prison with Plea 2007.

381. Ibid.

382. Ibid.

383. Corrigan 2006.

384. Berger, Searles, & Neuman 1995.

385. DeKeseredy & Schwartz 1998.

386. BJS 2000b; Brener, McMahon, Warren, & Douglas 1999.

387. Malamuth, Sockloskie, Koss, & Tanaka 1991.

388. Koss, Gidycz, & Wisniewski 1987.

389. Ouimette & Riggs 1998.

390. Carr & VanDeusen 2004.

391. Antioch College 1991.

392. Ibid.

393. Guskin 1994.

394. Hickman & Meuhlenhard 1999.
395. Legal Opinions Maryland Court of Appeals 2008.
396. Ibid.
397. Ibid.
398. Ibid.
399. Ibid.

## Chapter 8: Separating Fact from Fiction

400. BJS 2000.
401. Snyder 2000.
402. BJS 2006.
403. Levenson, Brannon, Fortney, & Baker 2007.
404. Kruttschnitt, Uggen, & Shelton 2000.
405. BJS 2003.
406. Zgoba & Simon 2005.
407. Meloy 2006.
408. Ibid.
409. Snyder 2000.
410. Hanson, Gordon, Harris, Marques, Murphy, Quinsey, & Seto 2002.
411. WSIPP 2007a.
412. BJS 2003.
413. Duwe & Donnay 2008.
414. Lieb & Nunlist 2008.
415. Levenson, Brannon, Fortney, & Baker 2007.
416. Ibid.
417. *Smith v. Doe* 2003.
418. Meloy 2006.
419. Levenson, D'Amora, & Hern 2007.
420. Adkins, Huff, & Stageberg 2000; Lewis 1988; Schram & Milloy 1995; Vasquez, Maddan, & Walker 2008.
421. Barnoski 2005; Zevitz & Farkas 2000a.
422. Duwe & Donnay 2008.
423. Meloy 2006: 87.
424. Bedarf 1995.
425. Meloy 2006.
426. Ibid.: 87.
427. Levenson, D'Amora, & Hern 2007.
428. Levenson & Cotter 2005b; Tewksbury 2005.
429. Human Rights Watch 2007.
430. Levenson & Cotter 2005b: 174.
431. Ibid.: 175.
432. Trailer Park Becomes Paradise for Sex Offenders 2007.
433. Many Sex Offenders are Often Homeless 2007.
434. Human Rights Watch 2007: 103.
435. Many Sex Offenders are Often Homeless 2007.
436. Ibid.
437. Ibid.
438. Iowa County Attorneys Association 2006.
439. Meloy 2006: 92.

440. Ibid.: 93.

441. Webster, Gartner, & Doob 2006.

442. Hanson, Gordon, Harris, Marques, Murphy, Quinsey, & Seto 2002.

443. Sheldon, Bluestone, Coleman, Cullen, & Melella 1985; Stone, Winslade & Klugman 2000; Wille & Beier 1989.

444. Seabloom, Seabloom, Seabloom, Barron, & Hendrickson 2003.

445. Mann 2004; Seabloom, Seabloom, Seabloom, Barron, & Hendrickson 2003; Wakeling, Webster, & Mann 2005.

446. McGrath, Cumming, Hoke, & Bonn-Miller 2007.

447. Peering Into the Minds of Sex Offenders 2008.

448. Ibid.

449. CSOM 2006.

450. Rosler & Witztum 2000.

451. Ibid.

452. Webster, Gartner, & Doof 2006.

# References

Abel, G. G., Becker, J. V., Cunningham-Rathner, J., Mittleman, M., & Rouleau, J. L. (1988). Multiple paraphilic diagnoses among sex offenders. *Bulletin of the American Academy of Psychiatry and the Law*, 16, 153–168.

Adkins, G., Huff, D., & Stageberg, P. (2000). *The Iowa sex offender registry and recidivism.* Des Moines, IA: Iowa Department of Human Rights, Division of Criminal and Juvenile Justice Planning and Statistical Analysis Center.

Adler, A. (2001). The perverse law of child pornography. *101 The Columbia Law Review 209.* Retrieved April 17, 2009, from http://cyber.law.harvard.edu/ilaw/Speech/Adler_full.html.

Administration on Children, Youth, and Families (ACYF). (2007). *Child maltreatment 2005.* Washington, DC: U.S. Department of Health and Human Services.

Admitted Flasher Sentenced. (2005, June 25). *Honolulu Star-Bulletin.* Retrieved October 17, 2008, from http://archives.starbulletin.com/2005/06/25/news/index7.html.

Ahern, Nancy R., & Kiehl, E. M. (2006). Adolescent sexual health & practice: A review of the literature implications for healthcare providers, educators, and policy makers. *Family and Community Health*, 29(4), 299–313.

American Psychiatric Association. (1994). *Diagnostic and statistical manual of mental disorders* (4th edition). Washington, DC: American Psychiatric Association.

Antioch College. (1991). *The Antioch College sexual offense prevention policy.* Retrieved November 7, 2008, from http://www.antioch-college.edu/Campus/sopp/index.html (site no longer active).

*Ashcroft v. Free Speech Coalition.* (2008). *Frontline.* Retrieved from http://www.pbs.org/wgbh/pages/frontline/shows/porn/prosecuting/supreme.html.

Barnoski, R. (2005). *Sex offender sentencing in Washington state: Has community notification reduced recidivism?* Olympia, WA: Washington State Institute for Public Policy.

Bean, J. L. (2002). Expressions of female sexuality. *Journal of Sex & Marital Therapy*, 28(s), 29–38.

Bedarf, A. (1995). Examining sex offender community notification laws. *California Law Review*, 83, 885–939.

Benedict, H. (1992). *Virgin or vamp: How the press covers sex crimes*. New York: Oxford University Press.

Berger, R. J., Searles, P., & Neuman, W. L. (1995). Rape-law reform: Its nature, origins, and impact. In P. Searles & R. J. Berger (Eds.), *Rape and society: Readings on the problem of sexual assault* (pp. 223–232). Boulder, CO: Westview Press.

Bernstein, E., & Schaffner, L. (Eds.). (2004). *Regulating sex: The politics of intimacy and identity*. New York, NY: Routledge.

Blumberg, E. S. (2003). The lives and voices of highly sexual women. *The Journal of Sex Research*, 40(2), 146–157.

Brecher, E. M. (2000). *The sex researchers*. San Francisco, CA: Specific Press.

Brener, N. D., McMahon, P. M., Warren, C. H., & Douglas, K. A. (1999). Forced sexual intercourse and associated health-risk behaviors among female college students in the United States. *Journal of Consulting Clinical Psychology*, 67, 252–259.

Briere, J. (1989). University males' sexual interest in children: Predicting potential indices of "pedophilia" in a nonforensic sample. *Child Abuse and Neglect*, 13, 65–75.

Brunsendorff, O., & Henningsen, P. (1961). *The complete history of eroticism*. Secaucus, NJ: Castle Press.

Bullough, V. L. (1998). Alfred Kinsey and the Kinsey Report: Historical overview and lasting contributions. *The Journal of Sex Research*, 35(2), 127–131.

Bureau of Justice Statistics (BJS). (2006). *Criminal victimization in the United States 2005: Statistical tables* (NCJ 215244). Washington, DC: U.S. Department of Justice.

Bureau of Justice Statistics (BJS). (2005). *Criminal victimization 2004* (NCJ 210674). Washington, DC: U.S. Department of Justice.

Bureau of Justice Statistics (BJS). (2003). *Recidivism of sex offenders released from prison in 1994* (NCJ 198281). Washington, DC: U.S. Department of Justice.

Bureau of Justice Statistics (BJS). (2000). *Sexual assault of young children as reported to law enforcement: Victim, incident, and offender characteristics* (NCJ 182990). Washington, DC: U.S. Department of Justice.

Bureau of Justice Statistics (BJS). (2000b). *The sexual victimization of college women* (NCJ 182369). Washington, DC: U.S. Department of Justice.

Bureau of Justice Statistics (BJS). (1997). *An analysis of data on rape and sexual assault: Sex offenses and offenders: An analysis of data on rape and sexual assault* (NCJ 163392).

Burick, L. T. (1968). An analysis of the Illinois Sexually Dangerous Persons Act. *The Journal of Criminal Law, Criminology, and Political Science*, 59(2), 254–266.

Califia, P. (1986). The obscene, disgusting, and vile Meese Commission report. *Cultronix*. Retrieved December 1, 2008, from http://cultronix.eserver.org/califia/meese/.

Career Flasher Sentenced to 13 Years for Indecent Exposure. (2007, August 16). *San Francisco Chronicle*. Retrieved November 2, 2008, from http://www.sfgate.com/cgi-bin/article.cgi?f=/n/a/2007/08/16/state/n073857D94.DTL.

Carlsmith, K. J., Monahan, J., & Evans, A. (2007). The function of punishment in the "civil" commitment of sexual violent predators. *Behavioural Sciences and the Law*, 25, 437–448.

Carr, J. L., & VanDeusen, K. M. (2004). Risk factors for male sexual aggression on college campuses. *Journal of Family Violence*, 19(5), 279–289.

Carringella-MacDonald, S. (1998). The relative visibility of rape cases in national popular magazines. *Violence Against Women*, 4(1), 62–80.

Center for Sex Offender Management (CSOM). (2006). *Understanding treatment for adults and juveniles who have committed sex offenses*. Washington, DC: U.S. Department of Justice.

Chenier, E. (2003). The criminal sexual psychopath in Canada: Sex, psychiatry and the law at mid-century. *Canadian Bulletin of Medical History*, 20(1), 75–101.

Child Porn Cartoon Conviction Upheld. (2008, December 19). *MSNBC Wire Services.* Retrieved December 18, 2008, from http://www.msnbc.msn.com/id/28319113/.

Cleary, S. (2004). *Sex offenders and self-control: Explaining sexual violence.* El Paso, TX: LFB Scholarly Publishers.

Cohen, S. (1972). *Folk devils and moral panics: The creation of the mods and rockers.* London: MacGibbon and Kee.

Cole, S. A. (2000). From the sexual psychopath statute to "Megan's Law": Psychiatric knowledge in the diagnosis, treatment, and adjudication of sex criminals in New Jersey, 1949–1999. *Journal of the History of Medicine, 55,* 292–314.

Connecticut Drops Felony Charges Against Julie Amero, Four Years After Her Arrest. (2008, November 21). *Hartford Courant.* Retrieved December 2, 2008, from http://blogs.courant.com/rick_green/2008/11/connecticut-drops-felony-charg.html.

Connell, R. W. (2005). Growing up masculine: Rethinking the significance of adolescence in the making of masculinities. *Irish Journal of Sociology, 12*(2), 11–28.

Cornwell, J. K. (2003). Sex offenders and the Supreme Court: The significance and limits of *Kansas v. Hendricks.* In B. J. Winick & J. Q. LaFond (Eds.), *Protecting society from sexually dangerous offenders: Law, justice, and therapy* (pp. 197-210). Washington, DC: American Psychological Association.

Corrigan, R. (2006). Making meaning of Megan's Law. *Law & Social Inquiry, 31*(2), 267–312.

Couple Busted in X-Rated Antics at Riverside Park. (2006, May 4). *New York Daily News.* Retrieved June 5, 2008, from http://www.nydailynews.com/archives/news/2006/05/04/2006-05-04_couple_busted_in_x-rated_ant.html.

Cowburn, M. (2005). Hegemony and discourse: Reconstructing the male sex offender and sexual coercion by men. *Sexualities, Evolution and Gender, 7*(3), 215–231.

Cullen, D., & Gotell, L. (2002). From orgasms to organizations: Maslow, women's sexuality and the gendered foundations of the needs hierarchy. *Gender, Work and Organization, 9*(5), 537–555.

Davenport, W. H. (1977). Sex in cross-cultural perspective. In F. A. Beach (Ed.), *Human Sexuality in Four Perspectives* (pp. 115–163). Baltimore, MD: John Hopkins University Press.

Debate on Child Pornography's Link to Molesting. (2007, July 19). *New York Times.* Retrieved on October 1, 2008, from http://www.nytimes.com/2007/07/19/us/19sex.html.

Defying U.S. Supreme Court, Kansas Court Upholds 17-Year Prison Sentence of Bisexual Teenager. (2004). *American Civil Liberties Union.* Retrieved January 2, 2009, from http://www.aclu.org/lgbt/discrim/11908prs20040130.html.

Deirmenjian, J. (1999). Stalking in cyberspace. *Journal of the American Academy of Psychiatry and the Law, 27*(3), 407–413.

DeKeseredy, W., & Schwartz, M. (1998). *Women abuse on campus: Results from the Canadian national survey.* Thousand Oaks, CA: Sage Publications.

DeMartino, M. F. (1979). *Human autoerotic practices.* New York: Human Sciences Press.

Denov, M. S. (2004). *Perspectives of denial on female sex offending: A culture of denial.* Aldershot: Ashgate Publications.

Department of Justice. (2007, October 16). DOJ announces ICAC task forces in all 50 states [Press release]. Washington, DC: Department of Justice.

Department of Justice. (2005, July 20). Department of Justice activates National Sex Offender Public Registry Web site [Press release]. Washington, DC: Department of Justice.

Diamond, L. M. (2006). Introduction: In search of good sexual-developmental pathways for adolescent girls. *New Directions for Child and Adolescent Development, 112,* 1–7.

Doniger, W. (2004). The mythology of masquerading animals, or, bestiality. *Journal of Social Research*, 71(3), 711-732.

Dorn, L. D., Dahl, R. E., Woodward, H. R., & Biro, F. (2006). Defining the boundaries of early adolescence: A user's guide to assessing pubertal status and pubertal timing in research with adolescence. *Applied Developmental Science*, 10(1), 30–56.

Doubts Rise as States Hold Sex Offenders After Prison. (2007, March 4). *New York Times*. Retrieved July 20, 2008, from http://www.nytimes.com/2007/03/04/us/04civil.html.

Dowler, K. (2006). Sex, lies, and videotape: The presentation of sex crime in local television news. *Journal of Criminal Justice*, 34, 383–392.

Dowler, K. (2002). *Off balance: Youth, race and crime in the news*. Berkeley, CA: Berkeley Media Studies Group, Public Health Institute, Vincent Schiraldi, Justice Police Institute.

Drifter Killed Adam Walsh in 1981. (2008, December 16). *CNN*. Retrieved January 1, 2009, from http://www.cnn.com/2008/CRIME/12/16/walsh.case.closed/index.html.

Duffield, G., Hassiotis, A. and Vizard, E. (1998). Zoophilia in young sexual abusers. *The Journal of Forensic Psychiatry*, 9(2), 294-304.

Duwe, G., & Donnay, W. (2008). The impact of Megan's Law on sex offender recidivism: The Minnesota experience. *Criminology*, 46(2), 411–446.

Dunsieth, N. W., Nelson, E. B., Brusman-Lovins, L. A., Holcomb, J. L., Beckman, D., Welge, J. A., Roby, D., Taylor, P. Jr., Soutullo, C. A., & McElroy, S. L. (2004). Psychiatric and legal features of 113 men convicted of sexual offenses. *Journal of Clinical Psychiatry*, 65, 293–300.

Eatontown to Repeal its Sex Offender Law. (2008, August 8). *Asbury Park Press*. Retrieved August 13, 2008, from http://www.asburyparkpress.com.

Epps, K. J. (1999). Causal explanations: Filling the theoretical reservoir. In M. C. Calder (Ed.), *Working with young people who sexually abuse: New pieces of the jigsaw puzzle* (pp. 7–26). Dorset, MA: Russell House.

Estrich, S. (1995). Is it rape? In P. Searles & R .J. Berger (Eds.), *Rape and society: Readings on the problem of sexual assault* (pp. 183–193). Boulder, CO: Westview Press.

FBI Agents Paid to Surf for Deviant Internet Porn. (2005, September 23). *The art of technology*. Retrieved September 1, 2008, from http://arstechnica.com/news.ars/post/20050923-5346.html.

Fehrenbach, P. A., & Monastersky, C. (1988). Characteristics of female adolescent sexual offenders. *American Journal of Orthopsychiatry*, 58, 148–151.

Fenichel, O. (1945). *The psychoanalytic theory of neurosis*. New York: W.W. Norton.

Ferguson, C. J., & Meehan, D. C. (2005). An analysis of females convicted of sex crimes in the state of Florida. *Journal of Child Sexual Abuse*, 14(1), 75–89.

Finkelhor, D. (1984). *Child sexual abuse: New theory and research*. New York: The Free Press.

Firestone, P., Kingston, D. A., Wexler, A., & Bradford, J. M. (2006). Long-term follow-up of exhibitionists: Psychological, phallometric, and offense characteristics. *The Journal of the American Academy of Psychiatry and the Law*, 34(3), 349–359.

Florida Executes Child Killer. (2008, July 1). *CNN*. Retrieved July 1, 2008, from http://www.cnn.com.

Foucault, M. (1978). *The history of sexuality: An introduction, volume I*. New York: Random House.

Freud, S. (1962). *Three essays on the theory of sexuality*. New York: Basic Book Publishers.

Frost, L. A. (1991). Pets and lovers: The human-companion animal bond in contemporary literary prose. *Journal of Popular Culture*, 25(1), 39-53.

Gebhard, P. H., Gagnon, J. H., Pomeroy, W. B., & Christenson, C. V. (1967). *Sex offenders: An analysis of types*. New York: Bantam Books.

Georgia Court Rejects Law on Sex Offenders. (2007, November 22). *Washington Post*. Retrieved November 20, 2008, from http://www.washingtonpost.com/wp-dyn/content/article/2007/11/21/AR2007112102091.html.

Glen Murphy, Jr. Pleads Guilty in Sex Assault Case. (2008, June 12). *Advance Indiana*. Retrieved December 1, 2008, from http://advanceindiana.blogspot.com/2008/06/glenn-murphy-jr-pleads-guilty-in-sex.html.

Gottfredson, M., & Hirschi, T. (1990). *A general theory of crime*. Stanford, CA: Stanford University Press.

Graber, J. A., &, Sontag, L. M. (2006). Puberty and girls' sexuality: Why hormones are not the complete answer. *New Directions for Child and Adolescent Development*, 112, 23–38.

Grayston, A. D., & DeLuca, R. V. (1999). Female perpetrators of child sexual abuse: A review of the clinical and empirical literature. *Aggression and Violent Behaviour*, 4, 93–106.

Green, R. (2008, November 21). Connecticut drops felony charges against Julie Amero, four years after her arrest. *Courant.com*. Retrieved April 23, 2009, from http://blogs.courant.com/rick_green/2008/11/connecticut-drops-felony-charg.html.

Greenhouse, L. (2007, October 31). Justices Hear Arguments on Internet Pornography Law. *New York Times*. Retrieved April 23, 2009, from http://www.nytimes.com/2007/10/31/washington/31scotus.html.

Greenwald, G. (2008, October 5). Porn producer invokes the Bush/Yoo defense—unsuccessfully. *Salon.com*. Retrieved April 23, 2009, from www.salon.com.opinion/greenwald/2008/10/05/porn/.

Greer, G. (1999). *The whole woman*. New York: Anchor Books.

Group for the Advancement of Psychiatry. (1977). *Psychiatry and sex psychopath legislation: The 30s to the 80s*. New York: Group for the Advancement of Psychiatry.

Guskin, A. E. (1994). *The Antioch response: Sex, you just don't talk about it*. Yellow Springs, OH: Antioch College.

Haas, L., & Haas, J. (1990). *Understanding sexuality*. Boston, MA: Mosby.

Hacker, F. J., & Frym, M. (1955). The Sexual Psychopath Act in practice: A critical discussion. *California Law Review*, 43(5), 766–780.

Haeberle, E. J. (1983). Introduction in *The birth of sexology: A brief history in documents*. Washington, DC: World Congress of Sexology. Retrieved from www.indiana.edu/~Kinsey/ resouces/sexology.html (not paginated).

Haeberle, E. J. (1982). *The sex atlas new popular reference edition*. New York: Continuum.

Hall, R., & Hall, R. C. W. (2007). A profile of pedophilia: Definitions, characteristics of offenders, recidivism, treatment outcomes, and forensic issues. *Mayo Clinic Proceedings*, 82(4), 457–471.

Hansen, C. (2007). To catch a predator: Protecting your kids from online enemies already in your home. New York: Dutton.

Hanson, R. K., Gordon, A., Harris, A. J. R., Marques, J. K., Murphy, W., Quinsey, V. L., & Seto, M. C. (2002). First report of the collaborative outcome data project on the effectiveness of psychological treatment for sex offenders. *Sexual Abuse: A Journal of Research and Treatment*, 14(2), 169–194.

Hanson, R. K., & Morton-Bourgon, K. (2004). *Predictors of sexual recidivism: An updated meta-analysis*. Ottawa, Canada: Public Safety and Emergency Preparedness Canada.

Haroain, L. (1994) Sexual development in children and adolescents (unpublished manuscript). San Francisco: Institute for Advanced Study of Human Sexuality.

Harris, C. (1946). Sex crimes: Their cause and cure. *Coronet*, 20(4), 3–9.

Hickman, S. E., & Muehlenhard, C. L. (1999). "By the semi-mystical appearance of a condom": How young women and men communicate sexual consent in heterosexual situations. *The Journal of Sex Research,* 36(3), 258–272.

Hirschi, T. (1969). *Causes of delinquency.* Berkeley, CA: University of California Press.

Hogg, C. (1999). The legal history of internet censorship and pornography in the United States. Retrieved October 2, 2008, from http://www.slais.ubc.ca/COURSES/libr500/fall1999/WWW_presentations/C_Hogg/unitedstates.htm.

Holmes, S. T., & Holmes, R. M. (2009). *Sex crimes: Patterns and behavior* (3rd ed.). Thousand Oaks, CA: Sage Publications.

Holmes, R. M., Tewksbury, R., & Holmes, S. T. (2004). Hidden JPGs: A functional alternative to voyeurism. *Journal of Popular Culture,* 32(3), 17–29.

Hudson, D. L. Jr. (2008). Pornography & obscenity: Overview. *First Amendment Center.* Retrieved January 1, 2009, from http://www.firstamendmentcenter.org/speech/adultent/topic.aspx?topic=pornography.

Human Rights Watch. (2007). *No easy answers: Sex offender laws in the U.S.* New York: Human Rights Watch.

Inside the Genarlow Wilson case. (2007, June 23). *The Citizen Online.* Retrieved December 17, 2008, from http://www.thecitizen.com/~citizen0/node/18008.

Iowa County Attorneys Association. (2006, December 11). Statement on sex offender residency restrictions in Iowa [Press release]. Des Moines: Iowa County Attorneys Association.

Janus, E. S. (2003). Examining our approaches to sex offenders and the law, Minnesota's sex offender commitment program: Would an empirically-based prevention policy be more effective? *William Mitchell Law Review,* 29, 1–37.

Jenkins, P. (1998). *Moral panic: Changing concepts of the child molester in modern America.* New Haven, CT: Yale University Press.

Jewkes, Y. (2004). *Media and crime.* Thousand Oaks, CA: Sage Publications.

Judge Tells Peeping Tom that Privacy Is Sacred. (2008, August 20). *Oregon Live.* Retrieved November 20, 2008, from http://www.oregonlive.com/portland/index.ssf/2008/08/judge_tells_peeping_tom_that_p.html.

Juvenile Sex Offender Laws Struck Down—For Now. (2008, April 6). *Las Vegas Sun.* Retrieved November 30, 2008, from http://www.lasvegassun.com/news/2008/apr/06/juvenile-sex-offender-laws-struck-down-now/.

*Kansas v. Hendricks,* 521 U.S. 346 (1997).

*Kansas v. Limon*: Case Background. (2005, October 21). *American Civil Liberties Union.* Retrieved June 6, 2007, from http://www.aclu.org/lgbt/discrim/11940res20050908.html.

Kinsey, A. C., Pomeroy, W. B., Martin, C. E., & Gebhard, P. H. (1953). *Sexual behavior in the human female.* Philadelphia: W.B. Saunders Company.

Kinsey, A. C., Pomeroy, W. B., & Martin, C. E. (1948). *Sexual behavior in the human male.* Philadelphia, PA: W.B. Saunders Company.

Kitzinger, J. (2007). *Framing abuse: Media influence and public understandings of sexual violence against children.* London: Pluto Press.

Koss, M. P., Gidycz, C. A., & Wisniewski, N. (1987). The score of rape: Incidence and prevalence of sexual aggression and victimization in a national sample of higher education students. *Journal of Consulting Clinical Psychology,* 55, 64–170.

Krafft-Ebing, R. V. (1922). *Psychopathia sexualis.* New York: Rebman Company.

Kruttschnitt, C., Uggen, C., & Shelton, K. (2000). Predictors of desistance among sex offenders: The interaction of formal and informal social controls. *Justice Quarterly,* 17, 62–87.

Lacoursiere, R. B. (2003). Evaluating offenders under a sexually violent predator law; The practical practice. In B. J. Winick & J. Q. LaFond (Eds.), *Protecting society from sexually dangerous offenders: Law, justice, and therapy* (pp. 75–97). Washington, DC: American Psychological Association.

LaFond, J. Q. (2000). The future of involuntary civil commitment in the U.S.A. after *Kansas v. Hendricks. Behavioral Sciences and the Law*, 18, 153–167.

Langstrom, N., & Seto, M. C. (2006). Exhibitionistic and voyeuristic behavior in a Swedish national population survey. *Archives of Sexual Behavior*, 35, 427–435.

Legal Opinions, Maryland Court of Appeals. (2008, May 5). *The Baltimore Daily Record.* Retrieved November 22, 2008, from http://findarticles.com/p/articles/mi_qn4183/is_/ai_n25393402.

Le Gall, A., Mullet, E., & Shafighi, S. R. (2002). Age, religious beliefs, and sexual attitudes. *The Journal of Sex Research*, 39(3), 207–216.

Levenson, J. S., Brannon, Y. N., Fortney, T., & Baker, J. (2007). Public perceptions about sex offenders and community protection policies. *Analysis of Social Issues and Public Policy*, 7(1), 1–25.

Levenson, J. S., & Cotter, L. P. (2005b). The impact of sex offender residence restrictions: 1,000 feet from danger or one step from absurd? *International Journal of Offender Therapy and Comparative Criminology*, 49(2), 168–178.

Levenson, J. S., D'Amora, D. A., & Hern, A. L. (2007). Megan's Law and its impact on community re-entry for sex offenders. *Behavioural Sciences and the Law*, 25, 587–602.

Levy, N. (2003). What (if anything) is wrong with bestiality? *Journal of Social Philosophy*, 34(3), 444–456.

Lewandowski, H. (1984/85). *The history of sexology.* Humboldt-Universitatzu Berlin. From http://www2.hu-berlin.de/sexology/GESUND/ARCHIV/LHIST.HTM (not paginated).

Lewis, C. F., & Stanley, C. R. (2000). Women accused of sexual offenses. *Behavioural Sciences and the Law*, 18, 73–81.

Lewis, R. (1988). *Effectiveness of statutory requirements for the registration of sex offenders: A report to the California state legislature.* Sacramento, CA: California Department of Justice.

Lieb, R., & Nunlist, C. (2008). *Community notification as viewed by Washington's citizens: A 10-year follow-up* (Document No. 08-03-1101). Olympia, WA: Washington State Institute for Public Policy.

Lieb, R., Quinsey, V., & Berliner, L. (1998). Sexual predators and social policy. *Crime and Justice*, 23, 2–49.

Lucken, K., & Bales, W. (2008). Florida's sexually violent predator program: An examination of risk and civil commitment eligibility. *Crime & Delinquency*, 54(1), 95–127.

Lucken, K., & Latina, J. (2002). Sex offender civil commitment laws: Medicalizing deviant sexual behavior. *Barry Law Review*, 15, 1–19.

Malamuth, N. M., Sockloskie, R. J., Koss, M. P., & Tanaka, J. S. (1991). Characteristics of aggressors against women: Testing a model using a national sample of college students. *Journal of Consulting Clinical Psychology*, 59, 670–681.

Mann, R. E. (2004). Innovation in sex offender treatment. *Journal of Sexual Aggression*, 10(2), 141–152.

Many Sex Offenders are Often Homeless. (2007, November 19). *USA Today.* Retrieved November 30, 2007, from http://www.usatoday.com/news/nation/2007-11-18-homeless-offenders_N.htm.

Marcus Dixon Rape Conviction Reversed. (2004, May 3). *TalkLeft: The Politics of Crime.* Retrieved December 20, 2008, from http://www.talkleft.com/story/2004/05/03/562/62659.

Marshall, W. L., Laws, D. R., & Barbaree, H. E. (1990). *Handbook of sexual assault: Issues, theories, and treatment of the offender.* New York: Springer Publications.

Mauro, T. (2001, October 31). High court tries to picture disputed virtual-porn law in practice. *Freedom Forum.* Retrieved April 23, 2009, from http://www.freedomforum.org/templates/document.asp?documentID=15270.

Mayer, A. (1992). *Women sex offenders: Treatment and dynamics.* Holmes Beach, FL: Learning Publications.

McGrath, R., Cumming, G., Hoke, S., & Bonn-Miller, M. (2007). Outcomes in a community sex offender treatment program: A comparison between polygraphed and matched non-polygraphed offenders. *Sexual Abuse: A Journal of Research and Treatment,* 19(4), 381–393.

McIlvenna, T. (February 2007). Lecture on the Socio-Sexual Response Cycle. Basic Lecture Series. Institute for Advanced Study of Human Sexuality, San Francisco, CA.

McIlvenna, T., & Haroian, L. (2001). Testimony of Rev. Dr. Ted McIlvenna and Dr. Loretta Haroian before the Attorney General's Commission on Pornography, October 16, 1985, Los Angeles, CA. *Workbook for Erotology Certificate Course of Study.* San Francisco: Institute for Advanced Study of Human Sexuality.

Meloy, M. L. (2006). *Sex offenses and the men who commit them: An assessment of sex offenders on probation.* Boston: Northeastern University Press.

Metzi, J. M. (2004a). From scopophilia to *Survivor:* A brief history of voyeurism. *Textual Practice,* 18(3), 415–434.

Metzi, J. M. (2004b). Voyeur nation? Changing definitions of voyeurism, 1950–2004. *Harvard Review of Psychiatry,* 12, 127–131.

Meyenburg, B., & Sigusch, V. (1977). Sexology in West Germany. *The Journal of Sex Research,* 13(3), 197–209.

Michels, S. (2008, October 10). Teen charged with sending nude pics of herself. *ABC News.* Retrieved April 23, 2009, from http://abcnews.go.com/TheLaw/story?id=5995084&page=1.

Michels, T. M., Kropp, R. Y., Eyre, S. L., & Halpern-Relsher, B. L. (2005). Initiating sexual experiences: How do young adolescents make decisions regarding early sexual activity? *Journal of Research on Adolescence,* 15(4), 583–607.

Miletski, H. (2001). Zoophilia—implications for therapy. *Journal of Sex Education,* 26(2), 85–89.

Miller, R. D. (2003). Chemical castration of sex offenders: Treatment or punishment? In B. J. Winick & J .Q. LaFond (Eds.), *Protecting society from sexually dangerous offenders: Law, justice, and therapy* (pp. 249–264). Washington, DC: American Psychological Association.

Morrison, S. R. (2008). *Creating sex offender registries: The Religious Right and the failure to protect society's vulnerable.* Boston: Steven R. Morrison.

Moser, C., & Madeson, J. J. (1996). *Bound to be free: The SM experience.* New York: Continuum Publishing Company.

Muraskin, R., & Domash, S. F. (2007). *Crime and the media: Headlines vs. reality.* Upper Saddle River, NJ: Prentice Hall.

Murray, J. (2000). Psychological profile of pedophiles and child molesters. *Journal of Psychology and Human Sexuality,* 134(2), 221–224.

My Space Deletes 146 Profiles of NE Sex Offenders. (2008, August 15). *KPTM Fox 42 News.* Retrieved August 18, 2008, from http://www.kptm.com.

National Adolescent Perpetrator Network (NAPN). (1993). The revised report from the National Task Force on Juvenile Sexual Offending. *Juvenile and Family Court Journal,* 44, 1–120.

Nine-Time Flasher Avoids Prison with Plea. (2007, December 12). *The News & Observer.* Retrieved November 21, 2008, from http://www.newsobserver.com/front/story/825222.html.

Noble, P., and Nadler, E. (1986). *United States of America vs. sex: How the Meese Commission lied about pornography.* New York, NY: Minotaur Press Ltd.

No Internet for Some Sex Offenders in New Jersey. (2007, December 27). *CNN.* Retrieved December 27, 2007, from http://www.cnn.com.

O'Dell, L. (2008). Child porn carton conviction upheld. *Fox News.* Retrieved April 23, 2009, from http://www.fox59.com/pages/landing/?Child-porn-cartoon-conviction-upheld-in-=1&blockID=167120&feedID=23.

Office of Juvenile Justice and Delinquency Prevention (OJJDP). (2001). *The decline in child sexual abuse cases* (NCJ 184741). Washington, DC: U.S. Department of Justice.

O'Neill, N., & O'Neill, G. (1973). *Open marriage a new life style for couples.* New York: Avon Books.

Ouimette, P. D., & Riggs, D. (1998). Testing a meditational model of sexually aggressive behavior in nonincarcerated perpetrators. *Violence Victims,* 13, 117–130.

Pallone, N. J. (2003). Without plea-bargaining, Megan Kanka would be alive today. *Criminology & Public Policy,* 3(1), 83–96.

Palmer, T., & Haffner, D. W. (2007). *A time to seek study guide on sexual and gender diversity.* Westport, CT: Religious Institute on Sexual Morality, Justice, and Healing.

Paul, R. (2005, September 23). FBI agents paid to surf for deviant internet porn. *Ars Technica.* Retrieved April 23, 2009, from http://arstechnica.com/old/content/2005/09/5346.ars.

Peering into the Minds of Sex Offenders. (2008, November 25). *WPTZ.* Retrieved November 30, 2008, from http://www.wptz.com/news/18143393/detail.html.

Peretti, P. O., and Rowan, M. (1982). Variables associated with male and female chronic zoophilia. *Social Behavior and Personality,* 10(1), 83–87.

Petrosino, A. J. and C. Petrosino. (1999). The public safety potential of Megan's law in Massachusetts: An assessment from a sample of criminal sexual psychopaths. *Crime and Delinquency* 45(1), 140–158.

Petrunik, M. (1994). *Models of dangerousness: A cross jurisdictional review of dangerousness legislation and practice.* Ottawa, Canada: Ministry of the Solicitor General of Canada.

Piemont, L. (2007). Fear of the empty self: The motivations for genital exhibitionism. *Modern Psychoanalysis,* 32(1), 79–93.

Pithers, W. (1990). Relapse prevention with sexual aggression: A method for maintaining therapeutic gain and enhancing external supervision. In W. L. Marshall, D. R. Laws, & H. E. Barbaree (Eds.), *Handbook of sexual assault: Issues, theories, and treatment of the offender* (pp. 343–361). New York: Plenum.

Ploscowe, M. (1960). Sex offenses and the American legal context. *Law and Contemporary Problems,* 15(3), 217–224.

Polygamist Guilty of Child Rape. (2002, June 24). *CBS News.* Retrieved November 21, 2008, from www.cbsnews.com/stories/2002/06/24/national/printables513227.shtml.

Polygamist Jailed for Child Rape. (2002, August 28). *BBC News.* Retrieved November 21, 2008, from http://news.bbc.co.uk/2/hi/world/americas/2218939.

Porn Producer Invokes the Bush/Yoo Defense—Unsuccessfully. (2008, October 5). *Salon.com.* Retrieved October 7, 2008, from www.salon.com/opinion/greenwald/2008/10/15/porn/.

Potter, G., & Kappeler, V. (2000). *Constructing crime: Perspectives on making news and social problems.* Long Grove, IL: Waveland Press.

Public Outrage Boosts Sentencing in Child Porn Cases. (2008, October 23). *ABA Journal–Law News Now.* Retrieved November 1, 2008, from http://abajournal.com/news/public_outrage_boosts_sentencing_of_child_porn_cases/.

Quayle, E., Vaughn, M., & Taylor, M. (2006). Sex offenders: Internet child abuse images and emotional avoidance: The importance of values. *Aggression and Violent Behavior,* 11(1), 1–11.

Quinsey, V., & Earls, C. (1990). The modification of sexual preferences. In W. L. Marshall, D. R. Laws, & H. E. Barbaree (Eds.), *Handbook of sexual assault: Issues, theories, and treatment of the offender* (pp. 279–295). New York: Plenum.

Raby, R. C. (2002). A tangle of discourses: Girls negotiating adolescence. *Journal of Youth Studies,* 5(4), 425–448.

Rape a Child, Pay with Your Life, Louisiana Argues. (2008, April 15). *CNN.* Retrieved April 15, 2008, from http://www.cnn.com.

Reinhardt, J. M., & Fisher, E. C. (1949). The sexual psychopath and the law. *Journal of Criminal Law and Criminology,* 39(6), 734–742.

Robinson, B. E., Manthei, R., Scheltema, K., Rich, R., & Koznar, J. (1999). Therapeutic uses of sexually explicit materials in the United States and the Czech and Slovak Republics: A qualitative study. *Journal of Sex & Marital Therapy,* 25, 103–119.

Rosler, A., & Witztum, E. (2000). Pharmaco-therapy of paraphilias in the next millennium.

Rydstrom, J. (2000). "Sodomitical sins are threefold": Typologies of bestiality, masturbation, and homosexuality in Sweden, 1880–1950. *Journal of the History of Sexuality,* 9(3), 240–276.

Sanghara, K. K., & Wilson, J. C. (2006). Stereotypes and attitudes about child sexual abusers: A comparison of experienced and inexperienced professionals in sex offender treatment. *Legal and Criminological Psychology,* 11, 229–244.

Sarrel, L. J., & Sarrel, P. M. (1979). *Sexual unfolding: Sexual development and sex therapies in late adolescence.* Boston, MA: Little, Brown and Company.

Sawhill, I. V. (2006). Teenage sex, pregnancy, and nonmarital births. *Gender Issues,* 23(4), 48–59.

Schram, D., & Milloy, C. (1995). *Community notification: A study of offender characteristics and recidivism.* Seattle, WA: Urban Policy Research.

Schulhofer, S. J. (1998). *Unwanted sex: The culture of intimidation and the failure of law.* Cambridge, MA: Harvard University Press.

Scully, D. (1994). *Understanding sexual violence: A study of convicted rapists.* New York: Routledge.

Seabloom, W. (1983). The family journal: A multigenerational sex education experience for families. Presented at the 6th World Congress of Sexology, Washington, DC.

Seabloom, W., Seabloom, M. E., Seabloom, E., Barron, R., & Hendrickson, S. (2003). A 14- to 24-year longitudinal study of a comprehensive sexual health model treatment program for adolescent sex offenders: Predictors of successful completion and subsequent criminal recidivism. *International Journal of Offender Therapy and Comparative Criminology,* 47(4), 468–581.

Sentencing Guidelines Commission. (2004). *Sex offender sentencing: Sentencing guidelines commission 2004.* Seattle, WA: State of Washington.

Sex Offenders Can Have More Freedom, Court Rules. (2008, July 15). *South Jersey News.* Retrieved August 12, 2008, from http://www.nj.com.

Sex Offenders Must Hand Over Online Passwords. (2008, December 30). *MSNBC.* Retrieved January 1, 2009, from http://www.msnbc.msn.com/id/28437829/.

Shanahan, M. J., Erickson, L. D., & Bauer, D. J. (2005). One hundred years of knowing: The changing science of adolescence, 1904 and 2004. *Journal of Research on Adolescence,* 15(4), 383–394.

Sheldon, T., Bluestone, H., Coleman, E., Cullen, K., & Melella, J. (1985). Pedophilia: An update on theory and practice. *Psychiatric Quarterly*, 57(2), 89–103.

Sher, J., and Carey, B. (2007, July 19). Debate on child pornography's link to molesting. *New York Times.*Retrieved April 23, 2009, from http://www.nytimes.com/2007/07/19/us/19sex.html?_r=4&hp=&oref=slogin&pagewanted=print.

Sieving, R. E., Eisenberg, M. E., Pettingell, S., & Skay, C. (2006). Friends' influence on adolescents' first sexual intercourse. *Perspectives on Sexual and Reproductive Health*, 38(1), 13–19.

Simon, L. (2000). An examination of the assumptions of specialization, mental disorder, and dangerousness in sex offenders. *Behavioural Sciences and the Law*, 18, 275–308.

Simon, L. (1997). The myth of sex offender specialization: An empirical analysis. *New England Journal on Criminal and Civil Confinement*, 23(2), 387–403.

Simon, L., & Zgoba, K. (2006). Sex crimes against children: Legislation, prevention and investigation. *Crime Prevention Studies*, 19, 65–100.

Smith, C. L. (2005, October 6). Horseplay. *Rolling Stone.* 984, 90.

Snyder, H. (2000). *Sexual assault of young children as reported to law enforcement: Victim, incident, and offender characteristics.* Washington, DC: Bureau of Justice Statistics, U.S. Department of Justice.

Society for the Scientific Study of Sexuality. (1987). The Board of Directors of the Society for the Scientific Study of Sex issues policy statements. *The Journal of Sex Research*, 23(2), 284–287.

Sprinkle, A. (1986, January 20). *Testimony before the Meese Commission hearing on pornography.* Retrieved December 29, 2008, from http://gos.sbc.edu/s/sprinkle2.html.

State of Louisiana. (2008, June 25). Governor signs chemical castration bill, authorizing the castration of sex offenders in Louisiana [Press release]. Baton Rouge, LA: Office of the Governor. Retrieved July 18, 2008 from http://gov.louisiana.gov.

*State of Ohio v. Lowe.* (2007). 112 Ohio St.3d 507, 2007-Ohio-606.

*State v. Robinson*, 496 A.2d 1067 (1985).

*State v. Way*, 297 N.C. 293 (1979).

Stone, H. T., Winslade, W. J., & Klugman, C. M. (2000). Sex offenders, sentencing laws, and pharmaceutical treatment: A prescription for failure. *Behavioral Sciences and the Law*, 19, 83–110.

Supreme Court Upholds Child Pornography Law. (2008, May 20). *New York Times.* Retrieved November 12, 2008, from http://www.nytimes.com/2008/05/20/washington/20scotus.html?_r=1.

Sutherland, E. (1950). The diffusion of sexual psychopath laws. *The American Journal of Sociology*, 56(2), 142–148.

Sutherland, E. (1939). *Principles of criminology* (3rd ed.). Philadelphia, PA: J.B. Lippincott.

Teen Charged with Sending Nude Pics of Herself. (2008, October 10). *ABC News.* Retrieved October 30, 2008, from http//:www.abcnews.go.com/TheLaw/story?id=5995084&page=1.

Ten-Year Old's Crime Tests Limits of Megan's Law. (2001, June 16). *New York Times.* Retrieved November 30, 2008, from http://www.nytimes.com.

Tewksbury, R. (2005). Sex offender registries as a tool for public safety: Views from registered sex offenders. *Western Criminology Review*, 7, 1–8.

Texas Officials: FLDS Raid about Child Abuse, Not Religion. (2008, December 23). *Chronicle.* Retrieved December 23, 2008, from http://www.chron.com/disp/story.mpl/metropolitan/6178975.html.

Texas Office of the Attorney General. (2001). Cybercrimes. *Criminal Law Update*, 8(3), 4–11.

The Other Matthew. (2007, February 20). *Boston Phoenix*. Retrieved June 6, 2007, from http://bostonphoenix.com/boston/news_features/other_stories/document/02704491.htm.

The Unknown Sex Fiend. (1950, February 13). *Time*. Retrieved December 1, 2008, from http://www.time.com/time/magazine/article/0,9171,811945,00.html?iid=digg_share.

Then and Now: Heidi Fleiss. (2005, June 19). *CNN.com*. Retrieved December 2, 2008, from www.cnn.com/2005/US/02/28/cnn25.tan.fleiss/.

Tokheim, R. (June 2005). Juvenile sex offenders can be changed, counselor contends. *Metro Lutheran* (www.metrolutheran.org).

Tonight on *Dateline* This Man Will Die. (2008, June 26). *Esquire*. Retrieved November 30, 2008, from http://www.esquire.com/features/predator0907.

Towery, M. (2007, June 19). Inside the Genarlow Wilson case. *Townhall.com*. Retrieved April 1, 2009, from http://townhall.com/Columnists/MattTowery/2007/06/19/inside_the_genarlow_wilson_case?page=full&comments=true.

Thompson, B. (1994). *Sadomasochism*. London: Cassell.

Trailer Park Becomes Paradise for Sex Offenders. (2007, October 18). *CNN*. Retrieved October 18, 2007, from http://www.cnn.com.

Travin, S., Cullen, K., & Protter, B. (1990). Female sexual offenders: Severe victims and victimizers. *Journal of Forensic Sciences*, 35, 140–150.

Two Men Plead Guilty to Sexual Misconduct at Overlook. (2008, August 22). *The Huntsville Times*. Retrieved December 18, 2008, from http://blog.al.com/breaking/2008/08/two_men_plead_guilty_to_sexual.html.

Uniform Crime Report (UCR). (2007). *Crime in the United States, 2006*. Washington, DC: U.S. Department of Justice.

U.S. Polygamist Gets Five Years. (2001, August 24). *BBC News*. Retrieved September 4, 2008, from http://news.bbc.co.uk/2/hi/americas/1508284.stm.

Vandiver, D. M., & Walker, J. T. (2002). Female sex offenders: An overview and analysis of 40 cases. *Criminal Justice Review*, 27(2), 284–300.

Vasquez, B. E., Maddan, S., & Walker, J. T. (2008). The influence of sex offender registration and notification laws in the United States: A time-series analysis. *Crime & Delinquency*, 54, 175–192.

Virtual Porn Case to Test High Court's Sexually Explicit Material Standard. (2001, January 26). *Freedom Forum*. Retrieved October 2, 2008, from http://www.freedomforum.org/templates/document.asp?documentID=12938.

Wakeling, H. C., Webster, S. D., & Mann, R. E. (2005). Sexual offenders' treatment experience: A qualitative and quantitative investigation. *Journal of Sexual Aggression*, 11(2), 171–186.

Wakeling, H. C., Webster, S., Moulden, H. M., & Marshall, W. L. (2007). Decisions to offend in men who sexually abuse their daughters. *Journal of Sexual Aggression*, 13(2), 81–99.

Wallmyr, G., & Welin, C. (2006). Young people, pornography, and sexuality: Sources and attitudes. *The Journal of School Nursing*, 22(5), 290–295.

Warren, J., Reboussin, R., & Hazelwood, R. (1998). Crime scene and distance correlates of serial rape. *Journal of Quantitative Criminology*, 14, 35–39.

Washington State Institute for Public Policy (WSIPP). (2007a). *Six-year follow-up of 135 released sex offenders recommended for commitment under Washington's sexually violent predator law, where no petition was filed* (No. 03-12-1101). Olympia, WA: Washington State Institute for Public Policy.

Washington State Institute for Public Policy (WSIPP). (2007b). *Comparison of state laws authorizing involuntary commitment of sexually violent predators: 2006 update, revised* (No. 05-03-1101). Olympia, WA: Washington State Institute for Public Policy.

Webster, C. M., Gartner, R., & Doob, A. N. (2006). Results by design: The artefactual construction of high recidivism rates for sex offenders. *Canadian Journal of Criminology and Criminal Justice*, 48(1), 79–93.

Weeks, D. (2002). Get your freak on: How black girls sexualize identity. *Sex Education*, 2(3), 251–262.

Weeks, J. (1986). *Sexuality.* New York: Routledge.

Weinberg, T. S. (1995). Sociological and social psychological issues in the study of sadomasochism. In Thomas S. Weinberg (Ed.), *S&M studies in dominance and submission* (pp. 289–303). Amherst, MA: Prometheus Books.

Wertham, F. (1938). Psychiatry and the prevention of sex crimes. *Journal of Criminal Law and Criminology*, 28(6), 847–853.

Wheatland, T. (2005). *Ashcroft v. ACLU*: In search of plausible, less restrictive alternatives. *Berkeley Technology Law Journal*, 20, 371–396.

Why is Genarlow Wilson in Prison? (2007, June 6). Retrieved June 8, 2007, from http://www.wilsonappeal.com/index.php (site no longer active).

Wille, R., & Beier, K. M. (1989). Castration in Germany. *Sexual Abuse: A Journal of Research and Treatment*, 2(2), 103–133.

Williams, L. (1989). *Hard core power, pleasure and the "frenzy of the visible."* Berkeley, CA: University of California Press.

Wireless Voyeur Appeals 56-Year Term. (2007, February 14). *CNET News.* Retrieved November 1, 2008, from http://news.cnet.com/Police-blotter-Wireless-voyeur-appeals-56-year-term/2100-1030_3-6158933.html.

Wolf, N. (1997). *Promiscuities: The secret struggle for womanhood.* New York: Random House.

Wolf, N. (1991). *The beauty myth.* Toronto, Canada: Random House of Canada Limited.

Young GOP Leader Accused in Gay Sex Crime. (2007, August 10). *The Advocate.* Retrieved December 1, 2007, from http://www.advocate.com/news_detail_ektid47960.asp.

Zahorsky, R. (2008, October 23). Public outrage boosts sentencing in child porn cases. *ABA Journal.* Retrieved April 25, 2009, from http://abajournal.com/news/public_outrage_boosts_sentencing_of_child_porn_cases/.

Zevitz, R. G., & Farkas, M. A. (2000a). *Sex offender community notification: Assessing the impact in Wisconsin.* Washington, DC: U.S. Department of Justice, National Institute of Justice.

Zgoba, K. J., & Simon, L. M. J. (2005). Recidivism rates of sexual offenders up to 7 years later. *Criminal Justice Review*, 30(2), 155–173.

Zilney, L. A. & Zilney, L. J. (2008). Sex offender laws. In Gregg Barak (Ed.). *Battleground: Criminal justice* (pp. 671–681). Westport, CT: Greenwood Press.

Zimring, F. E., Piquero, A. R., & Jennings, W. G. (2007). Sexual delinquency in Racine: Does early sex offending predict later sex offending in youth and young adulthood? *Criminology and Public Policy*, 6(3), 507–534.

Zonana, H. V., Bonnie, R. J., & Hoge, S. K. (2003). In the wake of *Hendricks:* The treatment and restraint of sexually dangerous offenders viewed from the perspective of American psychiatry. In B. J. Winick & J. Q. LaFond (Eds.), *Protecting society from sexually dangerous offenders: Law, justice, and therapy* (pp. 131–145). Washington, DC: American Psychological Association.

# INDEX

# About the Authors

LAURA J. ZILNEY is a sexologist with a private practice near Toronto, Ontario, Canada. She is a graduate of the University of Waterloo (Ontario), Carleton University (Ottawa, Ontario) and received her doctorate from the Institute for Advanced Study of Human Sexuality in San Francisco, California.

LISA ANNE ZILNEY is an associate professor in the Department of Justice Studies at Montclair State University in New Jersey. She holds a PhD from the University of Tennessee, an MS from Eastern Kentucky University, and a BA from the University of Windsor in Canada.